P9-DXC-487

Human Body

a visual encyclopedia

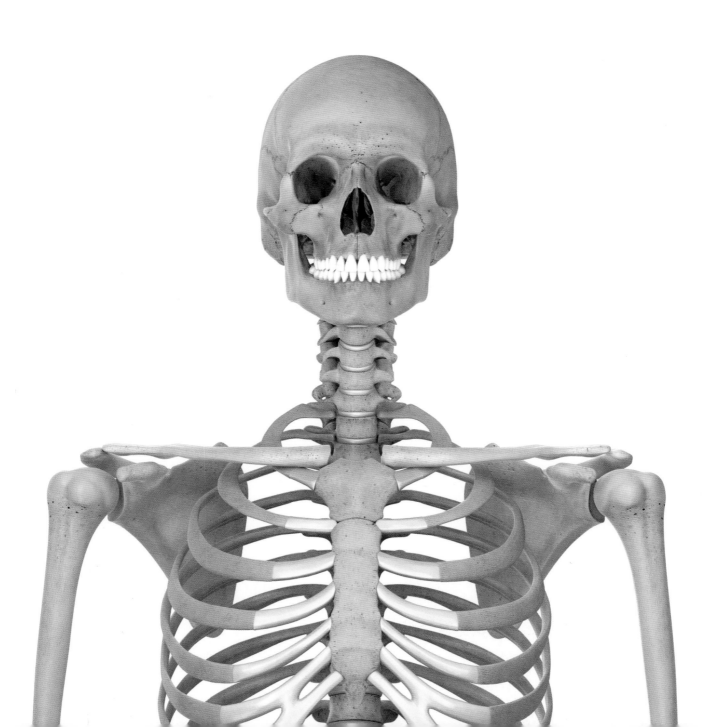

Human Body
a visual encyclopedia

DK PUBLISHING

**LONDON, NEW YORK,
MELBOURNE, MUNICH, and DELHI**

Written by Richard Walker, John Woodward,
Shaila Brown, Ben Morgan
Consultant for Mind chapter Kathrin Cohen Kadosh

Senior editors Shaila Brown, Ben Morgan
Project editor Ruth O'Rourke-Jones
Editorial assistant Damilare Olugbode
Project designer Hedi Hunter
Designer Daniela Boraschi
Production editor Ben Marcus
Managing editor Julie Ferris
Managing art editor Owen Peyton Jones
Publisher Sarah Larter
Associate publishing director Liz Wheeler
Art director Phil Ormerod
Publishing director Jonathan Metcalf

DK India
Managing editor Rohan Sinha
Deputy managing editor Alka Thakur Hazarika
Project editor Dharini Ganesh
Editors Suefa Lee, Parameshwari Sircar
Deputy managing art editor Mitun Bannerjee
Consultant art director Shefali Upadhyay
Project designer Amit Malhotra
Designers Rakesh Khundongbam, Pooja Pawwar,
Anuj Sharma, Vinita Venugopal, Shreya Anand Virmani
Production manager Pankaj Sharma
Senior DTP designer Jagtar Singh
DTP designers Arvind Kumar,
Arjinder Singh, Bimlesh Tiwary
DTP/CTS manager Balwant Singh
Picture researcher Sakshi Saluja

First American Edition, 2012

Published in the United States by DK Publishing
345 Hudson Street,
New York, New York 10014

16 10 9 8 7 6 5

037–181750–Jul/12

Published in Great Britain by Dorling Kindersley Limited.

A catalog record for this book is available from the Library of Congress.

ISBN 978-0-7566-9307-7

DK books are available at special discounts when purchased in bulk for
sales promotions, premiums, fund-raising, or educational use.
For details, contact: DK Publishing Special Markets,
345 Hudson Street, New York,
New York 10014 or SpecialSales@dk.com.

Printed and bound in China by Hung Hing

Discover more at
www.dk.com

Contents

BODY
BASICS

Just like a jigsaw puzzle, your body is made up of thousands of pieces. Beneath its protective covering of skin are trillions of tiny cells, neatly organized into the working tissues and organs that form you.

Finding out

The process of finding out how the incredibly complex human body works started thousands of years ago—long before there were medical schools and devices that enabled doctors to look inside the body. Even today, thanks to huge advances in technology, we are still making new discoveries about the workings of the body.

◄ CANOPIC JARS
The ancient Egyptians placed body organs in stone or ceramic vessels known as canopic jars. There was a different jar for each of four main organs—the lungs, stomach, liver, and intestines.

ANCIENT WISDOM

Many ancient cultures contributed towards a greater understanding of how the body works. The Egyptians, for example, realized that the heart was at the center of a system that drove the blood and that the pulse was related to the heartbeat. They also gained some knowledge about the body's internal organs during a process called mummification. This involved removing the major organs of the dead and preserving them in jars placed alongside the body in the tomb.

GLADIATORS' DOCTOR

Claudius Galen was an important Roman-Greek surgeon and philosopher. In the early 160s CE, he was put in charge of treating wounded gladiators. As a result, Galen learned much about the human body and although many of his ideas were wrong, he discovered that arteries carried blood and that urine was made in the kidneys.

◄ ROMAN MOSAIC *In ancient Rome, gladiators fought to the death, inflicting horrific wounds on each other.*

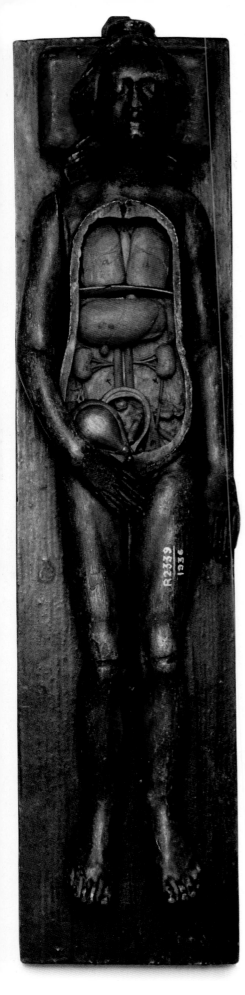

MEDIEVAL THINKING

In early medieval times, knowledge about the workings of the human body was still largely based on many of Galen's theories. It was not until the 1400s, when laws on dissecting corpses were relaxed in some countries, that anatomists could study the body and try to find out how the bones, muscles, and body systems worked.

◄ TEACHING ANATOMY *During the 1400s, wooden anatomical models, such as the ones show here, were used as medical teaching aids.*

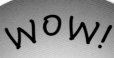
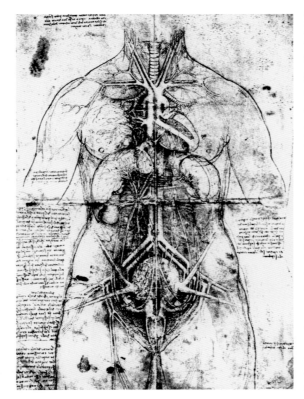

BODY ART

In the late 1400s, when Italian artist Leonardo da Vinci was given permission to dissect corpses, he used his skill to draw many anatomically precise pictures. But in an age when the printing press was still a new invention, Leonardo's drawings remained unseen. The breakthrough came in 1543, when Flemish doctor Andreas Vesalius published his book *On the Structure of the Human Body*, providing a valuable medical reference tool.

◄ THE GREAT LADY *This drawing by Leonardo, known as* The Great Lady, *shows the internal body organs in great detail.*

WAXWORKS OF ART

Detailed anatomical wax models became popular in the 1700s for teaching medical students about the human body. They were brightly colored and clearly showed the muscles, nerves, blood vessels, and internal organs in 3-D. The most famous and earliest collection of anatomical wax models is at the oldest scientific museum in Europe, La Specola in Florence, Italy.

◄ LIFELIKE LIMB *This wax model of an arm was made in Italy in the 1800s. Such models provided medical students with a fantastic tool for understanding the internal workings of the body.*

Looking inside

From the outside, the body rarely gives any clues about what is going on inside. One way of discovering how the body works is to use some of the astonishing medical technology that allows doctors to look inside a person without causing any harm. This also helps them spot any hidden injury or signs of disease.

X-RAY

When X-ray imaging was discovered in the late 1800s, doctors were able, for the first time, to see inside the living body without having to cut it open. This body imaging technique fires X-rays—a form of radiation—through a particular part of the body onto a photographic plate. Hard, dense parts of the body, such as bones, show up clearly since they absorb the rays. Softer body tissues are not visible since the X-rays pass right through them.

CT SCAN

In a CT (computed tomography) scan, beams of X-rays are sent through the body and are then analyzed by computer. This turns scans into images that show "slices" through the body. These slices can be built up into 3-D pictures to give an all-around view of an organ. CT scans are more revealing than ordinary X-rays because they show the soft tissues in greater detail.

Hard tissues such as bone show up as white areas.

Softer internal organs show up as gray or black areas in an X-ray.

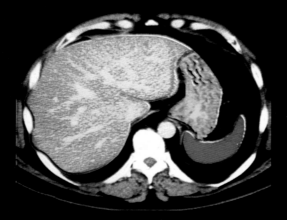

▲ CROSS-SECTION *This CT scan shows a slice through the abdomen, revealing the liver (orange), stomach (green), and spleen (pink).*

FAST FACTS

■ X-rays were once used in shoe stores to examine how well the new shoes fitted each customer's feet.

■ Patients undergoing an MRI scan have to remove any metal objects, such as jewelry, from their body because the scanner contains very strong magnets.

■ Ultrasound is used in medicine to clean teeth, break up kidney stones, and remove cataracts from the eyes.

ULTRASOUND

With ultrasound, high-pitched sound waves that we cannot hear are beamed into the body. These bounce off organs, producing echoes that are picked up and turned into pictures by a computer. Ultrasound is very safe, so it can be used to make sure that an unborn baby is growing normally.

▶ BABY REVEALED
This ultrasound scan shows the face and fingers of a seven-month-old baby inside its mother's womb.

Taken in 1895, an image of hand bones was the first ever X-ray.

MRI SCAN

A person having an MRI (magnetic resonance imaging) scan is put inside a tunnel-like scanner. When water molecules in the body are exposed to strong magnets they can be made to "flip" and give out tiny bursts of radio waves. These are picked up by a scanner and turned into an image.

◀ BRAIN SCAN *This MRI scan shows a slice through the head. Brain tissues are shown in different colors.*

ENDOSCOPE

An endoscope is a flexible tube with a camera at one end. It is pushed inside the body through an opening, such as the mouth. It has its own light source to light up body cavities, and a transmitter sends back images to be viewed on a screen.

◀ BODY FRAMEWORK
Bones show up best in an X-ray, as can be seen in this image of the incredibly flexible skeleton of a gymnast.

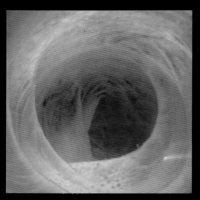

▶ INSIDE VIEW
An endoscope takes an inside look at the small intestine. This is an ideal way to check for blockages and growths.

Building blocks

Your body is made of trillions of cells. These are living building blocks that are really tiny. The cells shown here have all been photographed with the help of a powerful microscope to make them visible. Cells are constantly dividing to produce new cells that enable your body to grow and to repair itself.

Unlike other body cells, a stem cell does not have a distinctive shape because it does not have a specialized role.

THE CELL FACTORY

All cells inside your body are produced by stem cells. These stem cells are unique because they can change into the many different types of cells that make and shape your body, including skin, muscle, and blood cells. Cell production is a job that starts in the earliest days of life.

FAST FACTS

■ The body's biggest cells—egg cells or ova—are 0.004 in (0.1 mm) across and just visible without a microscope.

■ The smallest body cells are just 0.00016 in (0.004 mm) long and are found in the cerebellum (part of the brain).

■ Placed in a row, 40 average-sized cells would stretch across a period.

TYPES OF CELLS

There are more than 200 types of cell in the body, six of which are shown here. Each has its own specific shape and size, related to the job it does. Nerve cells, for example, are long and thin, ideal for carrying electrical signals. Fat cells, crammed with fat droplets, provide fuel for the body and help insulate and keep you warm.

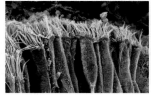

▲ EPITHELIAL CELLS
Protective epithelial cells—these are from an air passage—line flat surfaces and organs.

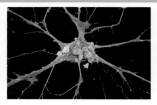

▲ NERVE CELL
Wirelike nerve cells (neurons) carry electrical signals and form the nervous system.

▲ FAT CELL
Also called adipocytes, these rounded cells store fat, one of the body's energy sources.

A cell membrane surrounds and protects the stem cell, holding the contents together.

MAKING NEW CELLS

Cells divide repeatedly to replace worn-out cells—a process known as mitosis. Before a cell divides, chromosomes, which carry the instructions needed to build and run a cell, copy themselves within the nucleus (control center) of the cell. Then the cell splits into two identical cells, each with a full set of instructions.

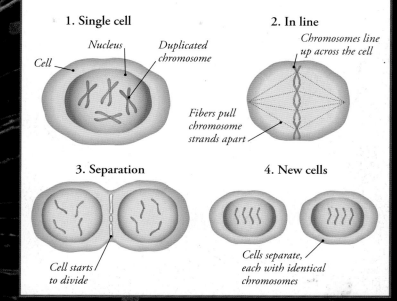

1. Single cell
Nucleus
Duplicated chromosome
Cell

2. In line
Chromosomes line up across the cell
Fibers pull chromosome strands apart

3. Separation
Cell starts to divide

4. New cells
Cells separate, each with identical chromosomes

▲ STEM CELL *We start life as a tiny embryo growing inside our mother. An embryo contains stem cells like this one that can develop into any one of the cells found inside the body.*

WOW!

The human body is built from 100 trillion cells and produces about 5 million cells every second to replace those that die.

SEEING SMALL

The invention of the microscope in the 1600s opened up a hidden world for English scientist Robert Hooke. He devised a microscope (shown above) to study tiny objects such as plants and insects. In 1665, Hooke recorded his findings in his groundbreaking book, *Micrographia* (meaning "small drawings"). He also invented the term *cell* to describe the basic unit of life.

▲ BONE CELL
This bone cell (osteocyte) maintains the bone tissue (brown) that surrounds it.

▲ MUSCLE CELLS
All movement is produced by muscle cells. These cardiac muscle cells make the heart beat.

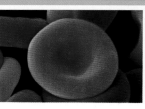

▲ RED BLOOD CELLS
These small, dimpled blood cells carry oxygen from the lungs to body tissues.

Inside cells

Right now, the trillions of cells inside your body are buzzing with activity. Inside each tiny cell there are many parts that make substances, release energy, and recycle worn-out materials. Although body cells come in many shapes and sizes, they all share the same basic structure.

IN CHARGE

Except for red blood cells, every cell in your body has a control center called the nucleus. It contains the essential instructions to build, maintain, and run the cell. Outside the controlling nucleus is the cytoplasm, a clear, jellylike liquid that contains cell parts called organelles ("tiny organs"). These organelles have their own specific task.

Ribosomes are tiny structures that make important substances called proteins, using instructions received from the nucleus.

The nucleus is the largest organelle within the cell.

Lysosomes break down and recycle worn-out organelles.

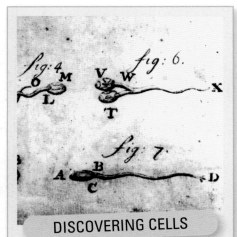

DISCOVERING CELLS

In the 1670s, Dutch textile merchant Antonie van Leeuwenhoek made some amazing discoveries using his simple but powerful microscope. His interest in studying living things led to the discovery of bacteria, red blood cells, and sperm (shown here in his drawing).

▲ CELL MEMBRANE *Guarding the contents of the cell is a protective layer called the cell membrane. It consists of various parts that help control the movement of substances into and out of the cell.*

▲ CLOSE-UP VIEW
This model of a typical cell shows the features that can be seen using a powerful electron microscope.

The cytoplasm, which consists mainly of water, helps move materials around the cell.

▲ POWERHOUSES
Mitochondria are the powerhouses of the cell, releasing energy to keep the cell alive.

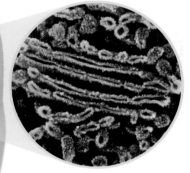

◀ PROTEIN FACTORIES
This organelle, called the endoplasmic reticulum, is the busiest area of the cell. It helps to move and store proteins made by tiny ribosomes on its surface.

Microtubules are fine rods that support and shape the cell, and also move organelles through the cytoplasm.

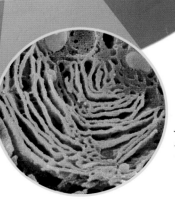

◀ PROCESS AND PACKAGE
The Golgi complex is a stack of flattened bags that processes and packages proteins for use inside and outside the cell.

FAST FACTS

■ Humans start life as a single cell, which divides and gives rise to the trillions of cells that make up a body.

■ All living things—including animals and plants—are made of cells. Some, such as bacteria, consist of a single cell.

■ The cells with the shortest lifespan are those lining the small intestine. They live for about 36 hours. Brain cells, however, may last a lifetime.

BODY BASICS

LOOK CLOSER: SEEING BIG

Invented in the 1930s, electron microscopes can magnify the insides of cells up to 200,000 times. Ordinary light microscopes have a maximum magnification of just 2,000 times, so they reveal much less detail.

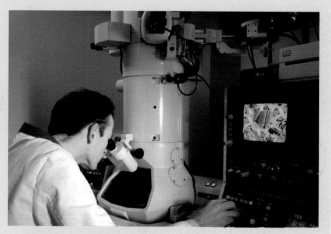

▲ ELECTRON MICROSCOPE *A scientist looks at a 3-D image created by a scanning electron microscope. The same image can be viewed on the monitor's screen.*

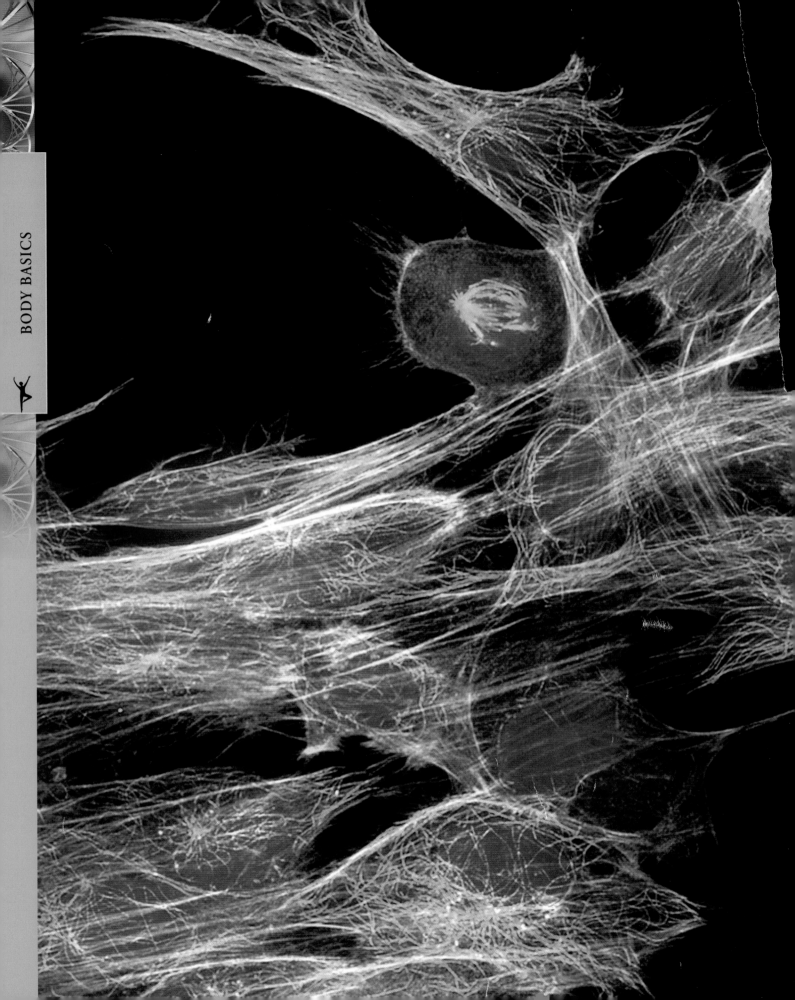

HOLDING IT TOGETHER
These highly magnified cells (blue),
each with a nucleus (purple), are called
fibroblasts. They play an important role
in the body by producing connective
tissues. These provide the scaffolding
for many organs, including the skin,
and also form the tendons that link
bones to muscles.

Body jigsaw

Your body's trillions of cells fit into an incredibly complicated jigsaw to give you shape and make your body work. If they didn't, you would be a squishy mass of random cells. Cells that have the same function are organized into working groups called tissues. When groups of tissues join together to do a particular job they are called organs—your heart, lungs, and brain are all body organs.

TISSUE TYPES

There are four basic types of tissues in your body. Epithelial tissues are sheets of cells that cover the inner surfaces of your organs and form your outer skin. Connective tissues are fibrous and hold organs and other body structures together. Muscle tissues make you move by contracting (pulling) and relaxing. A network of nerve tissues is used to send messages all around the body.

Your lungs are organs that take in oxygen from the air and pass it to your blood.

▶ MUSCLE TISSUE
Muscle cells form long and striped skeletal muscle tissue, which pulls on your bones to make you move.

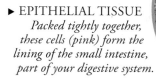

WOW!

Your body's biggest and heaviest organ is the one that covers all the other parts of your body— your skin!

Your bones are organs that are made mainly from hard connective tissues.

▶ EPITHELIAL TISSUE
Packed tightly together, these cells (pink) form the lining of the small intestine, part of your digestive system.

Made up of more than 100 billion nerve cells, the brain is your body's most complex organ, controlling nearly all your activities.

◀ NERVE TISSUE
These neurons (green) are cells that make up nerve tissue. They carry information in the form of electrical signals between your brain and the rest of your body.

The thyroid gland contains tissue that releases chemical messengers called hormones.

▼ CONNECTIVE TISSUE
This is cartilage, a type of tough, flexible tissue that covers the ends of your bones (where they form joints) to keep them from wearing out. It also gives your nose and ears their shape.

Your blood vessels are made up of connective, muscle, and epithelial tissues.

The stomach is the organ that churns food and breaks it down into smaller pieces.

Nerves carry electrical signals to all your body's organs.

GETTING ORGANIZED

For your body to work like clockwork, it has to be organized—from the tiniest cells, to tissues, organs, and finally into systems that have specific roles.

▲ CELL *A living human body cell cannot exist on its own. The more complex the cell is, the more it depends on other cells to survive. Simple cells are better at surviving on their own, but cannot perform complicated tasks.*

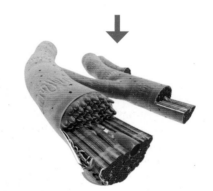

▲ TISSUE *These cardiac (heart) muscle cells form cardiac muscle tissue, which contracts (pulls) to make the heart beat.*

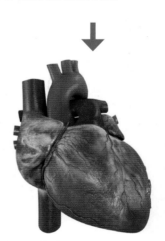

▲ ORGAN *The heart is an organ made from not only muscle tissue but also epithelial, connective, and nerve tissues. It is the main organ in your circulatory system, pumping the blood—liquid tissue—around your body.*

Working together

The human body is an incredible machine. It performs countless tasks effortlessly every second, every day. It supports and moves us, delivers food and oxygen to our cells, protects us from disease, gets rid of waste, enables us to reproduce, and allows us to think and feel. All these tasks are performed by the 12 body systems you can see below.

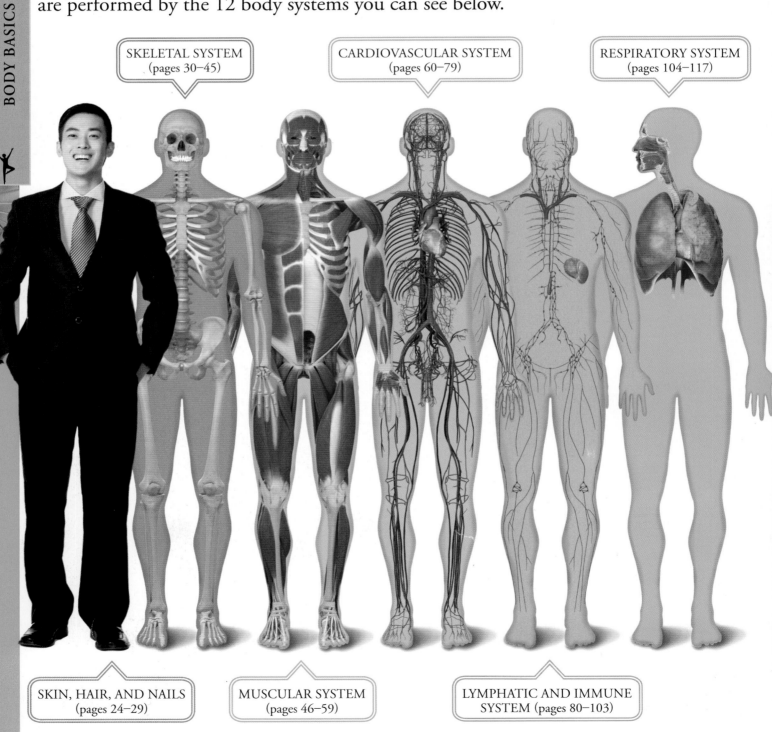

SKELETAL SYSTEM
(pages 30–45)

CARDIOVASCULAR SYSTEM
(pages 60–79)

RESPIRATORY SYSTEM
(pages 104–117)

SKIN, HAIR, AND NAILS
(pages 24–29)

MUSCULAR SYSTEM
(pages 46–59)

LYMPHATIC AND IMMUNE
SYSTEM (pages 80–103)

EXTRAORDINARY SYSTEMS

Each body system consists of a group of vital organs that carry out specific tasks. The systems do not operate alone, but work together to maintain a healthy and efficient body. For example, all systems require a constant supply of oxygen, which is taken in by the respiratory system and transported by the cardiovascular system.

FAST FACTS

■ Your outer layer of skin is completely replaced every month.
■ We use our respiratory system to take about 30,000 breaths a day, breathing out enough air to blow up 3,750 party balloons.
■ In an average lifetime, the urinary system makes and releases about 10,000 gallons (40,000 liters) of urine, enough to fill a small swimming pool.

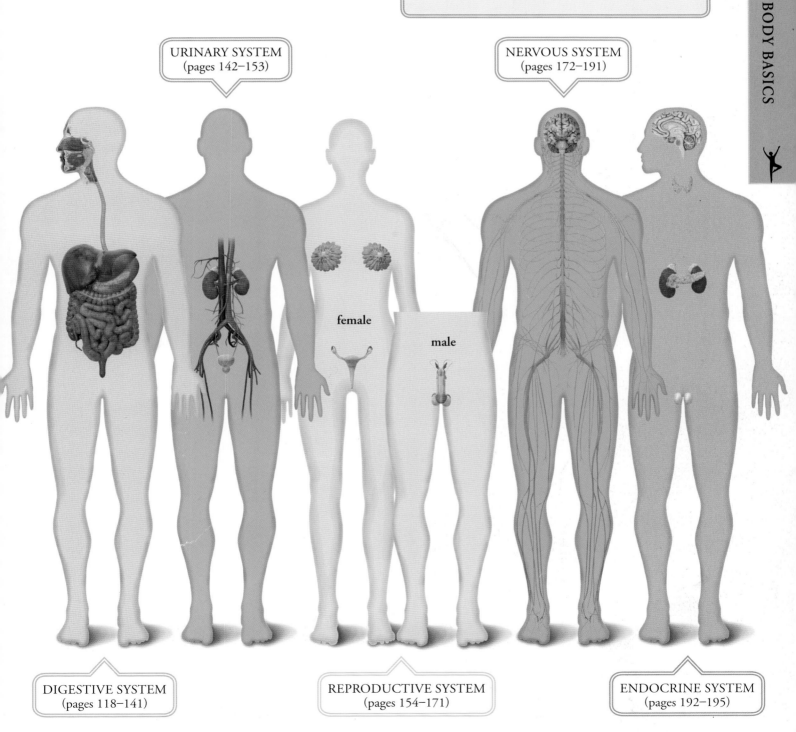

URINARY SYSTEM
(pages 142–153)

NERVOUS SYSTEM
(pages 172–191)

female

male

DIGESTIVE SYSTEM
(pages 118–141)

REPRODUCTIVE SYSTEM
(pages 154–171)

ENDOCRINE SYSTEM
(pages 192–195)

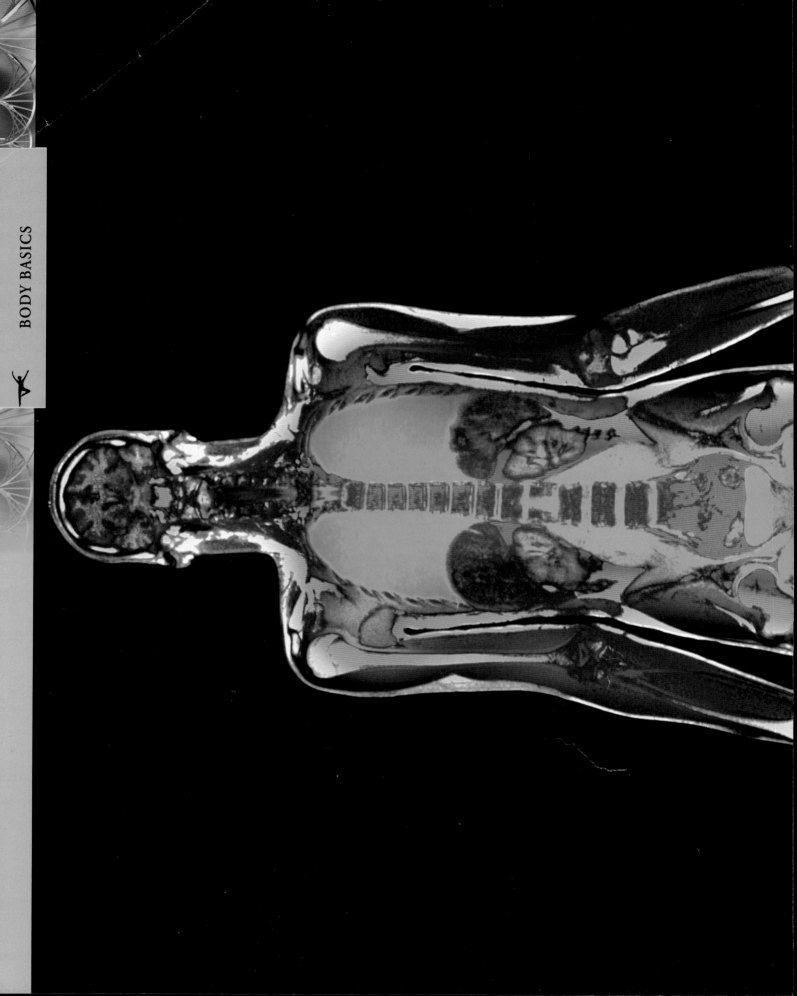

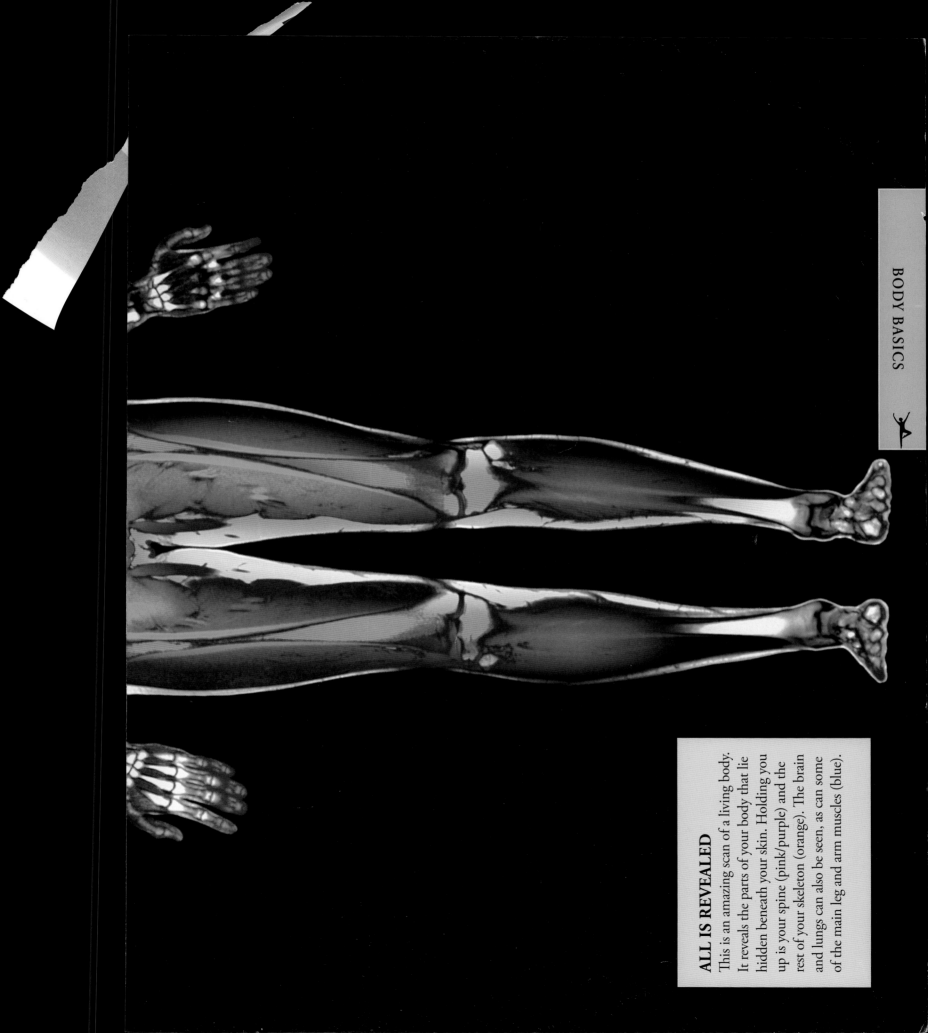

ALL IS REVEALED

This is an amazing scan of a living body. It reveals the parts of your body that lie hidden beneath your skin. Holding you up is your spine (pink/purple) and the rest of your skeleton (orange). The brain and lungs can also be seen, as can some of the main leg and arm muscles (blue).

Outer barrier

Wrapped around your body like a protective overcoat, your skin forms a barrier between the inside of your body and the outside world. Your skin is waterproof, keeps out germs, and repairs itself. It also filters out harmful rays in sunlight, enables you to feel your surroundings, and helps control your body temperature.

UNDER THE SKIN

The largest organ in your body, skin is just millimeters thick. It has two layers—the epidermis and dermis. Cells in the base of the epidermis divide constantly, producing cells that move to the surface, flatten, and fill with a tough, waterproof protein called keratin. The thicker dermis contains sweat glands, blood vessels, and other structures that perform the skin's many tasks.

The hair shaft sprouts above the skin's surface from a follicle.

The epidermis is the upper part of the skin. It has several layers.

The dermis is the lower part of the skin. It contains blood vessels.

Sebaceous glands release an oily substance, sebum, that softens hair and skin.

Arteries supply food and oxygen to skin cells.

Nerve carry signals from touch receptors toward the brain.

LOOK CLOSER: TEMPERATURE CONTROL

Skin performs a vital role in keeping your body temperature at a steady 98.6 °F (37 °C). In hot conditions, dermis blood vessels widen to lose extra heat, and sweat evaporates from the skin to cool the body. When it's cold, dermis blood vessels narrow to keep heat from escaping and tiny muscles pull body hairs upright in an effort to trap warm air, lifting the skin into goosebumps.

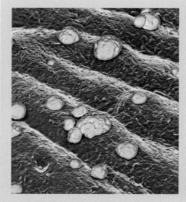

▲ SWEAT *This magnified view shows tiny sweat droplets on the surface of a fingertip.*

▲ GOOSEBUMPS *The skin's surface is covered in little bumps if we get too cold.*

WOW!

We lose about 50,000 skin flakes every minute, and 44 lbs (20 kg) of flakes in a lifetime.

◄ SKIN CELLS
Continually worn away, these dead, flat skin cells are replaced by cells that move to the surface from the lowest layer of the epidermis.

SUN PROTECTION

Sunlight contains harmful ultraviolet rays that can damage skin cells. As a defensive barrier, skin contains special cells called melanocytes. These cells produce melanin, a natural brown pigment (coloring substance) that passes into neighboring epidermis cells. Here, melanocytes form a screen that blocks ultraviolet rays. In sunny weather melanin production increases, producing a suntan.

Receptors detect touch, cold, heat, or pain.

Flat, dead cells on surface of epidermis

Melanin granules spread out in epidermis cells

This tiny muscle pulls the hair upright in cold conditions.

Epidermis cell   *Melanocyte*

A hair follicle is a narrow pocket in the skin from which a hair grows.

The fat layer under the skin stores energy and helps keep you warm.

Sweat glands release watery sweat onto the skin's surface to cool you down.

FINGERPRINTS

Packed with receptors, your fingers are incredibly sensitive. They also have tiny ridges that help you grip objects. On hard surfaces, such as glass, ridges leave behind patterns called fingerprints. There are three main types of patterns—loop, whorl, and arch—but each person's fingerprint is unique. That's why the police use them to identify criminals.

Loop

Arch

Whorl

Hair and nails

Made from dead cells packed with a tough substance called keratin, both hair and nails grow from the skin. Millions of hairs grow on your body. These include thicker hairs on your head and finer vellus hairs elsewhere. Nails cover the ends of your fingers and toes, and also help you grip small objects when you pick them up.

BODY PROTECTION

Hairs are flexible strands that have different protective roles according to where they grow. Scalp hairs, for example, protect the head from sunlight. Nails are hard plates that protect and support the sensitive tips of your fingers and toes. Both of these body protectors are made from dead cells, so it doesn't hurt when you get your hair cut or trim your nails.

▶ EYELASHES
These help protect the eyes by shading them from sunlight and trapping dust particles. Anything that touches the eyelashes triggers blinking.

▼ VELLUS HAIRS *These fine hairs make us more sensitive to touch. For example, if an insect lands on vellus hairs you will feel it, warning you that you may be bitten.*

STRAIGHT, WAVY, OR CURLY?

What type of hair you have depends on the shape of your scalp hairs. The shafts of straight hair are round, those of wavy hair are oval, while curly hair shafts are flat. A hair's shape depends on whether it grows from a round, oval, or flat follicle.

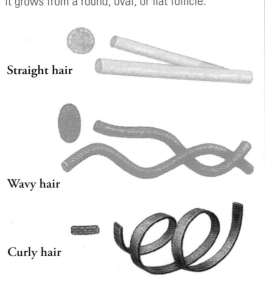

Straight hair

Wavy hair

Curly hair

▲ SCALP HAIRS *Growing from its follicle (pink), this is one of the 100,000 hairs on the scalp. Scales on the outside of the hair overlap, just like roof tiles.*

Each day, about 120 scalp hairs are lost and replaced.

HOW HAIR GROWS

Each hair grows from a narrow hole called a follicle. At the hair's base, living cells divide, pushing upward to make the shaft longer. As they do so, cells fill with keratin and die. After a phase of growth, a hair is pushed out by its replacement.

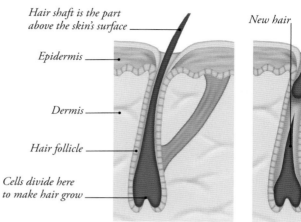

Hair shaft is the part above the skin's surface

Old hair is pushed out of the follicle by new hair

New hair

Epidermis

Dermis

Hair follicle

Cells divide here to make hair grow

Plug blocks opening to follicle

Red, inflamed tissue

White blood cells and bacteria form pus

Oily sebum

Sebaceous gland releases sebum

Hair follicle

GETTING PIMPLES

Sebum—the skin's natural oil—is released into hair follicles to soften hairs. But too much sebum can block hair follicles, causing pimples. Bacteria infecting the trapped sebum are attacked by white blood cells. This makes the follicle red, painful, and filled with creamy pus.

NAIL STRUCTURE

As this cutaway view shows, nails have a root, a body, and a free edge. Living cells in the matrix behind the root divide constantly. The new cells push the nail body forward, filling with keratin and dying as they do so. This makes the edge of the nail grow by about 0.11 in (3 mm) a month.

◄ NAILS *Seen under a microscope, these are the dead, flattened cells that nails are made of. Packed with keratin, the cells form plates that interlock to make nails really hard.*

Fat underneath skin

Nail matrix is where new nail is formed

Nail root

Body of nail

Free edge of nail

Finger bone

warm and moist, your skin makes a perfect home for millions of germs and bugs that are often too small to see with the naked eye. Unknowingly, we carry around these passengers day and night. Many feed on skin cells and oils; others suck blood. Luckily for us, these passengers are often harmless, and some even protect us from dangerous germs.

The needle-like sucking mouthparts withdraw when a louse is not feeding.

Head lice have gray-brown bodies, but after feeding on blood they can often look reddish. Hungry head lice can feed up to five times a day.

◄ HEAD LOUSE
In microscopic view, this head louse can be seen gripping on to a strand of hair.

HAIR GRIPPERS

With their flattened bodies and sharp, grasping claws, tiny head lice crawl through hair, piercing the scalp to suck blood. Between feeds they grip hairs, making it difficult to wash or comb them away. The wingless insects live for about 30 days. They mainly infect children and are passed on when heads touch.

A head louse relies on its two sensitive feelers (antennae) to detect movement and to smell.

The legs end in sharp, curved claws that are perfect for grasping hairs, preventing the louse from being dislodged.

A head louse egg, called a nit, is glued firmly to a scalp hair. A female head louse can lay up to 10 eggs a day.

BURROWING MITES

Eyelash mites are wormlike creatures that live head downward inside the eyelash follicles. Here they feast on oily sebum and dead skin cells. You cannot see or feel them, and they are often harmless. They emerge from their human homes at night and wander over the skin, as can be seen in this magnified view.

FRIENDLY GERMS

Millions of germs, such as these ball-shaped skin bacteria called *Staphylococcus* (meaning "bunches of grapes") live on your body, favoring damper, warmer places such as armpits. Many deter other harmful bacteria from settling on your body's surface. But if the skin is cut, bacteria can get inside the body, multiply rapidly, and cause infection.

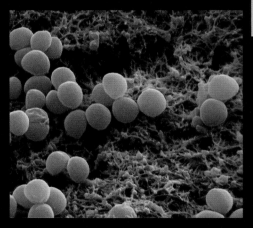

BED CRAWLERS

Wingless bedbugs find their victims by detecting body warmth. Most active at night, they emerge from their hiding places, pierce the skin of sleeping victims, and feed on blood, leaving itchy rashes and bite marks. After feeding for about five minutes, the blood-swollen bugs scurry back to their hiding places to digest their meal.

Bedbugs have flattened, oval bodies with three pairs of curved legs.

WOW!

If thousands of skin bacteria can fit onto the period at the end of this sentence, imagine how many are living on your skin.

BONES AND MUSCLES

 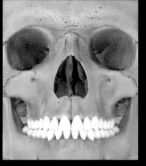 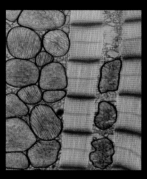

Find out how your bones, muscles, and joints work together to support and move your body—from throwing and kicking a ball, to shaping your facial expressions.

Supporting skeleton

Without the skeleton, your body would collapse into a shapeless heap. Built from hard, strong bones, the skeleton not only holds up your body but also allows it to move. It surrounds organs such as the brain and heart, and protects them from damage caused by everyday knocks and jolts. Your bones also make blood cells and store calcium, a mineral that is essential for healthy teeth.

TWO SKELETONS

The skeleton can be divided into two main parts. The axial skeleton (cream) consists of the backbone, skull, ribs, and breastbone. It runs down the center of the body and supports and protects important organs. The appendicular skeleton (blue) consists of the arms and legs and the girdles that attach them to the axial skeleton.

The shoulder (pectoral girdle) is formed by the clavicle and scapula bones.

The hip (pelvic girdle) is formed from two linked hipbones.

The kneecap (patella) protects the front of the knee joint.

The thighbone (femur) is the skeleton's biggest bone, and supports the weight of the upper body.

▲ BONE NUMBERS
Eighty bones make up the axial skeleton. The appendicular skeleton has 126.

Your skeleton makes up around 20 percent of your body's weight.

The shinbone (tibia) links knee to ankle and carries most of the body's weight.

The fibula is the smaller lower leg bone that forms part of the ankle.

The metatarsal is one of the five sole bones in the foot.

FLEXIBLE FRAMEWORK

An adult skeleton is made up of 206 bones, many of which you can see in this model. The framework that these bones create is not rigid. Movable joints, such as the knee joint between the thighbone and shinbone, make the skeleton flexible. They allow the body to move when bones are pulled by muscles.

The skull shapes the head and face, surrounds and protects the brain, and houses the eyes and ears.

▶ SMALLEST BONE *The size of a rice grain, the stirrup (stapes) is the body's smallest bone. It is one of three bones, called ossicles, found inside each ear.*

The ulna is the inner bone of the forearm.

The radius is the outer forearm bone that forms the elbow joint with the ulna and humerus.

The collarbone (clavicle) helps hold the shoulder and arm out to the side of the body.

The humerus is the upper arm bone that links the shoulder to the elbow.

The breastbone (sternum) provides an attachment point for the ribs and protects the heart.

The ribs are 12 pairs of curved bones that support the chest and play a role in breathing.

The shoulder blade (scapula) forms the shoulder joint with the humerus.

The backbone is a flexible column of bones (vertebrae) that holds the head and upper body upright.

WILHELM ROENTGEN

In 1895, German physicist Wilhelm Roentgen discovered X-rays. He found that when X-rays were projected through the body onto a photographic plate, they produced clear images of bones.

The hip girdle supports organs in the lower abdomen and forms a hip joint with each thighbone.

SEEING THE SKELETON

Doctors use X-rays to see the skeleton inside living bodies. X-rays help doctors to diagnose damaged or broken bones. X-rays also reveal how some bones, such as the ribs, perform an important role by surrounding and protecting soft organs.

◀ CHEST X-RAY *This X-ray shows a man's healthy lungs (dark areas) and heart (pale blue) enclosed by the ribs (pale bands).*

Inside bones

Just like your heart or eyes, your bones are living organs. Bones are made from cells as well as a mix of materials that make them hard and tough, but also slightly springy. Their structure makes them strong enough to support your body, but light enough not to weigh you down.

◄ COMPACT BONE
This outer part of the bone is made from cylinders of hard bone tissue that run along the length of the bone, making it strong. At the center are blood vessels (red).

ALL ABOUT BONES

Although all bones differ in shape and size, they have the same basic structure. A hard, tough outer layer of compact bone surrounds a lighter mass of spongy bone, while a network of blood vessels delivers the essential supplies that keep your bones alive. Some bones also have a central space filled with a jellylike material called bone marrow.

► INSIDE A BONE
Part of a long bone, this thighbone (femur) has been cut away so you can see its structure.

Vein

Yellow bone marrow stores fat rich in energy.

Artery

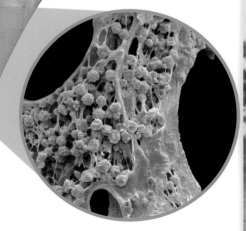

◄ SPONGY BONE
Despite its name, spongy bone is not soft but strong. Lighter than compact bone, it helps reduce the bone's total weight.

Spongy bone is thickest near the ends of the bone because it is here that your bone has to bear the most stress.

▲ RED BONE MARROW
This soft tissue fills the spaces in spongy bone. It produces all the different types of blood cells. This close-up image shows both red blood cells (red) and white blood cells (blue) in the bone marrow.

Long bones like this one are also found in your arms.

These blood vessels supply oxygen and nutrients to the bone and remove waste.

A tough membrane protects the bone's surface and provides an anchor for your muscles.

The shaft links the bone's two rounded heads.

Bone tissue contains calcium, a substance obtained from food such as milk and cheese.

LOOK CLOSER: BUILD OR BREAK

Your bones are constantly being broken down and built up to make sure they are as strong as possible. Two types of cells are responsible. These cells are known as osteoblasts and osteoclasts.

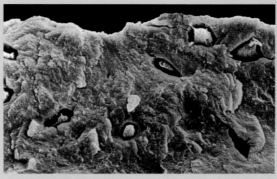

▲ OSTEOBLASTS *Found on the surface of the bone, osteoblasts are bone-building cells. They are surrounded here by the bone tissue (orange) they have just made.*

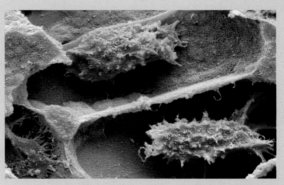

▲ OSTEOCLASTS *These cells (pink) break down worn-out bone. Here they are busy eating away at the surrounding tissue (cream).*

WOW!

Your red bone marrow makes red blood cells at a rate of about 2 million cells every second.

BUILT FOR STRENGTH

Your bones are far stronger and lighter than concrete or steel. If your skeleton was made from steel it would weigh five times as much, making it almost impossible for you to move around. The complex honeycomblike design of tiny struts and hollow spaces inside bones has been copied in many man-made structures.

The head of the thighbone carries the body's weight.

These criss-cross struts in spongy bone are arranged in a way that provides maximum support.

Compact bone is tough and dense so that it doesn't buckle under stress.

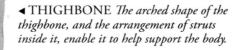

◄ THIGHBONE *The arched shape of the thighbone, and the arrangement of struts inside it, enable it to help support the body.*

▲ EIFFEL TOWER, FRANCE *The arch at the base of this tower supports its weight, helped by the criss-cross pattern of metal struts.*

Living bones

Your bones are not lifeless. Packed with blood vessels, nerves, and cells, they can bleed when cut and can grow and repair themselves. Bones appear a few weeks after a baby starts to develop in its mother's womb, and continue growing after birth, through childhood, and into early adulthood.

▼ IN THE WOMB *By 17 weeks, the bones in this skeleton have grown enough for the unborn baby to make movements.*

☐ Bone
☐ Cartilage

EARLY SKELETON

Babies are born with more than 300 bones, but these are not fully formed. As the baby grows, some of these bones fuse together to form bigger bones. A baby's skull is flexible to help the mother give birth.

The strong, flat bones of the skull protect the brain.

HOW BONES GROW

When bones first form, they are made of flexible cartilage, like the tissue that supports your ear. As the weeks and years pass, bone cells turn this soft cartilage framework into much harder bone. This process eventually finishes at the age of 20.

The spaces between a baby's skull bones allow the brain to grow.

Lower jaw

The upper arm bone (humerus) is one of the skeleton's long bones.

Shoulder blade

The curved ribs surround delicate organs to protect them from being crushed.

▶ CARTILAGE TO BONE
This sequence shows the development of a long bone.

The long bone is made of flexible cartilage.

Seven-week-old embryo

Hard, compact bone tissue has formed.

Cartilage

These blood vessels supply the bone cells.

Twelve-week-old fetus (unborn baby)

Strong but light spongy bone has formed.

Compact bone

The cartilage protects the ends of the bone.

The long bone has growth areas made from cartilage, which allows the bone to lengthen.

During childhood

HEALING BONES

If bones break or fracture, the healing process begins immediately. Within hours, as you can see in this section of a broken long bone, a blood clot forms to stop bleeding from vessels inside the bone. Then rebuilding begins. Cartilage is used to make a temporary repair and is gradually replaced by stronger bone cells. The whole process takes about 12 weeks, but is longer for leg bones that carry the body's weight.

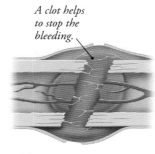

A clot helps to stop the bleeding.

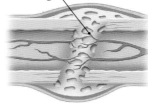

The new blood vessels start to grow through the cartilage.

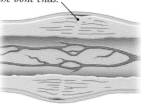

The new bone tissue connects the bone ends.

▲ THREE HOURS
Within hours a blood clot forms between the bone ends.

▲ THREE WEEKS
The cartilage replaces the clot to bridge the gap in the bone.

▲ THREE MONTHS
The bone replaces the cartilage and the break is repaired.

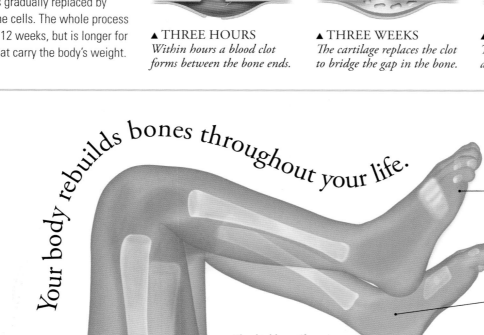

Your body rebuilds bones throughout your life.

In the womb, cartilage still makes up much of a baby's skeleton.

This cartilage will be replaced by the small, knobby bones known as short bones, as the baby grows.

The thighbone (femur) will become the longest bone in the body.

This part of the hip bone forms a flexible joint with the thighbone.

The chain of bones that makes up the backbone is made mostly of light spongy bone.

People most commonly break bones in their fingers, wrists, and arms.

WOW!

LOOK CLOSER: FIXING FRACTURES

When an arm or leg bone is broken, a doctor first takes an X-ray to see where the break is. Once realigned, the bones are wrapped in a rigid cast to make sure that they hold together and heal properly. If a fracture is really bad, doctors use metal pins and plates to fix the bones in place.

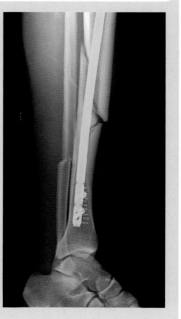

▶ PINNED BONES
This X-ray shows a small number of tiny pins and a plate (yellow) being used to hold the broken leg bones together.

Moving joints

Wherever two or more bones meet in your skeleton, they form a joint. Some of these joints are fixed and rigid. But most are free-moving joints that give your skeleton incredible flexibility, allowing you to run, write, and perform many other movements. Joints also provide stability by holding your bones together.

FLEXIBLE JOINTS

You have six main types of free-moving (synovial) joints in your body. Each joint has its own range of movement depending on how the bones fit together in the joint. The ball-and-socket joint in your hip, for example, allows you to move your leg in most directions, while the hinge joint in your elbow allows for movement in one direction only.

▶ PIVOT JOINT
In this joint, the rounded end of one bone fits within another, like a peg pushed through a hole. Found at the top of your neck, the joint allows you to turn your head from side to side.

▲ SADDLE JOINT
Your thumb has the only saddle joint in your body. It allows movement in two directions—from side to side and back and forth—making your thumb more flexible than your fingers.

HOW JOINTS WORK

This is an inside view of a synovial joint. It is held together by a tough fibrous capsule. The bone ends are covered by a flexible, rubbery tissue called cartilage and separated by synovial fluid, which helps oil the joint. Together they allow the joint to move smoothly.

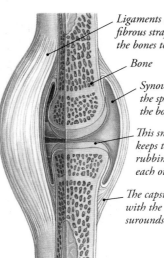

Ligaments are strong, fibrous straps that hold the bones together.

Bone

Synovial fluid fills the space between the bones.

This smooth cartilage keeps the bones from rubbing against each other.

The capsule, together with the ligaments, surrounds the joint.

WOW!
There are about 400 joints in the body, and more than 250 of these are free-moving, synovial joints.

▲ BALL-AND-SOCKET JOINT
This flexible joint is formed where the ball-like head of one bone fits into the shallow cup-shaped socket of another. It allows you to swing your arms and legs in most directions.

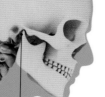

The joints in your skull are fused together to protect your brain.

A hinged joint in your jaw allows for movement.

▲ ELLIPSOIDAL JOINT
Found in your knuckles and in your wrists, a dome-shaped bone fits into the cavity of another bone, allowing up-and-down and side-to-side movements.

Lower leg bone

Heel bone

Sole bone

STRONG HOLD

Many joints, such as these between the foot and leg bones, are held together by tough straps of fibrous tissue called ligaments. These allow the joints to move but prevent the bones from being pulled apart.

More than a dozen ligaments are attached to your ankle, heel, and sole bones, providing both support and stability.

SUPER FLEXIBLE

People whose bodies are very flexible are sometimes called double-jointed. This doesn't mean that they have more joints than normal; rather, their ligaments are more stretchy, making their joints more flexible. Gymnasts in particular have unusually flexible joints, but they also need to maintain this flexibility by exercising.

▲ HINGE JOINT
Just like a door hinge that moves in one direction, this joint works in the same way, allowing you to bend or straighten your elbows, knees, fingers, and toes.

🔍 LOOK CLOSER: PULLED APART

Sometimes a sudden knock or blow can force bones out of their normal position. The joint between those bones is said to be dislocated. Doctors treat a dislocation by forcefully moving bones back into their correct position.

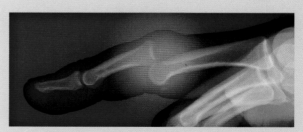

▲ DISLOCATED FINGER *This X-ray of the hand shows clearly how two finger bones have been pulled apart at a knuckle joint.*

▲ PLANE JOINT *This type of joint allows you to make small gliding movements only. It forms where two flat bone ends fit tightly together, such as in your ankle.*

Hardheaded

Your skull is the most complex part of your skeleton. It is made up of 22 bones, but only your lower jaw bone can move. The others are fused together to form a superstrong case that protects your brain and the main sense organs. It also forms a foundation for your face, shaping how you look.

WOW!

The U-shaped hyoid bone in your lower jaw is the only bone in the body that is not attached to another bone. It provides a moving base for the tongue.

Eight thin but incredibly strong bones form the domed part of your skull.

TIGHT FIT
The skull bones of a newborn baby are loosely joined by soft tissue. This allows the skull to expand as the baby's brain grows. By about the age of 18 months, the soft tissue is replaced by bony joints called sutures. These lock together like the pieces of a jigsaw puzzle to form a rigid case.

Each eye socket is a ball-shaped hollow area with a hole at the back for the optic nerve. This nerve carries information from your eye to your brain.

A triangular hole in the front of the skull leads to an air passage behind the nose called the nasal cavity.

An adult has a full set of 32 teeth, firmly rooted in the bones of the upper and lower jaws.

▲ SIDE VIEW
The sutures, where most of the skull bones are joined together, are clearly visible in this side view of a skull.

SKULL KIT

If you were to separate all the bones in a human skull, you would find that most of the biggest bones fit together to form the cranium—the strong bony case that surrounds and protects your brain. The others are the facial bones that contain your teeth and anchor the face muscles, which give you a wide range of facial expressions.

■ **Cranial bones**
☐ **Facial bones**

Your spinal cord passes through this big hole where the skull joins the spine.

Your upper jaw is made up of two bones that also form the base of each eye socket.

Small blood vessels that serve the brain pass through tiny holes in the bones.

Built for strength, your mobile lower jaw is a single bone, studded with 16 teeth.

◄ SEPARATE BONES
This view of the skull shows 20 of the 22 bones (the two tiny bones that sit on each corner of the eye are not shown). Most of the bones of the skull are paired to give your face shape.

The skull sutures form wavy lines where the bones interlock.

Each cheekbone arches out below the eye socket, rejoining the skull behind the jaw.

Your movable lower jaw enables you to breathe, speak, and eat.

DOUBLE PROTECTION

The brain is your body's control center. It has double protection against damage. First, the skull's rounded shape makes it extra strong, like a crash helmet, as can be seen in this image. Then, within the skull, there is a layer of shock-absorbing padding.

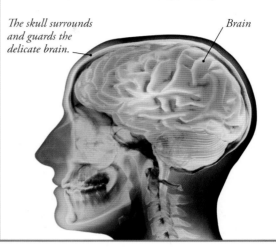

The skull surrounds and guards the delicate brain.

Brain

NOSE SUPPORTER

Most of your nose is not supported by bone, but by a tough, flexible material called cartilage. The same fibrous material supports your ears, which is why they are so bendable. Cartilage also forms springy pads in your joints to keep the ends of the bones from grinding together.

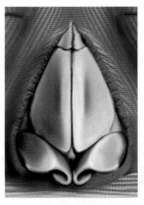

WEIGHT SAVERS

Some of the skull bones around your nose contain hollow, air-filled spaces called sinuses. These spaces help reduce the weight of your skull, and also act as sound boxes that add tone to your voice. They are connected to your nasal cavity through small openings, which may become blocked if you catch a bad cold.

Your sinuses are found on either side of your nose.

The hollow areas are like echo chambers.

41

Bending backbone

Running from your skull down to your hips is a long chain of bones, forming your backbone. This strong column of bones holds your head and body upright but at the same time allows your neck and back to twist and bend. Your backbone also protects your delicate spinal cord—a large bundle of nerve fibers that sends messages to and from your brain to the rest of your body.

▼ ATLAS AND AXIS
The atlas, the topmost bone, allows your head to nod. It also rotates on the axis bone beneath it so your head can turn from side to side.

STACK OF BONES

Twenty-six ring-shaped bones called vertebrae form your S-shaped backbone. There are seven neck bones supporting your head and 12 chest bones that are linked to your ribs. Your lower back has five lumbar bones that bear most of the weight of your upper body, and a group of small bones in the sacrum and cocyx are fused together to form the tail-end of your backbone.

FLEXIBLE SPINE

The joints between any two vertebrae allow only limited movements. But added together, these small movements make your backbone very flexible. It can bend forward, backward, from side to side, and twist and turn. The backbone's soft curve gives it the springiness to absorb jolts as you move.

Your backbone curves gently, protecting the spinal cord from snapping.

Atlas

Axis

Neck (cervical) bones

Chest (thoracic) bones

A hole through each bone forms a tunnel-like area for the spinal cord.

Nerve roots exit through narrow spaces along the backbone.

WOW!

You have the same number of neck bones as a giraffe—the difference being that a giraffe's neck bones are much longer.

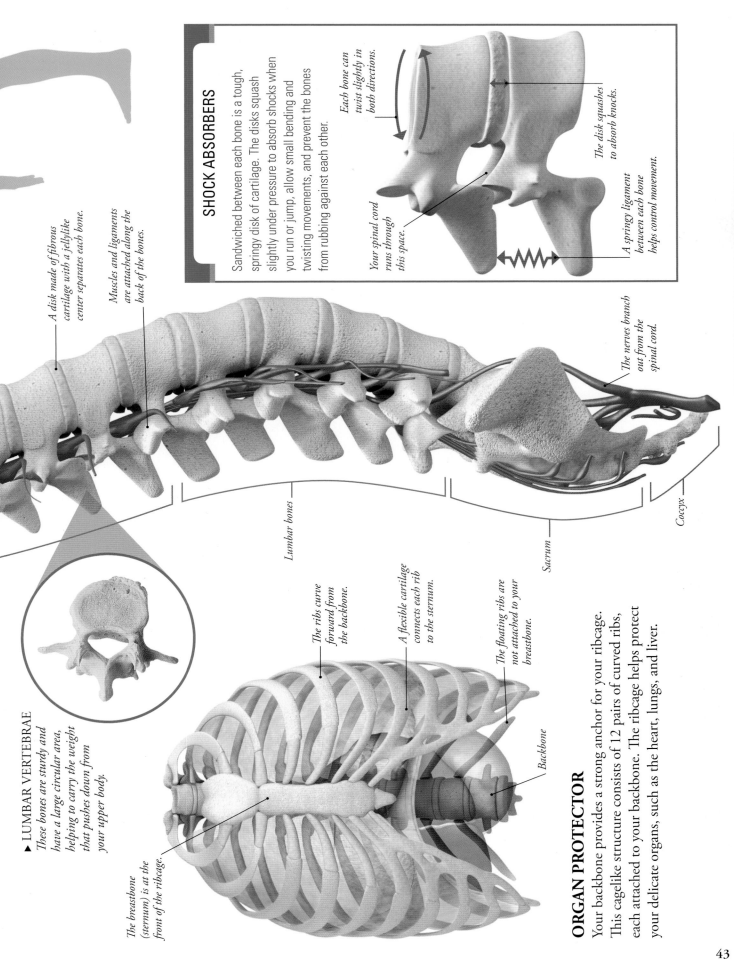

SHOCK ABSORBERS

Sandwiched between each bone is a tough, springy disk of cartilage. The disks squash slightly under pressure to absorb shocks when you run or jump, allow small bending and twisting movements, and prevent the bones from rubbing against each other.

Each bone can twist slightly in both directions.

The disk squashes to absorb knocks.

Your spinal cord runs through this space.

A springy ligament between each bone helps control movement.

A disk made of fibrous cartilage with a jellylike center separates each bone.

Muscles and ligaments are attached along the back of the bones.

The nerves branch out from the spinal cord.

Lumbar bones

Sacrum

Coccyx

▶ LUMBAR VERTEBRAE
These bones are sturdy and have a large circular area, helping to carry the weight that pushes down from your upper body.

The breastbone (sternum) is at the front of the ribcage.

The ribs curve forward from the backbone.

A flexible cartilage connects each rib to the sternum.

The floating ribs are not attached to your breastbone.

Backbone

ORGAN PROTECTOR

Your backbone provides a strong anchor for your ribcage. This cagelike structure consists of 12 pairs of curved ribs, each attached to your backbone. The ribcage helps protect your delicate organs, such as the heart, lungs, and liver.

43

SUPER STRETCHY

Contortionists are people who have unusually flexible joints and can twist their bodies into incredible shapes. They are often described as being double-jointed, but actually have the same number of joints as everyone else. Contortionists train hard to maintain and increase their flexibility.

Muscle machine

You can move because you have muscles—fleshy machines that turn fuel into motion by moving the bones of your skeleton. Some muscles are under your concious control, such as when you decide to move your hand and turn the page of this book. However, there are many other muscles working away without you knowing to keep your body alive, healthy, and upright.

MUSCLE TYPES

Your body has three types of muscle, seen here under a microscope. You use skeletal muscle to move your arms and legs, heart muscle to power your heart, and smooth muscle to move food along your digestive system.

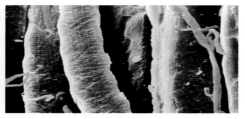

▲ SKELETAL MUSCLE *Made up of bundles of threadlike fibers, skeletal muscle shrinks and shortens to pull tight and move bones.*

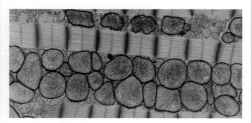

▲ HEART MUSCLE *This is a special type of muscle that never gets tired, because it has to keep your heart beating every day of your life.*

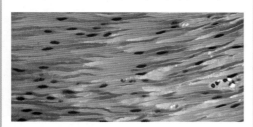

▲ SMOOTH MUSCLE *Made of long cells, often linked together in muscular sheets, smooth muscles form part of organs such as your stomach.*

The bulkiest muscle in your body pulls your leg straight at the hip.

AMAZING MUSCLES

The big muscles that cover your skeleton make up almost half your body weight. They form layers that work together to move all the parts of your body. About 640 of these skeletal muscles are under your conscious control. Some are very strong, like the ones at the tops of your legs, but others are built for precision rather than power.

The Achilles tendon connects your calf muscle to the heel bone.

The calf muscle pulls your heel up so you can walk, run, or stand on tiptoe.

Muscle

Tendon

◀ BONE CONNECTORS *Muscles are connected to your skeleton by tough, slightly stretchy straps of tendons. They allow muscles to move bones into position.*

Bone

This powerful neck muscle bends your head forward.

Muscles anchored to your skull work your jaw when you chew.

Your triceps straightens your arm at the elbow.

WOW! There are more than 14 muscles in your tongue, which is why it's so flexible!

Your chest muscles pull your arms in toward your body.

The biceps bends your elbow by pulling on the forearm.

There are no bones in your abdomen, so tough straps of muscle help strengthen this part of your body.

HOT WORK

Working muscles release heat—and the harder they work, the hotter they get. This image of a man exercising shows the hottest parts of his body in white, red, and yellow. His arms are hot because these muscles are working hard. But a lot of the heat is being carried away to the man's face, where it is more easily lost to the air. This keeps his body from overheating.

STAYING UPRIGHT

Some of your skeletal muscles are kept busy keeping you upright—especially your back and neck muscles. When you fall asleep, like this boy sleeping on a train, your muscles get the chance to relax and go floppy. Sleeping on a train is uncomfortable, but at night in your bed, the body is properly supported and your muscles get the rest they need.

>> FAST FACTS

■ You have three times as many muscles as bones in your body.
■ You use at least 12 muscles in your face just to smile at a friend.
■ The most powerful muscle is the masseter muscle in your jaw. You use it to chew food.

Body movers

Every movement you make depends on your muscles—from blinking and eating, to walking and riding a bike. Your movements are controlled by nerve signals from your brain, which instruct the muscles to work together to produce precise movements. To make these movements, your muscles need energy. This energy comes from food, which is delivered to your muscles by your blood.

Skeletal muscle

The blood vessels supply fuel and oxygen to your muscles.

Muscle fiber

This is one of the myofibrils inside a fiber.

There are thousands of filaments within a myofibril.

HOW MUSCLES WORK

Skeletal muscles, such as those found in your arms, are formed by bundles of muscle fibers. Each muscle fiber is made of smaller rod-shaped fibers called myofibrils, and within these are superthin fibers known as filaments. When the filaments slide together, all the muscle fibers shorten, so the whole muscle contracts, pulls on your bones, and moves your arm.

TEAMWORK

When a muscle is stimulated by a nerve signal, it contracts and gets shorter. It cannot make itself longer. This means that muscles can pull, but not push. Many muscles, such as the those in your upper arm, are arranged in pairs that work against each other, pulling in different directions. For instance, the biceps pulls your forearm up, and the triceps pulls it down again.

Bending your arm

A tendon links a muscle to the bone it pulls.

When your biceps contracts and gets shorter and thicker, your arm bends.

Located on the opposite side of the upper arm bone, your triceps relaxes and gets longer.

48

LOOK CLOSER: GETTING THE MESSAGE

Your muscles are told to contract by nerve signals. These signals are carried from your brain by neurons (nerve cells) inside the nerves linked to your muscles.

▲ NERVE-MUSCLE JUNCTION *This is the place where a neuron (green) makes contact with a muscle fiber (red) of a skeletal muscle.*

OUT OF BREATH

Exercising hard makes you feel out of breath. This is because your body uses energy released in a different way from normal for activities such as fast running. This process produces a substance that clogs up your muscles. This substance is removed by oxygen, and this is why you must breathe very hard to recover.

MUSCLE FOOD

If you want strong muscles, you need to exercise regularly and eat foods rich in muscle-building proteins. These include foods such as meat, fish, and eggs. You also need other foods that contain carbohydrates, such as bread, potatoes, and rice. These supply your muscles with the energy needed to move you.

Foods rich in protein

WOW!

The fastest muscles in the body are the ones that move your eyeballs. They shift your gaze in about two-hundredths of a second.

Straightening your arm

As your arm straightens, your biceps relaxes.

Your triceps pulls and gets shorter and thicker to make your arm straighten.

You were born with all your muscle fibers in place.

INSIDE MUSCLES

Shown here is a microscopic view of a bundle of skeletal muscle fibers (red). These muscles help shape and move your body. Without them you wouldn't be able to walk, talk, or stand upright. Altogether, there are about 640 skeletal muscles packed into your body.

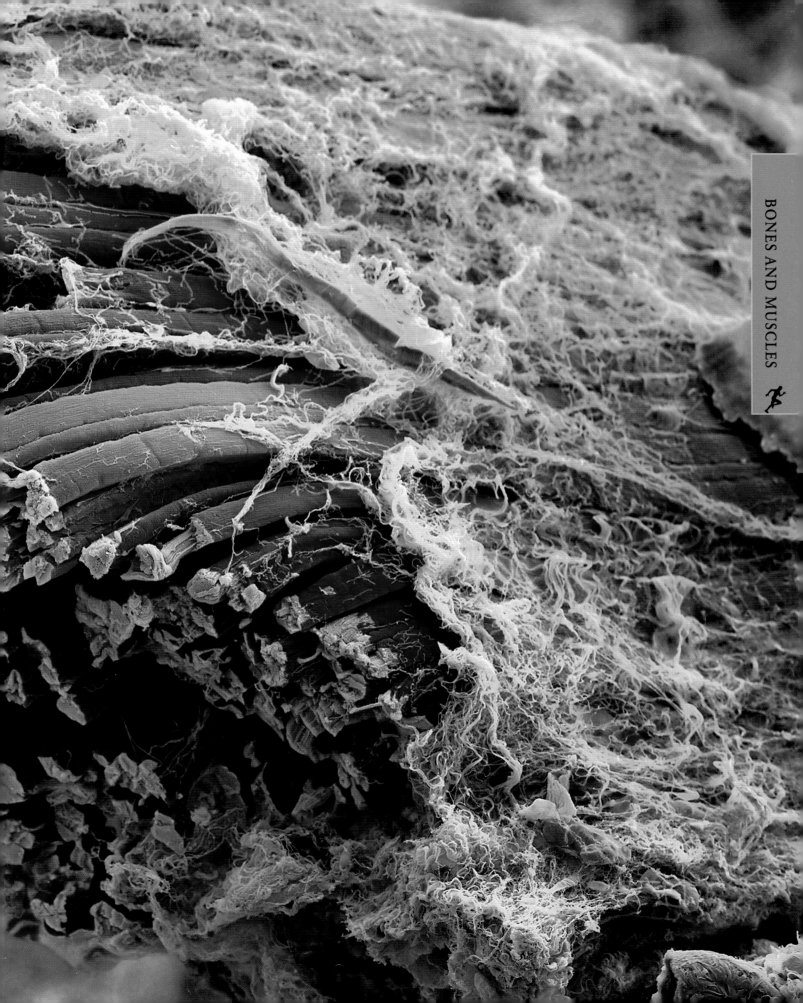

Making faces

Not all muscles pull on your bones to make you move. Controlled by signals from the brain, your facial muscles work with incredible precision, tugging on your skin to reveal what you are feeling without you even thinking about it. There are more than 7,000 different expressions, including those that last for a fraction of a second.

This flat forehead muscle raises the eyebrow and wrinkles the forehead.

The circular eye muscle helps close the eyelid.

The corner of your mouth is pulled upward and outward by this cheek muscle.

The muscle surrounding the mouth brings the lips together and also helps you shape the words when you speak.

This muscle pulls the corner of the mouth outward when you smile.

The corner of the mouth is pulled downward by this lower facial muscle.

◄ MAIN MOVERS *Shown here are some of the main muscles that produce facial expressions, along with the actions each performs.*

ALL IN THE FACE

Covering your face are thin elasticlike layers of muscle. Unlike skeletal muscles that are attached to bones, these facial muscles are attached at one end to your skull and at the other to your skin. A tiny, precise movement of one or more of these muscles pulls the skin and alters your expression.

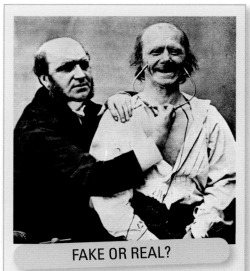

FAKE OR REAL?

In the 1860s, French doctor Guillaume Duchenne (left) studied the muscles that produced facial expressions. He used small electric shocks on his patients to trigger muscle movement, resulting in a variety of expressions, in this case a smile. During his investigation, Duchenne discovered the difference between a fake and a genuine smile—the latter involving muscle movement around the eye.

EXPRESSING FEELINGS

Your facial expressions reveal your emotions, communicating the way you feel to people around you. It is difficult to fake these expressions, because they are created automatically without us even thinking about it. The three examples shown below illustrate how different facial muscles work to reveal feelings of sadness, anger, and happiness.

◄ SADNESS
If you are feeling sad, the lips close, the lower facial muscles pull the mouth down at its corners, and the forehead muscles pull the eyebrows at their inner ends.

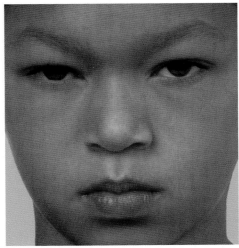

◄ ANGER
When you get angry, muscles pull the eyebrows down and wrinkle them. At the same time the circular eye muscles narrow the eyes, and the mouth muscles purse the lips.

◄ HAPPINESS
A smile is created by the muscles along the cheeks and those that lie along the side of the lips. These muscles stretch the mouth sideways and lift its corners upward.

REBUILDING FACES

Specialized artists combine skill in art with a detailed knowledge of anatomy to rebuild faces from the skulls of those who died recently or long ago. They use various materials to accurately rebuild layers of muscle and skin on the skull. The re-created face can then be used by historians, for example, to provide information about people from our past.

▲ MUSCLE LAYER *A forensic artist uses clay to reconstruct facial muscles on a skull.*

A USEFUL TOOL

Did you know you can use facial expressions to get what you want? Unable to talk, babies use a range of expressions such as gurgling, crying, or widening their eyes to help them get attention or food. Some pets, too, appear to mimic human expressions as a way of communicating.

WOW!

From smiles to scowls, basic facial expressions are understood by people all over the world.

Reaching out

Your body has the perfect tools for carrying out a variety of daily tasks, from holding a pen with delicate precision to throwing a ball with great force. The intricate framework of small bones in your hands is worked by the many muscles in your arms and together they are able to perform a multitude of movements.

BONES AND MUSCLES

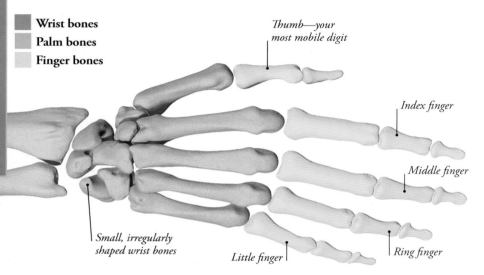

Wrist bones
Palm bones
Finger bones

Thumb—your most mobile digit

Index finger

Middle finger

Small, irregularly shaped wrist bones

Little finger

Ring finger

MOVE THOSE FINGERS

It takes about 30 muscles in each hand to move your fingers and thumbs. Most are located in your forearm, not your hand, and are attached to your hand bones by tough cordlike straps called tendons. Muscles on the top of your forearm straighten the fingers. Those on the underside of your arm and in the palm bend the fingers inward, so you can grasp and grip objects.

FLEXIBLE FRAMEWORK

Each hand is made up of 27 bones divided into three groups—eight wrist bones, five palm bones, and 14 finger (digit) bones. Some people are born with an extra digit, usually next to the little finger. The record is seven fingers on each hand!

Long, tough straps called tendons attach muscles to bones.

This joint allows you to move your wrist in all directions.

There is no muscle layer on the top of the hand, only tendons that move your fingers.

GETTING TO GRIPS

One of the most important features of your hand is your thumb. This digit has a unique joint that enables you to move it across your palm to touch the tips of your fingers. In addition to letting you pick up small objects, the thumb enables you to perform delicate and precise tasks. Try picking up a pencil without using your thumb and you'll see how much you rely on this digit.

▲ HOLDING A BRUSH *Small muscles in the hand press the thumb and fingers together to form a secure grip on an object.*

The muscles of the palm pull your fingers and thumb together.

The triceps works against your biceps to straighten the arm.

The fingers and wrist are straightened by this long, thin muscle.

These muscles stabilize and help straighten your elbow.

The arm is bent at the elbow by your biceps.

HANDY TOOLS

Having two arms that can both reach out and fold inward, along with hands that can grasp objects, enables us to perform a number of powerful movements. These include throwing a ball, swimming, and playing tennis.

▶ THROWING A BALL
This sequence shows the different muscles you use when you throw a ball. First, the muscles pull your arm back (green), then others lift it up (brown). Once the ball is released, the muscles pull your arm down (red).

WOW!

Between them, your two hands contain more than a quarter of your body's 206 bones.

SHOULDER JOINT

The shoulder joint is one of the most mobile joints in your body. The round end of the upper arm bone fits into a curved pocket in the shoulder blade. Known as a ball-and-socket joint, this allows you to move your arm in all directions. Your shoulder joint is held together by tough straps called ligaments.

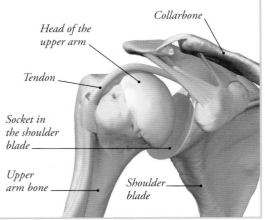

Collarbone

Head of the upper arm

Tendon

Socket in the shoulder blade

Upper arm bone

Shoulder blade

On the move

Your legs are the longest, strongest, and heaviest parts of your body. They need to be, since they hold you upright when you stand still and also provide the power to make you move. At the same time, your feet form a secure base, which supports your body weight, and push against the ground to help you walk or run.

FAST OR SLOW

Moving around on two legs requires strength. Much of the power comes from the thigh and buttock muscles, which also help keep you balanced when one foot is off the ground. Leg muscles are a mixture of fast fibers that can produce quick bursts of speed and slow fibers that work for longer periods without tiring.

The thinner lower leg bone is called the fibula.

Your hamstring muscles pull the thigh back and bend the knee.

This muscle lifts the foot upward and supports the foot arch when you walk or run.

This long muscle straightens your toes.

Your calf muscle bends your foot downward.

The Achilles tendon— a tough ropelike strap— attaches the calf muscle to the heel bone, enabling you to stand on your toes.

The muscles running along the sole move your toes and help cushion your foot.

The shinbone (tibia) is the largest bone in the lower leg.

The big toe has two bones—unlike the other toes, which have three bones each.

These long, thin sole bones form the arch of the foot.

FOOT WORK

The bony framework of your foot is stronger but less flexible than your hand because it has to support your body weight. Each foot has 26 bones—14 toe bones, five sole bones, and seven ankle bones.

The ankle bones work together to provide stability.

Sticking out from the back of the foot is your heel bone, the largest bone in your foot.

Ankle bones
Sole bones
Toe bones

A group of four powerful muscles— the quadriceps— straighten your knee when you kick.

These strong tendons keep the kneecap in place and allow your leg to flex and twist.

Your kneecap protects your knee joint.

ONE STEP AT A TIME

With each step you take, you push down first through your heel, then the springy sole, and finally your big toe, which lifts your body off the ground. This sequence of footprints shows the weight shift from heel to toe. The darker the green color, the more body weight is pushing downward.

Sole

Big toe

Pressure passes along the arch

Heel

WOW!

The average person will walk about 80,000 miles (128,000 km) in a lifetime. That's the same as walking around the world three times.

ON TIPTOE

When you stand on tiptoe, the calf muscles at the back of your lower leg pull the heel bone upward so that your foot is supported only by the toes. Dancing *en pointe* (on tiptoe) like a ballet dancer exerts a lot of pressure on your toes because your whole body weight presses down on a very small area of your body.

▶ EN POINTE *In this ballet position, the tendons on top of the foot are stretched to a maximum.*

IN ACTION

Your legs are the most muscular parts of your body. If you exercise or play sports, these muscles can become incredibly powerful. A professional soccer player, for example, can kick a ball with enough force to make it travel at about 70 mph (110 kph).

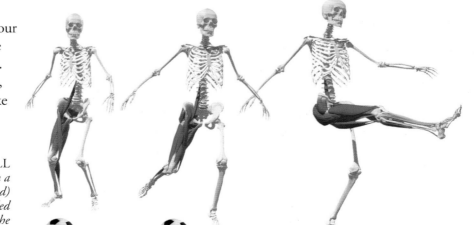

▶ KICKING A SOCCER BALL
This sequence shows what happens when a ball is kicked. Your hamstring muscles (red) pull the leg back. Then the thigh is pulled forward by the quadriceps (green), so that the lower leg can flick forward to kick the ball.

In space

When Yuri Gagarin made the first space flight in 1961, doctors had no idea what effect space travel would have on his body. Since then, nearly 700 people have flown in space, and we have discovered a lot about how the human body reacts to this extraordinary experience.

This visor has a thin layer of gold to shield the eyes from the Sun's harmful rays.

UPSIDE DOWN

On Earth, you know which way is up or down because gravity pulls your feet toward the ground. But in space there is no gravity. Your body floats around. Trainee astronauts can experience weightlessness (zero gravity) by taking flights in a specially designed aircraft known as the Vomit Comet.

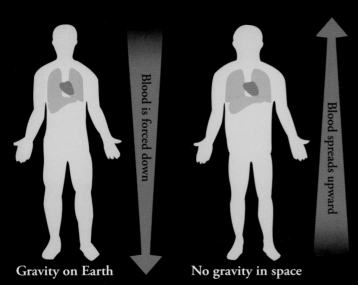

Gravity on Earth   Blood is forced down   No gravity in space   Blood spreads upward

FAST FACTS

■ Astronauts grow up to 2 in (5 cm) taller. This is because their backbone lengthens in space. But their height returns to normal when they come back to Earth.

■ Bones become weaker in space because they are not supporting the weight of the body, and without regular exercise, astronauts are prone to broken bones.

FAT FACE

On Earth, blood is drawn toward your feet by gravity. In space, your blood drifts upward, making your face fatter and your legs thinner—a condition known as bird's legs. Fluid collecting in your head also gives you a stuffy feeling, like having a cold.

BODY PROTECTION

Out in space, astronauts are exposed to all kinds of hazards. These include space debris, extreme cold, and lack of air. Inside the spacecraft, astronauts are protected from most of these dangers. However, they must wear special survival suits if they leave their spacecraft to make essential repairs to equipment or when exploring space such as during the Moon landings.

WOW!

Lying in bed for a long time has much the same effect on the body as being completely weightless in space.

In space, astronauts sneeze as much as 30 times an hour.

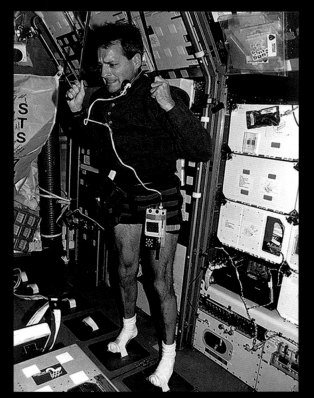

▲ SPACEWALK
The spacesuit protects the body, while the backpack provides vital air supplies during a spacewalk.

SPACE GYM

Astronauts use special equipment to exercise their bodies in the weightless conditions of space. Exercise helps relieve the effects of blood flowing to the head and gives muscles a workout that prevents them from wasting away through lack of use. This astronaut has his feet secured under straps to stop him from floating upward while exercising.

BACK TO EARTH

Returning to Earth is a strange experience, especially after many days of weightlessness. Weaker muscles and bones make it difficult for an astronaut to walk. In 2003, China's first astronaut Yang Liwei is carried from his spacecraft, as he gets used to the effects of Earth's gravity.

HEART AND BLOOD

See how your heart beats relentlessly 100,000 times a day. This hardworking organ pumps blood along an endless network of vessels, delivering essential supplies to each of your body's cells.

Around the body

To work efficiently, your body's trillions of cells need nonstop supplies of oxygen and food. This delivery service is provided by your blood, which flows continuously through an incredible branching network of tubes called blood vessels. The driving force behind this delivery service is your heart. Together the heart, blood, and blood vessels make up the circulatory system.

SUPER-FAST

Weaving through every part of your body are arteries and veins. These blood vessels are linked by capillaries, which are too small to be seen here. The shortest return journey that blood makes is from the heart to its own muscles, which takes a matter of seconds. The longest journey—to the toes and back—takes no more than a minute. Arteries carry blood away from the heart, while veins carry blood toward it.

NEVER-ENDING JOURNEY

Blood travels around your body in one direction through two loops. Linked by the heart, the shorter loop (blue arrows) carries blood to the lungs, where it picks up fresh oxygen. It then returns to the heart, taking oxygen-rich blood to the rest of your body along the longer loop (yellow arrows).

● Oxygen-rich blood
● Oxygen-poor blood

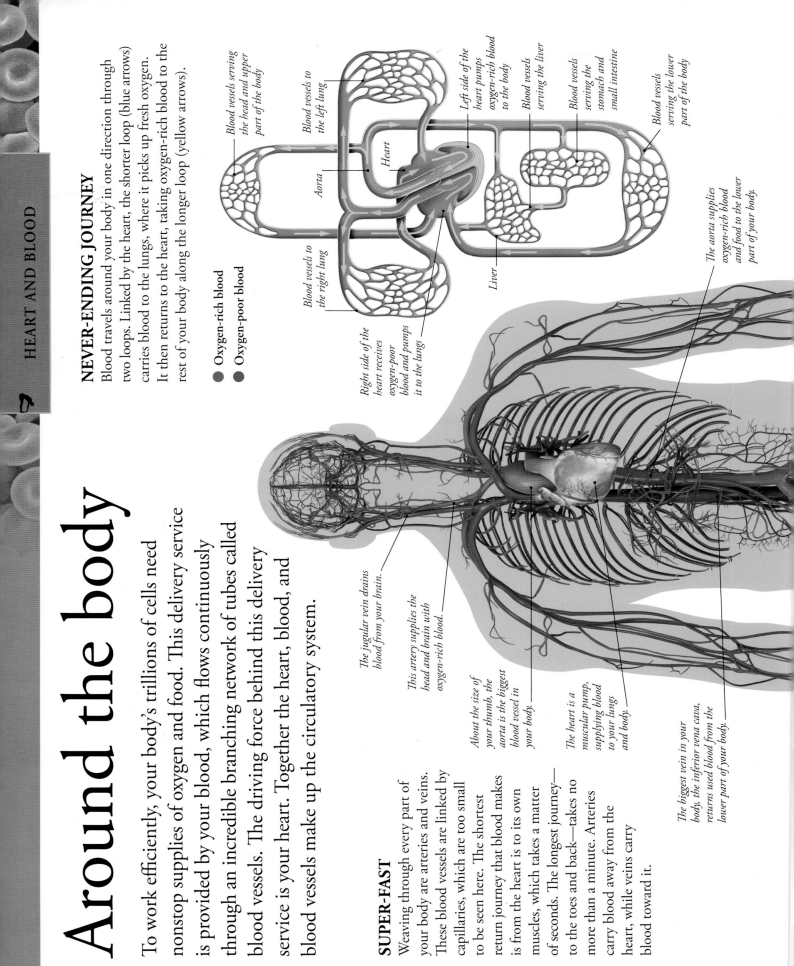

Blood vessels serving the head and upper part of the body

Blood vessels to the left lung

Left side of the heart pumps oxygen-rich blood to the body

Blood vessels serving the liver

Blood vessels serving the stomach and small intestine

Blood vessels serving the lower part of the body

Aorta

Heart

Liver

Blood vessels to the right lung

Right side of the heart receives oxygen-poor blood and pumps it to the lungs

The aorta supplies oxygen-rich blood and food to the lower part of your body.

The jugular vein drains blood from your brain.

This artery supplies the head and brain with oxygen-rich blood.

About the size of your thumb, the aorta is the biggest blood vessel in your body.

The heart is a muscular pump, supplying blood to your lungs and body.

The biggest vein in your body, the inferior vena cava, returns used blood from the lower part of your body.

Blood vessels stretch into every corner of your hand, forming a loop for the return journey to the heart.

The femoral vein drains blood from your thigh, carrying it to your heart.

BLOOD TRANSFUSIONS

Every day, lives are saved by the transfer, or transfusion, of blood from healthy donors to patients who have lost blood. Early blood transfusions often resulted in death. Only when doctors became aware of blood types (page 69) did the process become safer.

▲ EARLY TRANSFUSION *This 17th-century picture shows a transfusion of blood from a dog (far right) to a man, whose right arm is being bled.*

The femoral artery is the main artery in the upper leg, and lies close to your thighbone.

The longest vein in the body is called the saphenous vein, which rises from your foot to the top of your thigh.

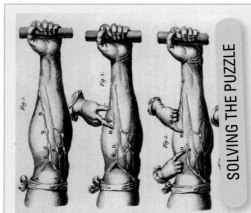

SOLVING THE PUZZLE

Since ancient times, no one knew how the heart and blood worked. The riddle was finally solved in the 1600s by English doctor William Harvey. He carried out various experiments, including tying a tight band around a person's upper arm and studying blood flow through the veins (shown above). Harvey discovered that blood circulated around the body, pumped by the heart.

WOW!

The blood flowing around your body gives the skin a pinkish tinge.

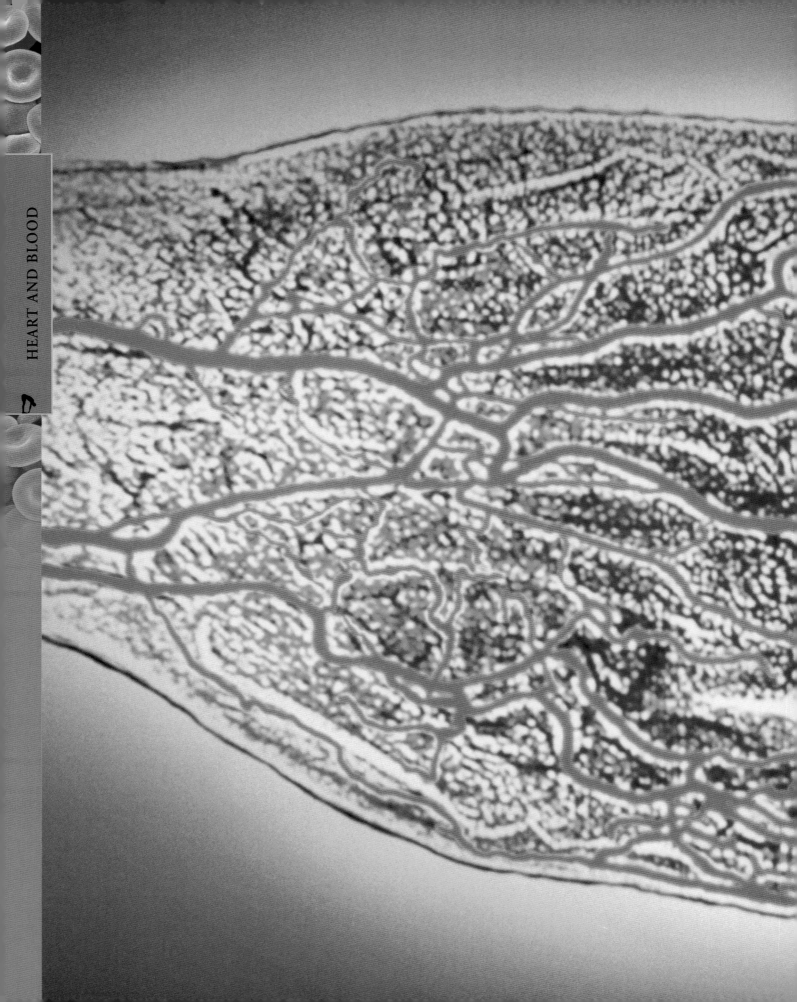

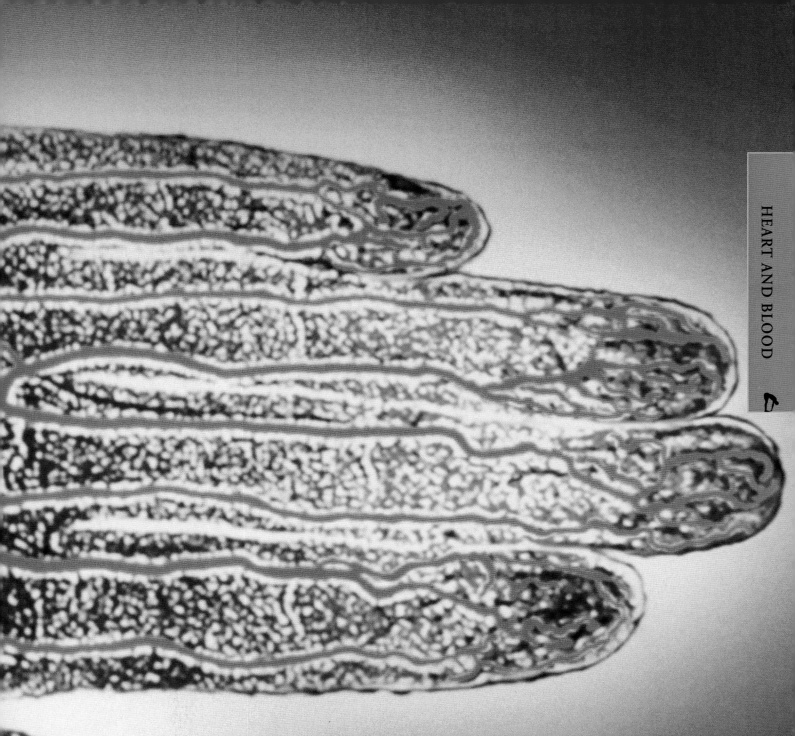

IN YOUR HANDS

This picture shows how your arteries form an incredible mazelike structure through your hand. It was taken by injecting dye into the arteries and X-raying them. Each finger is supplied by two arteries, which branch at the tips to deliver supplies to the skin cells under your nails.

Liquid life

Your blood is made of trillions of cells floating in a watery liquid called plasma—it is the red cells in your blood that give it its color. Every drop of blood goes on an incredible journey around your body thousands of times a day, carrying out vital tasks to keep your body working properly.

THE INGREDIENTS

Most of your blood is made from plasma—a clear liquid. The rest consists of red blood cells, white blood cells, and tiny cell pieces called platelets. Each ingredient carries out a specific task.

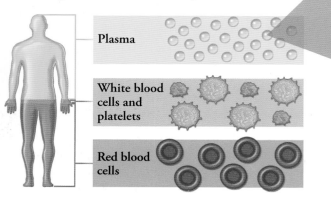

Plasma

White blood cells and platelets

Red blood cells

▲ PLASMA *This liquid carries the nutrients needed to keep your body cells alive.*

▶ BLOOD VESSEL *This cutaway view of a blood vessel shows the different blood cells carried in plasma.*

SUPER SERVICE

Transported by a network of tubes called blood vessels, blood delivers fuel and oxygen to your cells and takes away waste that would otherwise be harmful. Blood also distributes heat, keeping your body at a constant temperature. Its white blood cells form the first line of defense against germs that get into your body, while an army of platelets spring into action when it's time to heal wounds.

White blood cells defend your body by destroying germs. They are the largest of the blood cells.

WOW!

A pinhead-sized drop of blood contains about 2.5 million red blood cells, 3,750 white blood cells, and 160,000 platelets.

A blood vessel has a smooth lining so that blood flows through it easily.

TESTING BLOOD

Doctors often use blood tests to detect anything unusual in your blood, which might explain why you are feeling unwell. Here, a patient's finger has been pricked using a lancet and a sample of blood is collected on a test strip that detects specific substances.

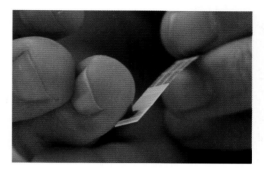

Red blood cells carry oxygen from your lungs to every cell in your body.

Platelets help heal a wound by forming a plug and by making blood clot.

MAKING RED BLOOD CELLS

All blood cells are made in red bone marrow. When you are young, nearly all bones contain red bone marrow. In adults, this is found only in the skull bones, ribs, shoulder blades, hipbones, and the ends of long bones.

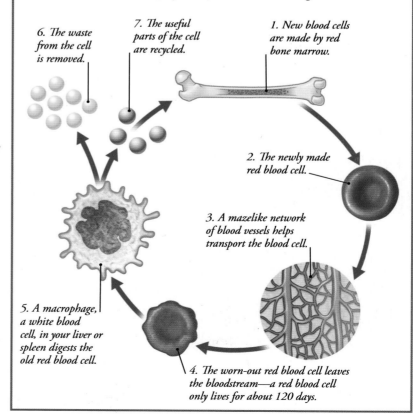

6. The waste from the cell is removed.

7. The useful parts of the cell are recycled.

1. New blood cells are made by red bone marrow.

2. The newly made red blood cell.

3. A mazelike network of blood vessels helps transport the blood cell.

5. A macrophage, a white blood cell, in your liver or spleen digests the old red blood cell.

4. The worn-out red blood cell leaves the bloodstream—a red blood cell only lives for about 120 days.

Oxygen carriers

Red blood cells are by far the most numerous cells in your body. These amazingly hardworking cells have the endless task of carrying oxygen to all your body cells to keep them alive. This demanding activity means that about two million red blood cells wear out every second, so your body has to make new cells at the same rate to replace them.

WOW!

You have about 25 trillion red blood cells circulating around your body.

▶ INSIDE THE CELL
Red blood cells are the only cells in the body that have no nucleus. Instead, they are packed with hemoglobin—the reddish protein that gives them their color.

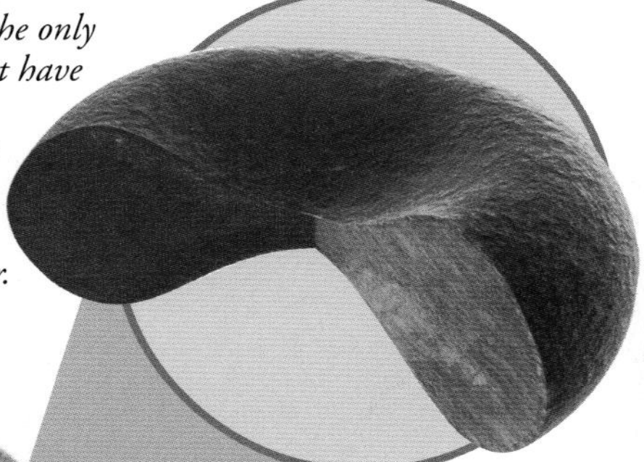

HARD AT WORK

Red blood cells are filled with the oxygen-carrying protein hemoglobin. As your blood flows through your lungs, hemoglobin picks up oxygen. Your blood transports this fresh supply of oxygen to all of your body's tissues, where hemoglobin releases the oxygen so that it can be used by your cells. Your red blood cells then return to your lungs to collect fresh supplies.

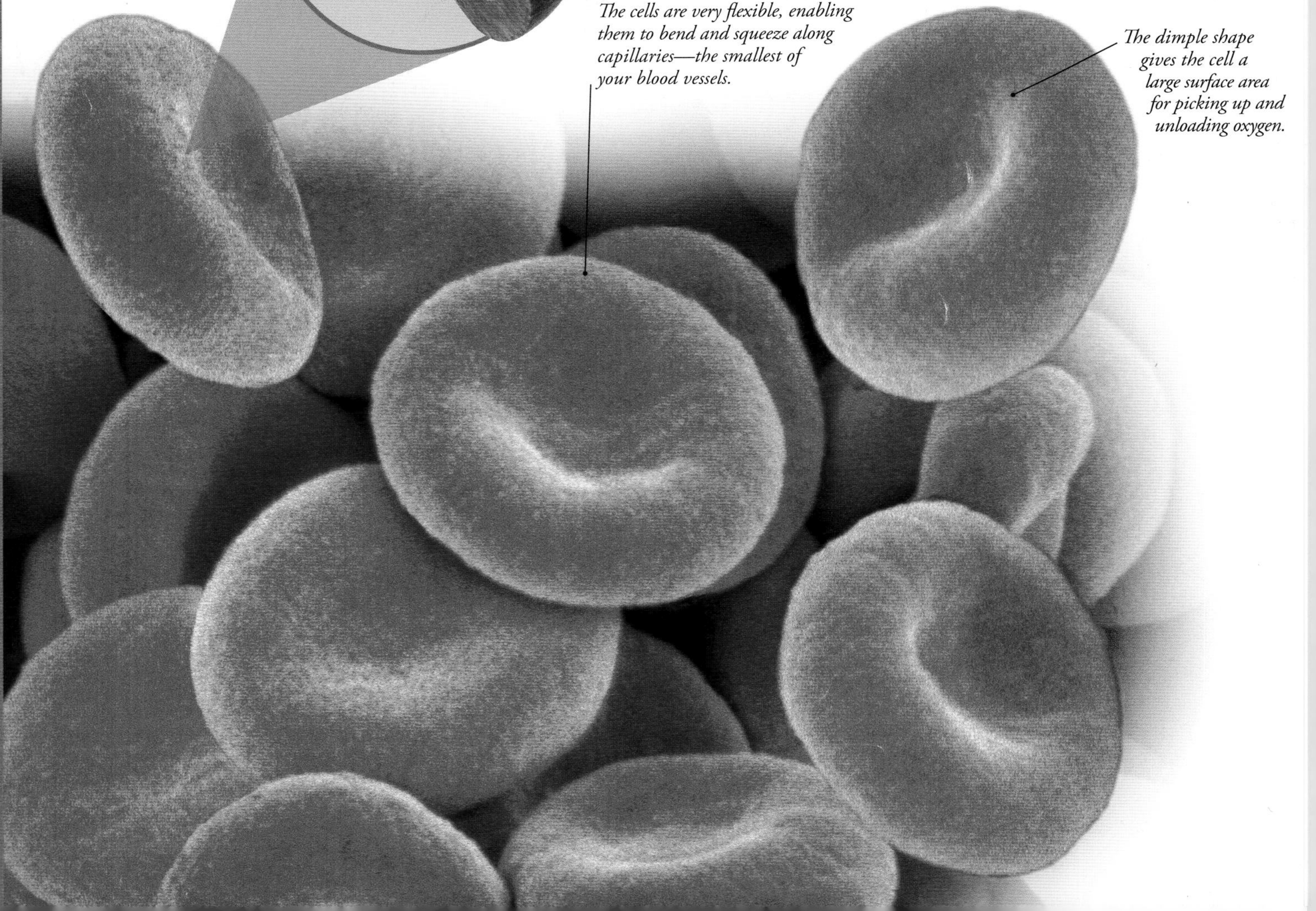

The cells are very flexible, enabling them to bend and squeeze along capillaries—the smallest of your blood vessels.

The dimple shape gives the cell a large surface area for picking up and unloading oxygen.

7

YOUR BLOOD TYPE

There are four main blood types—A, B, AB, and O. Which type you belong to depends on the presence of markers called antigens. These are found on the surface of red blood cells. The markers help your body identify blood cells that do not belong to you. Your blood plasma may also contain antibodies (proteins) that stick to blood cells carrying foreign antigens.

▲ BLOOD TYPE AB
There are no antibodies in type AB blood, so you can receive blood from any type.

A antigen

B antigen

▲ BLOOD TYPE O
These blood cells carry no antigens so type O blood can be donated to anyone.

anti-A antibody

anti-B antibody

▲ BLOOD TYPE A
Red blood cells in type A blood carry A antigens as markers.

A antigen

anti-B antibody

▲ BLOOD TYPE B
Red blood cells in type B blood carry B antigens as markers.

B antigen

anti-A antibody

▲ BLOOD TRANSFUSION *Blood can be donated to a patient who needs blood. However, a transfusion of the wrong blood type can make the blood cells clump together and block the blood vessels, so it is important to find the correct match.*

Oxygen-rich blood is bright red.

Oxygen-poor blood is dark red.

CHANGING COLOR

Your blood's color alters as it travels around your body. This is because the hemoglobin inside red blood cells changes color as it picks up or releases oxygen. After red blood cells have collected oxygen in your lungs, the blood flowing along arteries is bright red. After red blood cells have released oxygen in the tissues, blood traveling along veins is a dark purple-red.

KARL LANDSTEINER

Until the early 1900s, very little was known about why blood transfusions failed. The breakthrough came in 1901, when Austrian scientist Karl Landsteiner experimented on himself and his team and discovered the four main blood types. Blood could now be transfused safely from a donor to a recipient who shared the same blood type, saving countless of lives.

69

Super network

Delivering food and oxygen to all your hardworking cells and removing their wastes is a 24-hour task and one that requires a superefficient transportation system. This is exactly what your body has—an astonishing network of living tubes called blood vessels that transport the vital supplies. Altogether, about 60,000 miles (100,000 km) of blood vessels fit into your body and keep your cells working.

PERFECT MATCH

You have three types of blood vessels—arteries, veins, and capillaries. Each is perfectly built for its role as a blood transporter. Your arteries, for example, carry oxygen-rich blood from your heart to the rest of your body and can withstand the full force of the high pressure of blood that surges through them. Your veins, however, return oxygen-poor blood back to your heart and carry blood under lower pressure, while your capillaries deliver the fuel and oxygen to individual cells.

▶ VEIN *A vein is similar in structure to an artery, but some veins also have valves that prevent blood from flowing backward.*

▶ CAPILLARY *This is the smallest, the most numerous, and the most fragile of your blood vessels.*

A valve opens and closes like a trapdoor to keep blood flowing in the right direction.

The thin wall of a capillary is just one cell thick.

Inner lining of vein

▶ ARTERY *Thick muscle and elastic layers allow arteries to withstand the high blood pressure created when the heart beats.*

A smooth inner lining allows blood to flow through easily.

This elastic layer allows the artery to expand and bounce back as blood surges through it.

Elastic layer

Thin muscle layer

Tough, thick muscle layer

Protective coat

Protective coat

WOW!

If all your blood vessels were laid out end-to-end, they would wrap around the Earth twice.

LOOK CLOSER: SIDE BY SIDE

Arteries and veins run side by side throughout your body, forming an amazingly complex network of tubes. These blood vessels divide continuously, so that they can reach every part of your body.

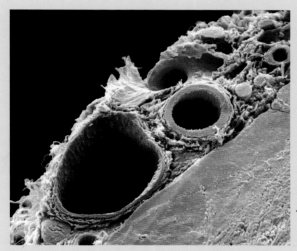

▲ ARTERIES AND VEINS *This cross-section of an organ shows a thin-walled vein (purple) alongside a thicker-walled artery (red). They are held in place and supported by connective tissue.*

CAPILLARY NETWORK

Your arteries and veins are the main highways of the circulatory system. Your capillaries are like the side streets and back alleys that link those highways. As the arteries get closer to their destination, they get smaller and form a capillary network. This ensures that every cell gets supplies of food and oxygen from a capillary. Once their deliveries are made, capillaries merge again to form tiny veins.

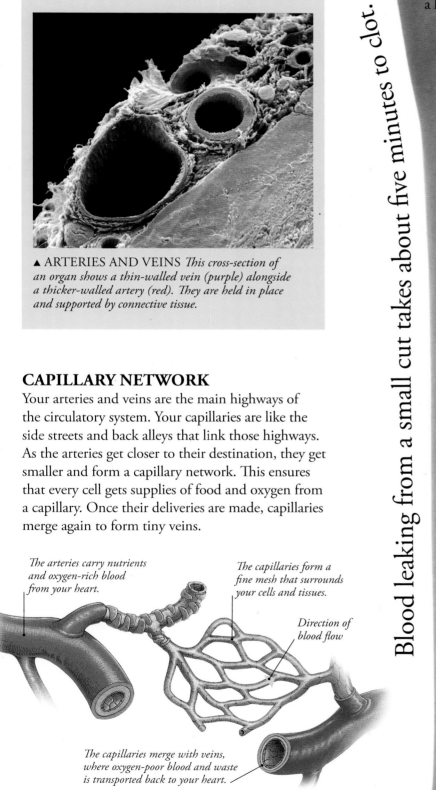

The arteries carry nutrients and oxygen-rich blood from your heart.

The capillaries form a fine mesh that surrounds your cells and tissues.

Direction of blood flow

The capillaries merge with veins, where oxygen-poor blood and waste is transported back to your heart.

WOUND HEALING

When a cut in the skin damages a bl[...] body reacts to prevent infection and [...] As white blood cells move in to dest[...] germs, platelets form a plug to stop [...] leaking out. They also create a net of [...] blood cells to make a jellylike clot. This dries to form a hard scab, which protects the wound while it heals.

Blood leaking from a small cut takes about five minutes to clot.

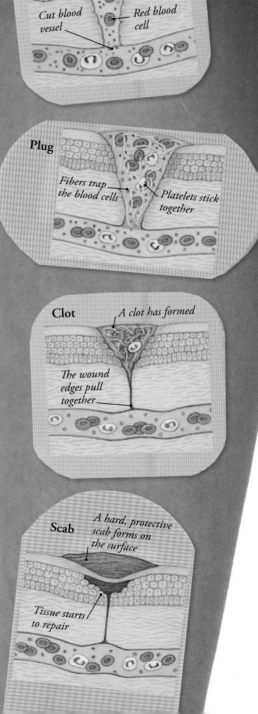

Injury White blood cell
Cut blood vessel — Red blood cell

Plug Fibers trap the blood cells — Platelets stick together

Clot A clot has formed
The wound edges pull together

Scab A hard, protective scab forms on the surface
Tissue starts to repair

71

A TIGHT SQUEEZE

Ten times narrower than strands of hair, capillaries form vast networks around your body, weaving through every tissue. This magnified image shows how a red blood cell has to squeeze its way through this system of tiny blood vessels.

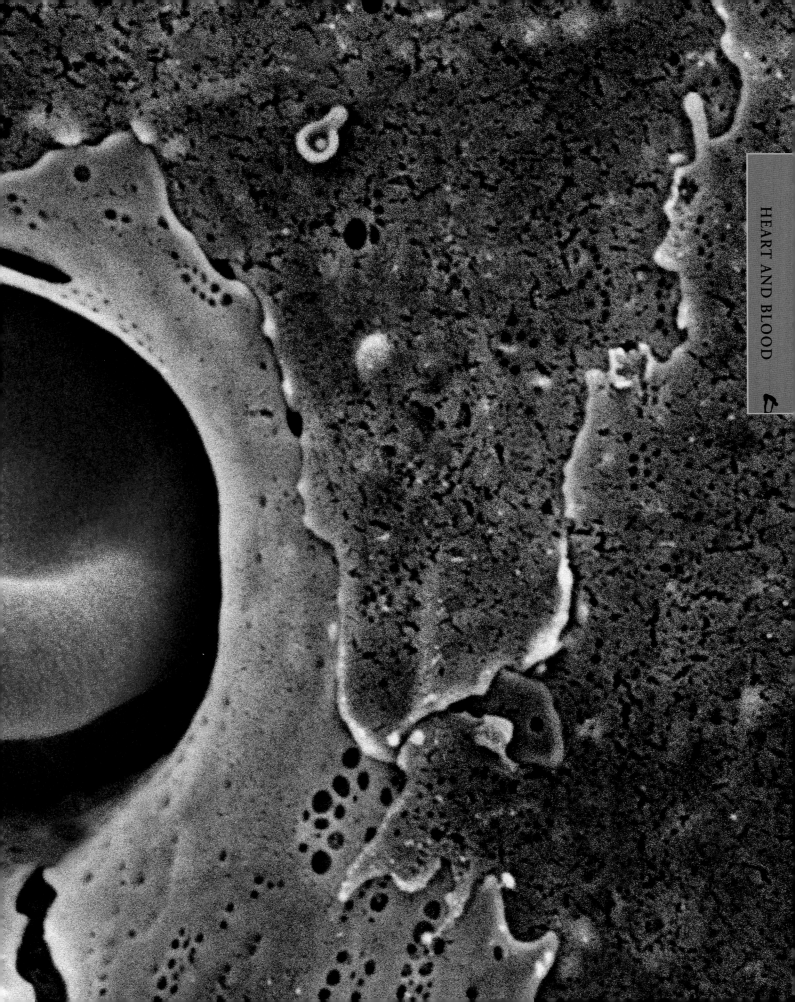

Engine room

At the center of your circulatory system is your heart, a fist-sized powerful pump that beats every second. With every beat, your heart pushes about a cupful of blood around your body and refills in time for the next beat. Made from a special kind of muscle, your heart never gets tired.

INSIDE THE HEART

Your heart lies in the middle of your chest, sandwiched between your two lungs and protected by the ribcage. It has two sides, each with a smaller, upper space (the atrium), and a lower, larger one (the ventricle). The right side of your heart pumps blood to your lungs, while the left side receives blood from your lungs and pumps it to every part of your body.

Right side

▲ VALVES *These open and close during each heartbeat to make sure that blood always flows in the right direction and never backward.*

Right atrium

Valve

Right ventricle

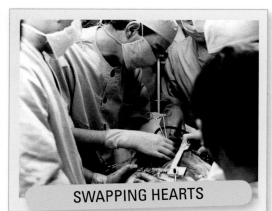

SWAPPING HEARTS

Before the 1960s, heart transplants were thought to be impossible because of the high risk of death. But in 1967, history was made when a pioneering South African surgeon, Christiaan Barnard (center), carried out the world's first successful heart transplant. He removed the damaged heart from his patient and replaced it with a healthy heart from a donor. Today, heart transplants are performed all the time.

▶ HEARTSTRINGS *These thin cords anchor the valve between each atrium and ventricle. When the heart beats, the heartstrings keep the valve from turning inside out.*

The inferior vena cava, your body's biggest vein, carries oxygen-poor blood from the lower body.

Blood races through this large artery, called the aorta, on its journey around your body.

The pulmonary artery is the only artery in your body that carries oxygen-poor blood.

Left side

WOW!

Each day, enough power is produced in the heart to drive a car 20 miles (32 km).

Blood from your lungs enters through these pulmonary veins.

Left atrium

The left ventricle has a thicker muscular wall because it has to pump blood farther than the right ventricle.

A wall of muscle divides the heart into right and left halves.

This tough double membrane surrounds and protects the heart.

🔍 LOOK CLOSER: BLOOD SUPPLY

Hardworking cardiac muscle cells demand constant supplies of food and oxygen to give them the energy needed to keep the heart beating. However, these cannot be supplied by the blood gushing through the heart. Instead, the heart has its own special network of blood vessels to supply its needs.

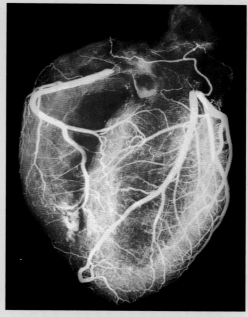

▲ ANGIOGRAM *This special type of X-ray shows the main blood vessels, called coronary arteries, that supply the heart's muscular wall with blood.*

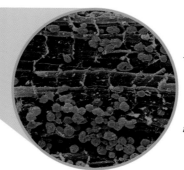

◄ CARDIAC MUSCLE *The thick walls of the heart are made with cardiac muscle cells (green). These are packed with mitochondria (red), which supply the heart's muscle cells with the energy they need to keep on beating.*

≫≫ FAST FACTS ≫≫

■ The first heartbeat happens during the fourth week of pregnancy, when the baby is no bigger than the size of your fingernail.
■ The heart is the first organ to receive oxygen-rich blood.
■ On average, an adult heart beats about 70 times a minute, when at rest.

75

Working pump

Every minute of your life, your powerful heart keeps pumping blood around your body to supply it with oxygen and nutrients. This amazing natural pump works in phases, first sucking in blood through one set of tubes, then forcing it out through a different set. The heart relaxes and then repeats the action—over and over again, day after day.

YOUR BEATING HEART

Your heart is like two pumps in one. The right side pumps oxygen-poor blood into your lungs, where it picks up fresh supplies of oxygen, while the left side pumps oxygen-rich blood to every part of your body. This heartbeat is made up of three stages, and it only takes about a second to complete the whole cycle.

● Oxygen-rich blood
● Oxygen-poor blood

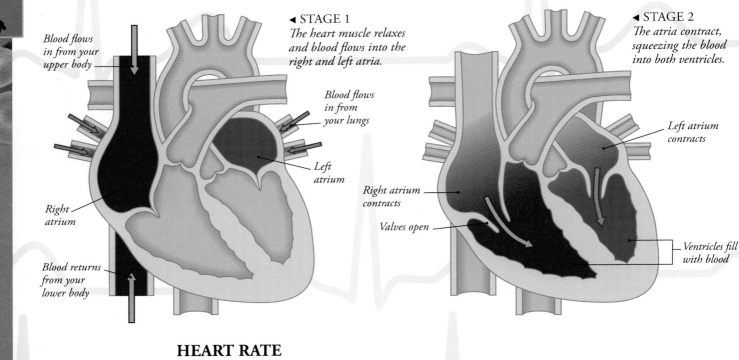

◀ STAGE 1
The heart muscle relaxes and blood flows into the right and left atria.

◀ STAGE 2
The atria contract, squeezing the blood into both ventricles.

Blood flows in from your upper body

Blood flows in from your lungs

Left atrium

Left atrium contracts

Right atrium

Right atrium contracts

Valves open

Blood returns from your lower body

Ventricles fill with blood

HEART RATE

Your heartbeat cycle is controlled by a special heart muscle in the right atrium that acts as a natural pacemaker. The muscle sends out electrical signals to your atria and ventricles to make them contract. The signals can be detected by an electrical heart monitor, called an ECG. By looking at the signals, a doctor can check whether your heart has a normal rhythm.

This peak shows the ventricles contracting to pump blood out of the heart.

▶ ECG RECORDING
A graphlike recording is made by an ECG. This reading shows a regular heart rhythm.

This flat line shows when the heart muscle is relaxed.

HEART VALVES

The heart is equipped with a set of valves to ensure that blood always flows in the right direction. On each side of the heart, a valve divides the upper atrium and the lower ventricle. This keeps the contracting ventricle from forcing blood back up into the atrium. Instead, it forces the blood through a semilunar (meaning "half-moon") valve (right), and into one of the arteries leaving the heart. The valve closes when the ventricle relaxes.

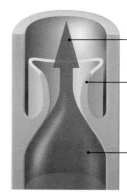

The blood surges forward.

The semilunar valve is forced open by the pressure of blood from behind.

The pressure of blood is high as the heart pumps.

The blood cannot flow backward.

The semilunar valve is forced to close by the pressure of blood in front of the valve.

The pressure of blood drops as the heart rests between beats.

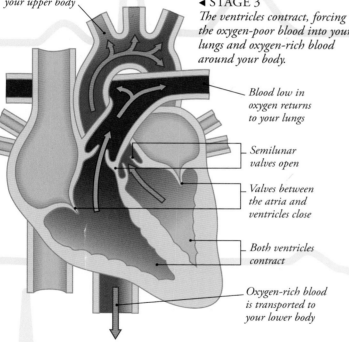

Blood rich in oxygen flows to your upper body

◄ STAGE 3
The ventricles contract, forcing the oxygen-poor blood into your lungs and oxygen-rich blood around your body.

Blood low in oxygen returns to your lungs

Semilunar valves open

Valves between the atria and ventricles close

Both ventricles contract

Oxygen-rich blood is transported to your lower body

HEARING HEARTBEATS

A doctor can check if your heart is working well by using an instrument called a stethoscope to listen to the sound of its valves closing. When the valves between the atria and the ventricles close they make a long, loud "lub" sound, and when the semilunar valves slam shut they make a shorter, sharper "dup" sound.

FEELING A PULSE

As your heart pumps blood through your arteries, they expand and then spring back in time with every heartbeat. We call this a pulse. It is most obvious where an artery passes over a bone near the surface, such as in your wrist or neck. You can feel your pulse by pressing down on the artery on the inside of your wrist.

Heartbeat

During an average lifetime, the human heart beats tirelessly about 2.5 billion times. Each heartbeat pumps blood around the body to deliver fuel and other vital supplies, and carry away waste products. The more active you are, the more fuel your body needs, so your heartbeat automatically changes to match what you are doing.

WOW!

While you are resting, your blood races out of your heart and into the main arteries at a rate of about 2 in (5 cm) per second.

READY FOR ACTION

If you are scared or very excited, your body releases a special chemical called adrenaline into your bloodstream. Within seconds, adrenaline triggers a number of actions including making your heart beat faster. This sends extra blood to your muscles and brain so that your body has the energy it needs to run away from danger or to fight back.

▶ ROLLER COASTER
Going on a roller coaster ride releases a rush of adrenaline that enables your body to cope with this nerve-racking experience.

When you are resting, your heart pumps about 10 pints (5 liters) of blood around your body every minute.

SWITCHING OFF

Your body is at its most relaxed when you are sleeping, but your heart keeps ticking away. It usually beats more slowly than when you are awake and resting. This means that your heart might slow from about 64 to 52 beats per minute as you fall asleep. But it speeds up again if you are dreaming.

Within 10 minutes of falling asleep, your heart rate starts to slow down.

AT REST

When you are sitting quietly, your body is resting. A normal resting heart rate can be anything from 40 to 100 beats per minute. The rate varies with your age, but also with your level of fitness. The higher your fitness level, the slower your resting heart rate will be.

Even watching a scary movie can make your heart beat faster.

WORKING OUT

Physical activity puts more demands on your body, so your heart rate speeds up to supply the extra fuel and oxygen your body needs. The harder you exercise, the faster your heart beats, and you can often feel your heart pounding away in your chest. But if you exercise regularly and get in shape, your heart doesn't have to work so hard to achieve the same result.

When you are exercising, your heart rate can go up to about 200 beats per minute.

DISEASE
DEFENSES

Your body is always under attack. Tiny organisms called germs are constantly trying to get inside you, which can make you sick. Fortunately, the body has complex defenses for fighting off these invaders.

Germs and disease

Every time you breathe in or touch something, your body picks up tiny organisms that are too small to see—microorganisms. Most microorganisms do no harm, but some try to invade your body and multiply inside you, which can make you sick. These harmful microorganisms are called germs. Germs affect the body in many ways, some causing nothing more than a sneeze and others causing dangerous diseases.

VIRUSES

The tiniest germs of all are viruses. A virus is little more than a packet of genes inside a protective coat. To reproduce, it must invade one of the cells in your body, which it then hijacks and turns into a virus-making factory. Such invasions can result in colds, flu, warts, and measles.

◀ COLD VIRUS *The virus that causes the common cold is called a rhinovirus. It spreads from person to person in droplets that are sneezed or coughed out.*

BACTERIA

Much bigger than viruses, bacteria are single-celled organisms. Many are harmless or even helpful to your body, but some cause diseases, including food poisoning, typhoid, and plague. Invading bacteria trigger disease by releasing poisons called toxins.

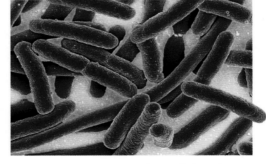

▲ BACTERIA CELLS *These rod-shaped bacteria are called* E. coli *and live inside your intestines. Some types of* E. coli *cause diarrhea.*

WORMS

Tapeworms and roundworms are types of worms that can live inside the human body. Tapeworms live in the intestines and steal nutrients from the food you eat. They can grow to 33 ft (10 m) in length—as long as a bus.

◀ TAPEWORM *The head of a tapeworm is equipped with suckers and hooks, which attach it firmly to the intestine wall.*

► ATHLETE'S FOOT *This close-up view shows filaments (orange) of the athlete's foot fungus growing between flakes of skin. Athlete's foot causes soreness, itching, and cracked skin.*

WOW!

The smallest viruses are so tiny that 400 million of them would fit inside a period.

FUNGI

Mushrooms and molds belong to a category of organisms called fungi. Most fungi grow in soil or on rotting matter, but a few types can grow on or inside the human body. Athlete's foot is a disease caused by fungi that grow as a network of tiny threads through damp skin.

MALARIA

The bloodsucking bite of certain types of mosquitoes can lead to the deadly disease malaria. This disease is caused by a single-celled organism called *Plasmodium*, which lives inside mosquitoes. Malaria kills up to a million people a year worldwide.

VIRUS SHAPES

There are millions of different viruses. Scientists classify them according to their size and their shape, both of which are amazingly varied. Some look like tubes, boxes, or golf balls. Others are more complex and look like tiny, man-made machines. Three important types of virus are shown below.

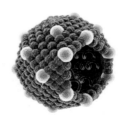

▲ SPIRAL *This virus has a corkscrew shape, with the virus's DNA coiled up inside. Measles is caused by a spiral virus.*

▲ ICOSAHEDRAL *Responsible for causing colds and polio, these viruses have a coat made of twenty triangular faces.*

▲ COMPLEX *Resembling tiny spacecraft, complete with landing gear to settle on cells, these viruses attack bacteria.*

Body barriers

Germs such as bacteria and viruses are always trying to get into your body. Fortunately, the human body is well protected. The first line of defense against invaders is the body's surface, which acts as a barrier to germs. The surface includes not only the tough, outer layer of skin but also the delicate surface of your eyes and the soft tissues lining your mouth, nose, throat, and stomach.

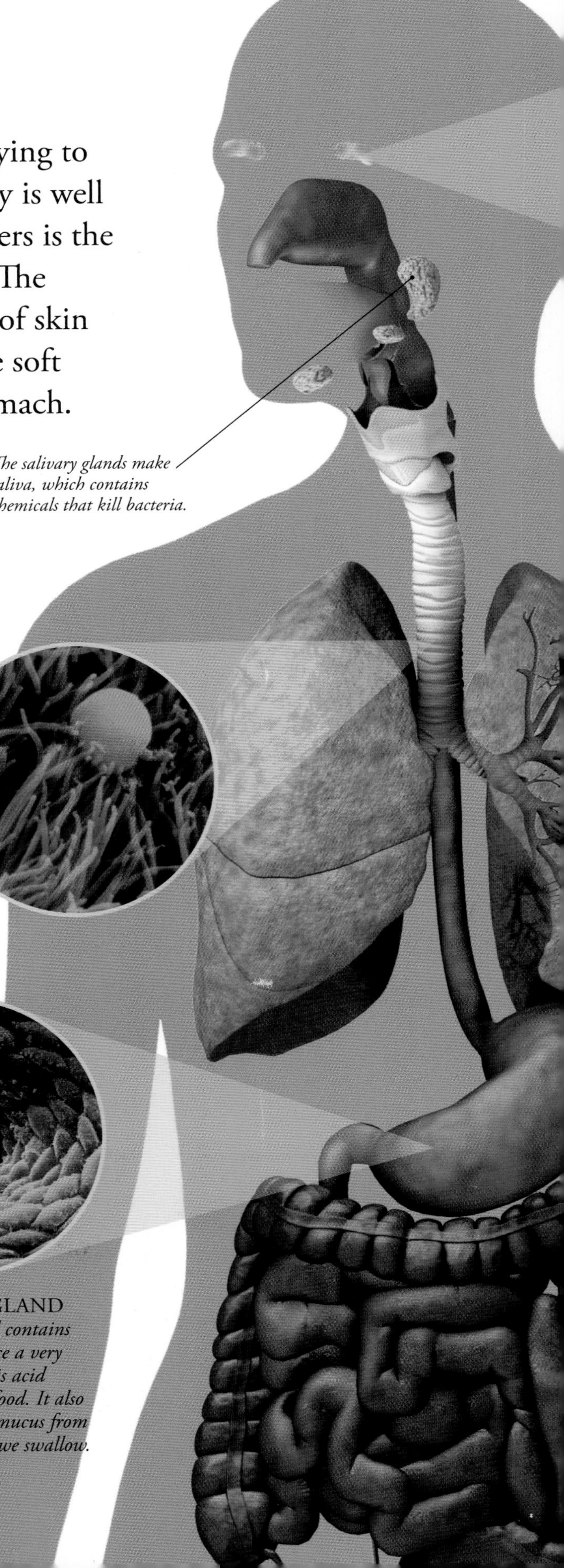

INNER BARRIERS

Germs can enter your body through the air you breathe in or through the food you eat. To stop these germs from getting any farther, the cells lining inner passages such as the throat and airways are packed together to form a germproof wall. This wall is covered in protective fluids such as saliva, mucus, and stomach acid.

The salivary glands make saliva, which contains chemicals that kill bacteria.

▶ STICKY STUFF *A sticky fluid called mucus, seen here magnified (green) covers the inner walls of airways leading to the lungs. Germs that land on mucus get stuck. Tiny hairs (pink) beat back and forth to push the mucus up to the throat, where it gets swallowed.*

LOUIS PASTEUR

French scientist Louis Pasteur (1822–95) was the first person to realize that disease can be caused by tiny organisms—germs. Before Pasteur, most people thought diseases were a punishment from God.

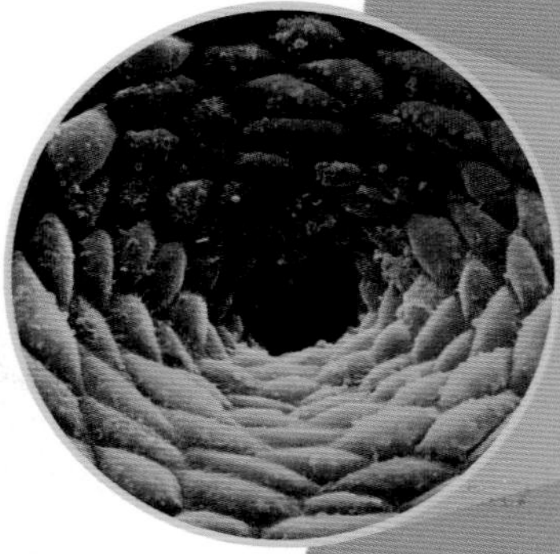

▲ STOMACH GLAND
The stomach's wall contains glands that produce a very powerful acid. This acid destroys germs in food. It also kills the germs in mucus from the throat, which we swallow.

84

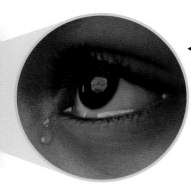

◀ TEARS *With every blink, watery tears wash bacteria off the surface of your eyes. Tears also contain lysozyme, a chemical that destroys the cell walls of bacteria.*

WOW!

Not all bacteria are bad. Your skin is home to millions of friendly bacteria that help protect you from the bacteria that cause disease.

Your skin's outer layer consists of dead cells packed tightly together, forming a very tough barrier. Germs cannot get through this unless your skin is cut.

In your intestines, any germs that survive the stomach's acid bath are attacked by the digestive juices that break down food.

FEVER

When harmful bacteria or viruses multiply inside you, they cause what doctors call an infection. Your body reacts to infections by heating up, raising your temperature above the normal 98.6 °F (37 °C). This reaction, called fever, helps stop the germs from multiplying. It also boosts the activity of germ-killing white blood cells.

▲ MEASURING TEMPERATURE *A mother uses a digital thermometer to check whether her daughter's temperature is higher than normal, indicating that she may have an infection.*

SWELLING UP

If your skin gets cut, germs can get into your body. To block their path and limit damage, the skin reacts by becoming inflamed (swollen). Blood vessels under the skin become wider and let blood leak out, so that germ-eating white blood cells can kill the germs. The area around the cut becomes swollen and red. The skin feels painful and hot as the wound is healing.

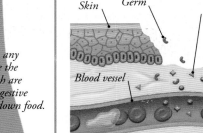

Skin *Germ* *Chemicals released by damaged cells*

Blood vessel

▲ DAMAGE *A cut in the skin allows germs to invade. Damaged cells release chemicals that attract germ-destroying white blood cells.*

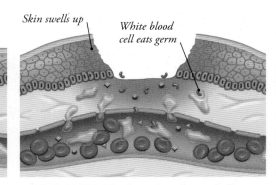

Skin swells up *White blood cell eats germ*

▲ RESPONSE *Blood vessels widen and allow blood cells to pass out. White blood cells flock into the wound to seek out and destroy the germs.*

White blood cells

The human body contains about 50 billion white blood cells. These are the body's defenders—they wander through blood and other body fluids seeking out germs such as bacteria and viruses and killing them. Some also seek and destroy the faulty body cells that cause cancer.

DEFENSE FORCE

There are several different types of white blood cells, each suited to attacking particular types of germs. Most are made in bone marrow, a jellylike tissue found in the hollow spaces inside bones. White blood cells live for only 3–4 days each. When you're sick, the number of white blood cells rises as your body fights the disease.

Killer cell

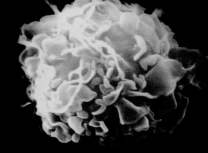

◄ BIG EATERS
Macrophage cells eat and kill germs such as bacteria. They also swallow up flecks of dirt and debris in injured tissue, helping to clean up wounds.

◄ FIRST DEFENSE
Neutrophils are the most common type of white blood cell. They are first on the scene to destroy invading germs when your skin is cut. They collect by the thousand in wounds, forming a yellowish substance called pus.

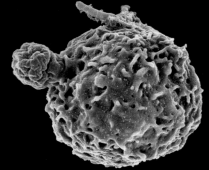

◄ SPECIALIZED KILLERS
Instead of attacking any invader, a lymphoctye learns to attack just one specific type of germ. Lymphocytes kill germs in various ways. Some stick to germs and flood them with poison. Others release chemicals called antibodies, which stick to germs and attract other types of white blood cells.

EATING GERMS

Macrophages and neutrophils destroy germs in the same way. Roaming through blood and other body fluids, they hunt invading microbes, particularly bacteria, by following their chemical trails. Once in contact with a bacterial cell, they confirm the target as "foreign" by examining the chemicals on its surface. Then the defender surrounds the enemy cell, which takes only a second, and digests it. This process of capture and destruction is called phagocytosis.

FIGHTING CANCER

Natural killer cells are white blood cells that defend the body against cancer and viruses. When a natural killer cell finds a cancer cell, it punches holes in its prey and injects poisons that kill the cancer cell from the inside.

◄ CANCER KILLER *A natural killer cell (green) makes contact with a cancer cell (orange). The killer cell identifies the cancer cell as abnormal by analyzing chemicals on its surface.*

Cancer cell

The killer cell attaches to the cancer cell prior to destroying it.

WOW!

A single drop of blood may contain as many as 25,000 white blood cells.

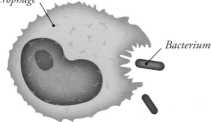

▲ CAPTURE *A macrophage identifies a bacterium as foreign and rapidly alters shape to surround and swallow its prey.*

Macrophage

Bacterium

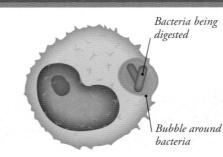

▲ DIGEST *The captured bacteria are enclosed in a kind of bubble (a vesicle) and doused in powerful enzymes that kill and digest them.*

Bacteria being digested

Bubble around bacteria

▲ EXPEL *Undigested waste is expelled from the macrophage, which then continues its search for more harmful bacteria.*

Waste particles expelled

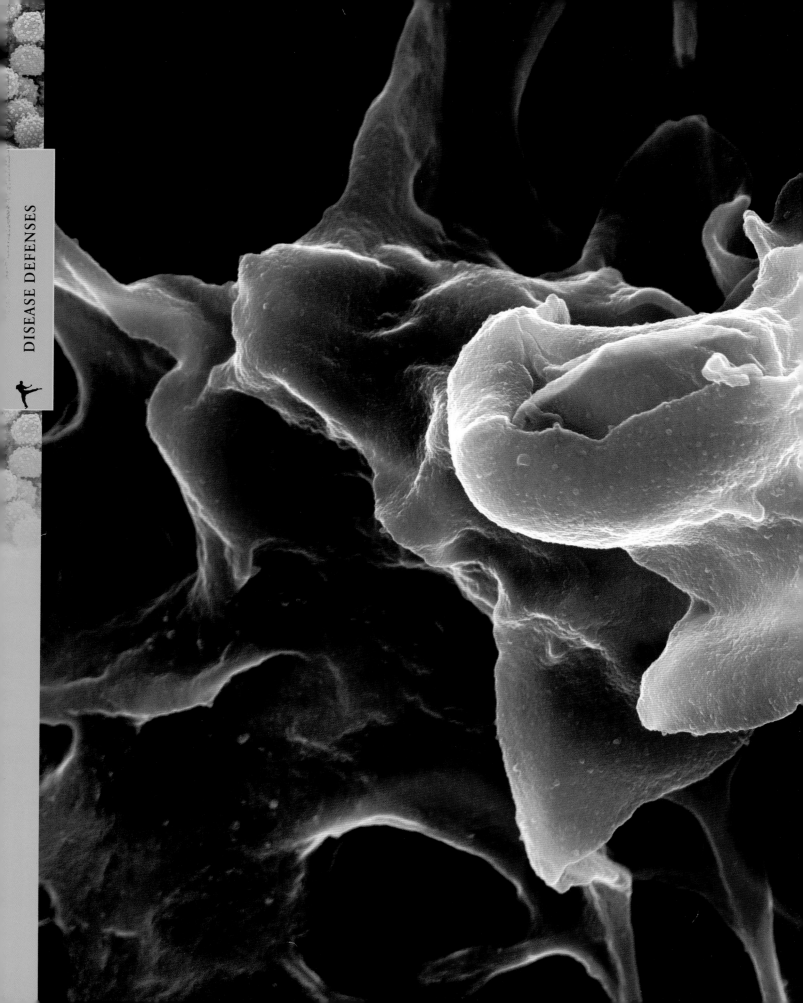

GERM DESTROYER

Seen magnified thousands of times, a type of white blood cell called a macrophage (brown) swallows a group of bacteria (green) before killing them. These bacteria cause a deadly disease called tuberculosis, which attacks a person's lungs.

Filtering germs

Germs that break through the body's barriers and invade internal tissues do not usually survive for long. The human body contains a network of tiny vessels that collect fluid from every type of tissue and carefully filter it for germs, which are then swiftly destroyed.

LYMPHATIC SYSTEM

Fluid from body tissues is collected by the vessels of the lymphatic system. As it flows along lymphatic vessels, the fluid passes through swellings called lymph nodes. These are packed with white blood cells called lymphocytes, which identify germs and kill them.

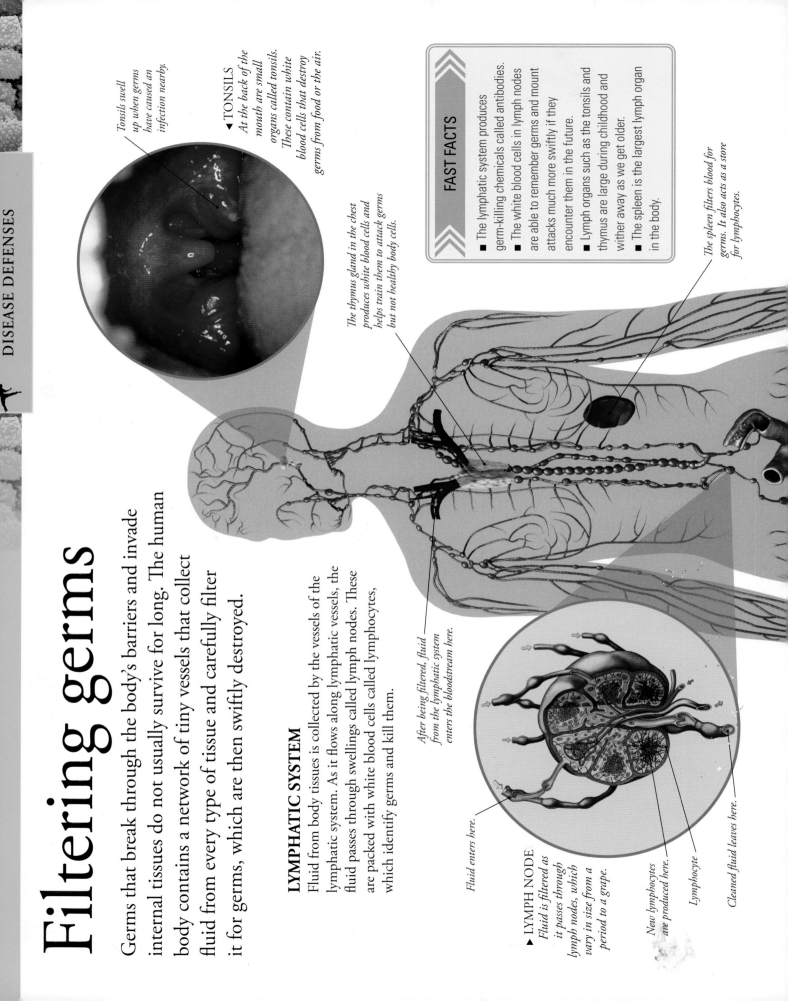

Tonsils swell up when germs have caused an infection nearby.

▶ TONSILS
At the back of the mouth are small organs called tonsils. These contain white blood cells that destroy germs from food or the air.

The thymus gland in the chest produces white blood cells and helps train them to attack germs but not healthy body cells.

The spleen filters blood for germs. It also acts as a store for lymphocytes.

After being filtered, fluid from the lymphatic system enters the bloodstream here.

▶ LYMPH NODE
Fluid is filtered as it passes through lymph nodes, which vary in size from a period to a grape.

New lymphocytes are produced here.

Fluid enters here.

Lymphocyte

Cleaned fluid leaves here.

FAST FACTS

- The lymphatic system produces germ-killing chemicals called antibodies.
- The white blood cells in lymph nodes are able to remember germs and mount attacks much more swiftly if they encounter them in the future.
- Lymph organs such as the tonsils and thymus are large during childhood and wither away as we get older.
- The spleen is the largest lymph organ in the body.

INVADING WORMS

In some tropical countries, the bite of a mosquito can introduce tiny worms into the human body, causing a disease known as elephantiasis. The worms block lymphatic vessels in the legs, causing fluid to build up. Over time, the legs and feet swell up enormously until they look like the legs of an elephant. Scientists are trying to wipe out this disfiguring disease and think it will be eradicated completely by 2020.

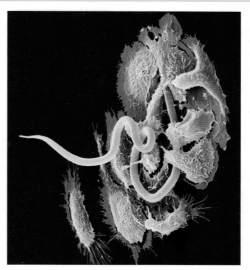

▲ UNDER ATTACK *Seen through a microscope at ×900 magnification, white blood cells (colored yellow) attack the worm that causes elephantiasis.*

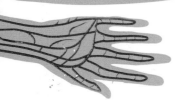

ONE-WAY FLOW

The fluid that the lymphatic system collects and filters is known as lymph. Unlike blood, lymph isn't pumped along by the heartbeat. Instead, it's pushed along more slowly whenever body movements squeeze lymphatic vessels. Valves inside the vessels make sure the fluid moves in one direction only.

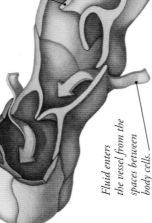

Valves open when the fluid flows the right way but shut if it tries to move backward.

Fluid enters the vessel from the spaces between body cells.

SWOLLEN NODES

If a doctor feels the sides of your neck or the underside of your chin, you're being checked for swollen lymph nodes (also called "swollen glands," though they aren't glands). When your body is fighting an infection, your lymph nodes become more active and swell up.

Immune system

Most germs fail to break through the body's barriers, but a few succeed and multiply inside us, causing an infection. When this happens, our immune system fights back. The immune system identifies new germs as enemies and then targets them specifically. It also remembers them for the future, giving us immunity to the diseases they cause.

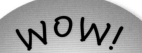

WOW!
Some sneaky germs continually change their surface markers to escape detection by the immune system.

◄ ANTIBODY CELL
Antibodies are made by specialized white blood cells called B-cells.

HOW ANTIBODIES KILL GERMS

Antibodies are chemicals that stick to germs such as bacteria, flagging them for destruction. There are millions of different types of germs, and each type of antibody recognizes only one of them. Fortunately, the human body can produce ten billion different types of antibodies, ensuring there's an antibody to match every germ you ever encounter.

1. INFECT *A germ invades the body and begins to multiply. It gets carried by body fluids to a lymph node.*

Germ

Antibody cells

2. DETECT *Inside the lymph node, many different antibody cells touch the germ to try and identify the unique molecules on its surface. Eventually, a cell with matching molecules recognizes the germ as an enemy and sticks to it.*

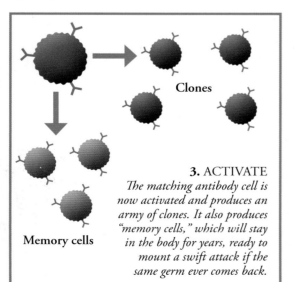

Clones

Memory cells

3. ACTIVATE
The matching antibody cell is now activated and produces an army of clones. It also produces "memory cells," which will stay in the body for years, ready to mount a swift attack if the same germ ever comes back.

4. SEEK *The clones make antibodies to match the unique molecules on the germ's surface. The antibodies are released into the blood and travel throughout the body. Wherever they find matching germs, they stick to them.*

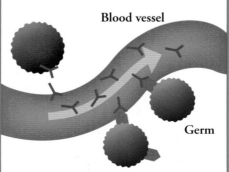

Blood vessel

Germ

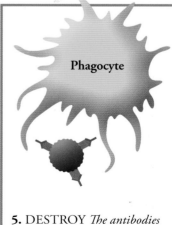

Phagocyte

5. DESTROY *The antibodies act as beacons to white blood cells called phagocytes, which swallow and destroy the germs.*

HOW KILLER CELLS WORK

Killer cells work like antibody cells, but instead of releasing antibody molecules into the blood, they travel through the bloodstream themselves and attack their targets directly. While antibodies attack bacteria, killer cells specialize in attacking cancer cells and body cells hijacked by viruses.

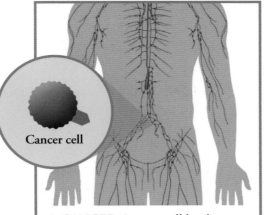

1. CANCER *A cancer cell breaks off a tumor and is carried by body fluids to a lymph node.*

Cancer cell

2. DETECT *In the lymph node, killer cells touch the cell and try to identify the molecules on its surface. Eventually, a cell with matching molecules recognizes the cancer cell as an enemy and sticks to it.*

Killer cells

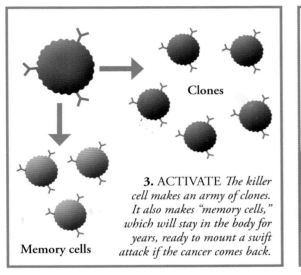

Clones

Memory cells

3. ACTIVATE *The killer cell makes an army of clones. It also makes "memory cells," which will stay in the body for years, ready to mount a swift attack if the cancer comes back.*

4. SEEK *Large numbers of the cloned cells leave the lymph node and travel through the body, on the lookout for cancer cells that match their surface molecules.*

Clones

5. DESTROY *When killer cells find cancer cells, they stick to them and kill them with poison.*

Cancer cell

Killer cell

VACCINATIONS

Your body normally becomes immune to infections only after it has overcome them. However, you can also become immune by being given a vaccination. Vaccines contain altered germs that can't make you sick but still trigger the immune system, which then builds up reserves of memory cells.

▲ ON THE ATTACK
Four killer cells attack a cancer cell. They will flood the cell with poison to destroy it.

◄ VACCINE INJECTION
Vaccines are usually given as injections, but some can be swallowed instead.

BIRD FLU VIRUS
This electron microscope image shows the bird flu virus magnified 500,000 times. The virus is found in wild birds but can also infect humans, causing a deadly form of influenza. Each virus consists of little more than a packet of genes in a protein shell (pink) and an envelope of fat (orange).

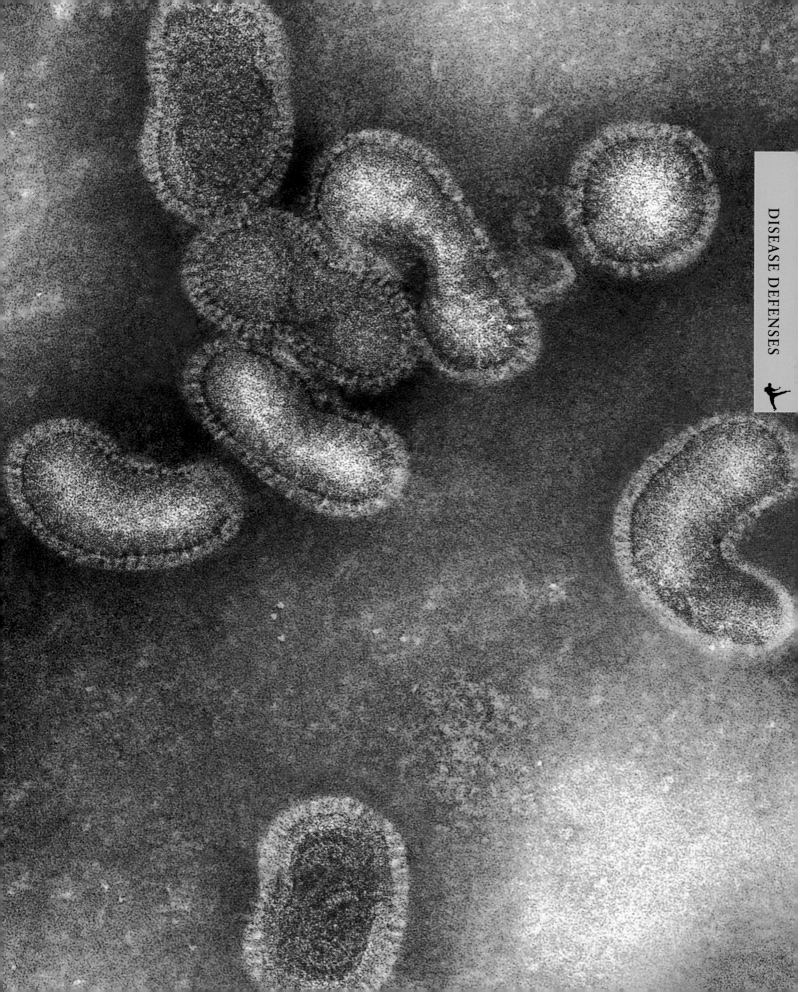

Allergies

The immune system protects the body by attacking foreign materials such as germs. In some people, however, it can misfire and attack harmless foreign substances. We call this overreaction an allergy. Allergies range from mild conditions, such as the runny nose of hay fever, to a life-threatening reaction called anaphylaxis.

TRIGGERS

Things that trigger allergies are known as allergens. Common allergens include nuts, pollen (a powder made by flowers), and animal hairs. Allergens can cause a reaction if they are swallowed, breathed in, or even touched. The affected part of the body often becomes red and swollen as though infected by germs.

WOW!

Allergic reactions can be triggered by exercise, perfume, chocolate, gold, household dust, cell phones, and even water.

▶ POLLEN GRAINS *Released by flowers, pollen grains can cause allergies such as hay fever.*

HOW ALLERGIES WORK

Allergens work by activating certain types of white blood cells that normally respond only to germs. Allergen molecules bind to chemicals called antibodies on the surface of the white blood cells. In response, the white blood cells burst and release a chemical called histamine, which causes body tissues nearby to swell up and become sore.

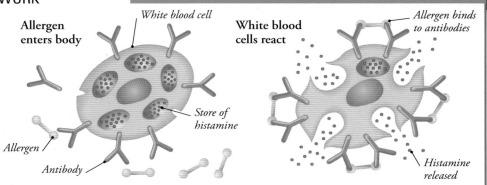

Allergen enters body

White blood cell

Allergen

Antibody

Store of histamine

White blood cells react

Allergen binds to antibodies

Histamine released

ASTHMA

This allergy is triggered by allergens in the air and it affects the airways leading to the lungs. During an asthma attack, muscles in the walls of the airways suddenly tighten, making breathing harder. The airway walls also become inflamed and produce thick mucus, making matters worse.

▶ INHALER *An asthma sufferer uses an inhaler to deliver a drug to his lungs. The drug relaxes muscles in the lungs, making breathing easier.*

RARE BUT DEADLY

In some people, allergic reactions are so severe that they affect the whole body and may even stop the heart. This rare but life-threatening reaction is called anaphylaxis and can be triggered by insect stings. Some people with an allergy to insect stings carry emergency medication at all times for use during an anaphylactic reaction.

TESTING FOR ALLERGIES

Some people suffer allergic reactions without knowing what the cause is. To identify the culprit, doctors carry out skin tests. A range of potential allergens—such as pollen, pet fur, or a foodstuff—are put on the skin. The skin is then monitored to see if it swells, reddens, or itches.

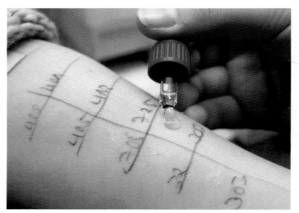

▶ SKIN TEST
A drop of fluid containing a potential allergen is put on a marked patch of skin.

Fighting disease

Your body has powerful defenses to fight off the germs that cause disease, but sometimes you might need extra help from doctors to get well. Doctors use a range of techniques to determine what kind of illness you might have and how best to treat it.

IDENTIFYING GERMS

The doctor's first job is to make a diagnosis, which means determining what kind of disease you have. If the doctor thinks the disease is caused by germs, you may need to provide a sample. This will be sent to a laboratory, which will identify any germs present.

◄ TAKING SAMPLES
While examining a young girl, a doctor takes a sample of saliva from her mouth with a cotton swab. The sample is then sent to a lab.

◄ SAMPLE PLATE
In the lab, the sample is smeared across a plate of jelly. The jelly contains nutrients that encourage bacteria from the sample to grow and multiply.

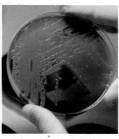

◄ CULTURE
Over several days, each bacterium from the sample multiplies to form a colony of thousands, forming a visible spot on the sample plate.

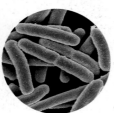

◄ IDENTIFY
The bacteria can now be identified. Viewing them with a microscope reveals their distinctive size, shape, and color.

HYGIENE
Dirty hands can spread disease from person to person. This picture shows colonies of bacteria that were allowed to grow from a dirty handprint. The bacteria are *E. coli*, which can cause food poisoning if they get into food. Good hygiene can help prevent the spread of disease. For example, washing your hands after using the bathroom reduces the risk of passing harmful bacteria to others.

GERM KILLERS
Diseases caused by bacteria are treated with drugs called antibiotics. These attack and destroy bacterial cells without harming body cells. There are many kinds of antibiotics, each active against particular kinds of bacteria. For diseases caused by viruses, doctors may prescribe antiviral drugs instead.

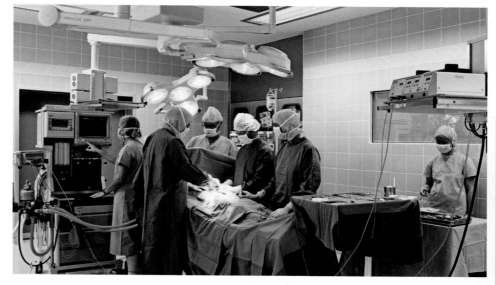

Each spot is a colony of thousands of bacteria that grew from a single bacterium in the dirty handprint.

WOW!

Given warmth and sufficient food, a single bacterium can divide and give rise to 5 billion trillion offspring in just one day.

SURGERY

If disease or injury damages an organ inside the body, doctors may need to perform surgery to repair the damage. Patients are first given drugs called anesthetics to make them fall asleep and to prevent pain. The surgeon then makes precise cuts in the skin in order to open up the body and gain access to the damaged area. Surgeons work in spotlessly clean operating theaters to prevent germs from entering the patient's body during an operation.

FIGHTING CANCER

Sometimes body cells stop working properly and begin to multiply out of control like germs, forming lumps known as tumors. This deadly disease is called cancer. Cancer is difficult to treat because drugs that attack cancer cells also harm healthy body cells. To help destroy tumors, doctors fire beams of powerful radiation at them—a treatment called radiotherapy.

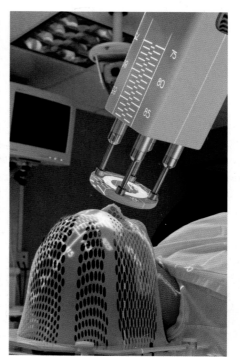

▶ RADIOTHERAPY *This patient is being treated for skin cancer. A beam of radiation is pointed at a tumor from several different angles, killing the cancer cells without harming the healthy tissue around it.*

Spare parts

In the past, losing an important part of the body due to disease or injury led to death or severe disability. Today, doctors can repair many parts of the body with artificial replacements. In years to come, they may be able to replace organs with fresh new ones grown in a lab from your own body cells. This technology would allow us to live decades longer than today.

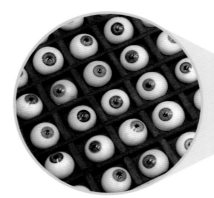

▲ GLASS EYES *Artificial eyes look realistic but they do not restore vision. However, scientists are developing implants that could restore some form of vision to people who are blind.*

REBUILDING THE BODY

Some of the artificial parts that doctors use to repair damaged bodies are mechanical or electrical devices made of metals and plastics. Others, such as artificial skin or transplanted organs, are made of living tissue. Most of these spare parts do not work as well as the organs they replace.

► NEW SKIN *Scientists have discovered how to grow sheets of artificial skin from a person's skin cells. Although they're very thin, these sheets may soon be used to repair damage caused by severe burns.*

▼ HIP JOINT *Damaged by age or disease, some joints, such as the hip, can be repaired with an artificial replacement.*

STEM CELLS

Some of the cells in the human body have an amazing ability: They can multiply and develop into any kind of tissue, such as skin, blood, or nerves. Such cells are known as stem cells. Scientists are trying to harness this ability of stem cells and create new tissues or organs to repair or replace body parts that are injured or diseased.

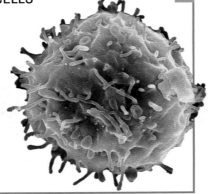

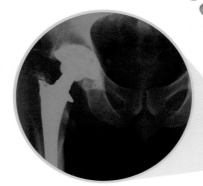

▲ EAR IMPLANT *A cochlear implant picks up sound and transmits it to the inner ear, giving some sense of hearing to people who are deaf.*

BLADE RUNNER

South African athlete Oscar Pistorius lost the lower part of both his legs when he was a baby. He now walks and runs on J-shaped artificial feet made of carbon fiber. These are so good that Pistorius, nicknamed "Blade Runner" by his fans, is able to compete against able-bodied athletes, as in the 2011 World Athletics Championships, shown below.

A computer controls the motors that make the arm and hand move.

PACEMAKER ▲
Implanted into the chest wall, a pacemaker sends an electric signal along a wire to the heart, controlling the rate at which it beats.

◀ ROBOTIC ARM
This high-tech mechanical arm is controlled by thought alone. Sensors on the shoulder pick up nerve signals inside the wearer's body and relay them to a computer, which controls the arm's movements.

A motor inside the elbow makes the arm bend.

ORGAN TRANSPLANTS

The most common way of replacing a damaged internal organ is to use a healthy organ from a donor—an organ transplant. Transplants can save lives and make people healthy again, but recipients must take powerful drugs to stop their bodies from rejecting the new organs.

◀ NEW BLADDER *The bladder is one of the few organs that scientists can grow in a lab, using a patient's own body cells.*

▲ KIDNEY TRANSPLANT *Surgeons prepare a donated kidney before implanting it into a recipient.*

101

Ancient remedies

Before the age of science, people used all sorts of weird and wacky remedies to try and cure diseases. Many people visited witch doctors or priests in search of magical cures. Others made their own medicines, following traditional old wives' recipes. Many of the ancient remedies were useless or even dangerous, but a few really did work and are still used today.

HERBAL MEDICINE

Plants have been used as medicines all over the world for thousands of years and they are still popular today. Some of our modern drugs were discovered thanks to ancient herbal remedies. The painkiller aspirin, for instance, comes from the bark of willow trees, which people once used to make a pain-relieving tea.

▶ BROKEN ARM
This engraving from the 1500s shows how a man's broken arm was treated. Turning the screw pulled the arm straight, moving the broken bones back into position.

CUPPING

The ancient practice of cupping was once widely believed to help cure diseases by encouraging blood flow. Small cups are heated and placed on the skin. As the air inside a cup cools, it contracts, sucking up an area of skin and drawing blood to the surface. Red rings and sometimes bruises are left afterward.

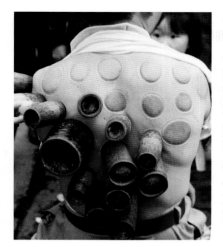

A HOLE IN THE HEAD

Stone age people believed that diseases were caused by evil spirits. The cure, they thought, was to drill a hole in the skull to release the spirit— a technique called trepanning. Some prehistoric skulls found by archaeologists have as many as 40 holes drilled in them.

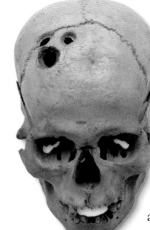

BARBER SURGEONS

In medieval Europe, all operations from tooth extraction to mending broken arms were performed by barbers. Surgery was often deadly since barbers had little idea how to stop wounds from getting infected. And patients had to stay awake during treatment since general anesthetics didn't exist.

BLOODLETTING

Removing blood, or bloodletting, was a very common medical practice for centuries. It was thought to put body fluids back into balance. Blood was drawn by cutting the skin, by piercing veins and arteries, or by using bloodsucking leeches.

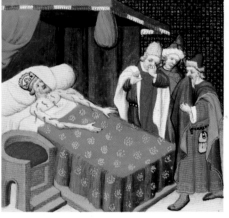

▲ BLOODSUCKERS
The Roman Emperor Galerius was treated with leeches to cure an "abominable stench."

MUD BATHS

Bathing in pools of mud, hot springs, or mineral water has long been a popular treatment for joint pain (arthritis), skin complaints, and other conditions. Even today, people travel great distances to visit famous spa towns and "take the waters."

LUNGS AND BREATHING

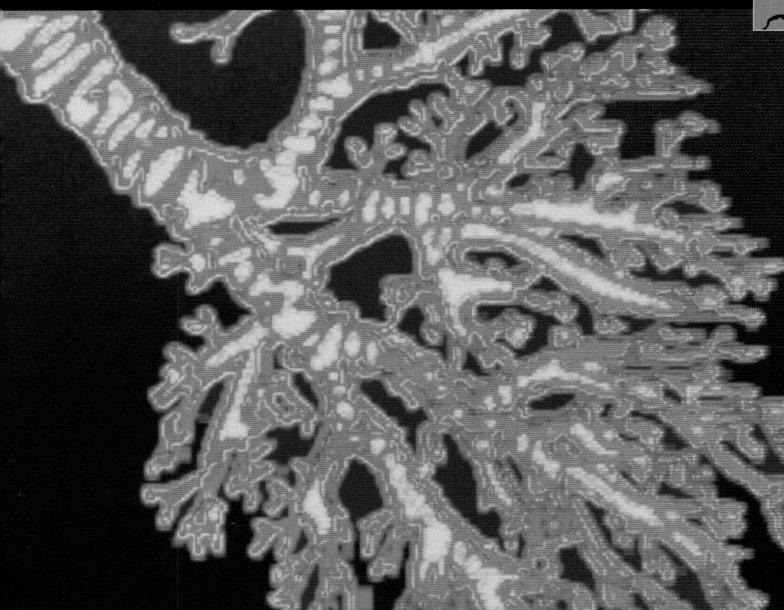

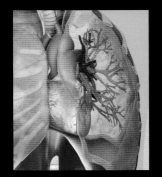
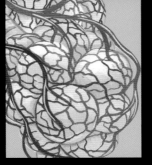

The cells in your body can't survive without a continual supply of oxygen from the air. Your lungs take in air with every breath, bringing oxygen to your blood to be carried around the body.

Airways

We never really think about breathing because it is such an automatic process, but it is vital to our survival. Every inward breath brings a new supply of air into the network of tubes that make up the respiratory system. These take air deep into the lungs, where the gas oxygen, which is vital for life, passes into the blood to be carried all around the body.

Air is warmed and cleaned as it passes through the nasal cavity.

The epiglottis is a flap at the front of the voice box.

The voice box, or larynx, produces sounds.

THE RESPIRATORY SYSTEM

Your lungs and the airways that carry air in and out of your body are located in your head and chest. The airways include the nasal cavity, the throat, the larynx (voice box), and the branching passages inside your lungs. Incoming air is cleaned as it travels through your nose and trachea to remove dirt and germs that could block or damage the delicate lungs.

▶ THIS WAY
TO THE LUNGS
The ridged appearance of the trachea is produced by rings of rubbery cartilage that hold it open during breathing and stop it from closing up.

Oxygen

OXYGEN SUPPLY

We breathe in oxygen and breathe out waste carbon dioxide. So why doesn't our oxygen supply run out? Plants ensure there is a steady supply in the air by releasing oxygen during photosynthesis, the process that uses sunlight and carbon dioxide to make food.

Carbon dioxide

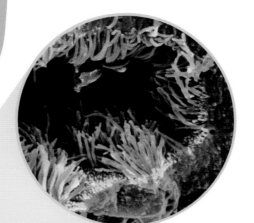

NO CHOKING

Every time you swallow food or drink, your breathing stops. A flap of tissue called the epiglottis drops over the entrance to your voice box to stop food from getting into the airway to your lungs and making you choke. If this happens, however, coughing forces food out of the airway and back into your throat.

▲ AIR CLEANERS

The trachea is lined with sticky mucus that traps dirt and germs in the incoming air. Tiny cilia (green) move the dirty mucus to the throat, where it is swallowed.

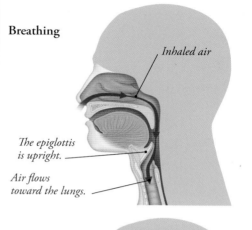

Breathing

Inhaled air

The epiglottis is upright.

Air flows toward the lungs.

Swallowing

Food is pushed into the esophagus.

Esophagus

The epiglottis folds over to cover the entrance to the voice box.

Air is carried to and from the lungs by the trachea.

Curved ribs form a protective cage around the lungs.

The airways become more finely branched as they penetrate deeper into the lung.

The heart pumps blood to the lungs to pick up oxygen.

Protective membranes cover the lungs.

A sheet of muscle called the diaphragm helps inflate the lungs.

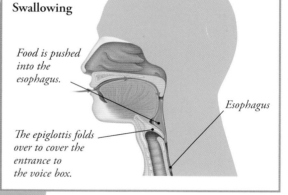

WOW!

Every day, you swallow about a glassful of slimy mucus produced by your airways.

In and out

Your body cells need constant supplies of oxygen. They also need to get rid of waste carbon dioxide gas. This exchange of gases happens in your lungs. Breathing in and out ensures that fresh supplies of oxygen are brought in and stale air containing carbon dioxide is removed. The lungs cannot move by themselves, so the process relies on muscles in the chest to suck air in and push it out.

WHAT IS AIR?

Air is a mixture of gases that surrounds our planet. As you can see from this balloon diagram, air is mostly nitrogen (about 78 percent) and oxygen (about 21 percent), plus small amounts of other gases. Oxygen is the only part of the gas mixture that your body uses.

Nitrogen

Oxygen

Other gases

AIR IN

Air is drawn into the body by the movement of the rib muscles and the diaphragm—a sheet of muscles under the lungs. When you breathe in, the diaphragm tightens and pulls down. At the same time, your rib muscles tighten and pull your ribcage upward and outward. As a result, your chest gets larger and your lungs suck in air through your mouth and nose.

You take in about 40,000 breaths of air every day.

Oxygen (20.8%)

Nitrogen and water vapor (79.16%)

Carbon dioxide (0.04%)

The ribcage moves upward and outward as the rib muscles contract.

The lungs get bigger and suck in air.

The diaphragm flattens and pulls downward.

AIR OUT

When you breathe out, your diaphragm relaxes and springs back into its natural, curved shape, pushing up against your lungs. At the same time, your rib muscles relax and let your ribcage drop back downward and inward. As a result, your lungs are squeezed and air is pushed out through your mouth and nose. The air you breathe out contains less oxygen and more carbon dioxide than the air you breathed in.

CONTROL CENTER

You don't have to think about breathing. The brain stem (orange) at the base of your brain (green) automatically controls your breathing rate. This control center monitors the amount of carbon dioxide in your blood. If the carbon dioxide level rises, during exercise for example, your breathing rate goes up to supply more oxygen to your muscles and to flush out the excess carbon dioxide.

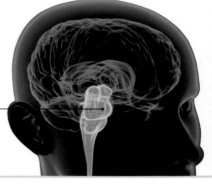

The brain stem controls the body's breathing rate.

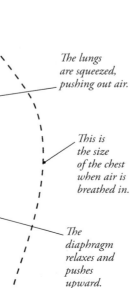

80.4% Nitrogen and water vapor

15.6% Oxygen

4% Carbon dioxide

The ribcage moves downward and inward as the rib muscles relax.

The lungs are squeezed, pushing out air.

This is the size of the chest when air is breathed in.

The diaphragm relaxes and pushes upward.

FAST OR SLOW?

At rest, we breathe in and out between 12 and 15 times a minute. During exercise, such as running, our breathing rate can more than double and we breathe more deeply. This is because our muscles are working harder and need more oxygen to release the energy required for movement. They also produce more carbon dioxide, which must be removed.

BREATHING UNDERWATER

A continual supply of oxygen from the air is vital for the human body. Without it, brain cells start dying in large numbers after only five minutes. Scuba divers breathe air underwater from a compressed-air tank carried on the back. One tank has enough air to last 45 minutes.

Inside the lungs

Packed into your chest are a pair of soft, spongy lungs. Their job is to get oxygen into, and carbon dioxide out of, your blood. This transfer is made possible by millions of tiny air bags inside the lungs that are supplied by a rich network of blood vessels.

The trachea carries air to and from the lungs.

Blood is carried into the lung by the pulmonary artery.

Blood is carried out of the lung by the pulmonary vein.

LUNG STRUCTURE

Air is carried to the lungs by a tube called the trachea. This branches into two tubes called bronchi, which branch further into smaller and smaller tubes called bronchioles. At the end of the tiniest bronchioles are 150 million little air bags, called alveoli, which swap oxygen for carbon dioxide.

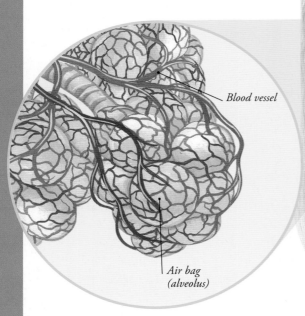

Blood vessel

Air bag (alveolus)

▲ AIR BAGS *The bronchioles end in tiny, lumpy air bags called alveoli. Oxygen from the air inside alveoli passes into the blood capillaries that surround them.*

Bronchioles

The right bronchus carries air to and from the right lung.

112

BRONCHIAL TREE

The branching network of airways inside the lungs is sometimes called the bronchial tree. As you can see here, it looks like an upside-down tree with the trachea as the trunk, bronchi as the branches, and the tiny bronchioles as twigs.

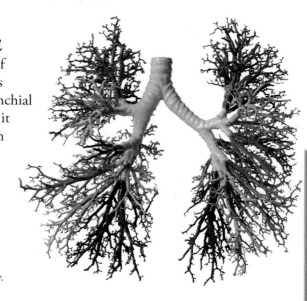

The left bronchus carries air to and from the left lung.

The left lung opened up to show its structure.

The heart fits into this space.

Slippery membranes surround the lungs.

🔍 LOOK CLOSER: DUST GOBBLERS

When you breathe in air, most dust particles, pollen grains, and germs are trapped by sticky mucus in the nose and airways. But some of them travel deep into the lungs. Before they can do any harm, they are gobbled up by wandering macrophages.

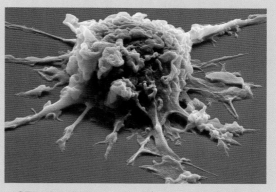

▲ GERM EATER *A macrophage is a type of white blood cell. It moves by extending its narrow "arms," which it also uses to grab foreign particles.*

INTO THE BLOOD

This is a close-up view of what happens at the junction between an alveolus and a capillary. Oxygen travels from the alveolus into the blood, and carbon dioxide moves in the opposite direction.

Oxygen passes into the blood.

Blood cell

Inside of alveolus

Carbon dioxide passes out of the blood into the alveolus.

Coughs and sneezes

Your lungs and airways are always at work, taking in fresh air and pushing out stale air, and most of the time you don't notice them doing it. Occasionally, however, they might surprise you with an unexpected cough, sneeze, yawn, or hiccup. These processes mostly play a vital role in keeping you healthy, but some are a bit of a mystery.

WOW!

You can't cough, sneeze, yawn, hiccup, or laugh when you're dreaming, since most of your muscles are paralyzed during dreams.

SNEEZING

If something itchy gets in your nose, your body clears it out with a deafening blast of air: a sneeze. After a sharp intake of breath, your eyes close and your rib muscles tighten to squeeze your lungs and blast air out, often with a brief scream. Your tongue rises to direct air into your nose, but most of the blast often comes out of the mouth.

Sneezes clear germs out of your nose but spread them to other people.

HICCUPS

Hiccups happen when your diaphragm muscle twitches. The sudden movement of the diaphragm causes a very sharp intake of breath, and the rush of air makes the vocal cords at the top of the trachea snap shut, blocking the air and producing a "hic" sound. Hiccups have no known purpose and can start for no apparent reason. They usually stop after a minute or two, but in rare cases they last longer. One man had a bout of hiccups that lasted 68 years.

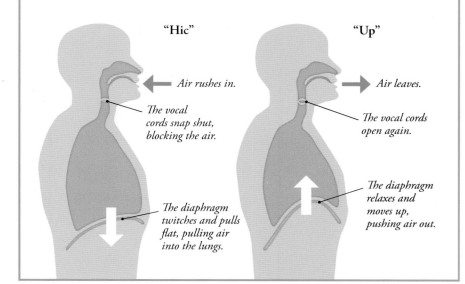

"Hic"

Air rushes in.

The vocal cords snap shut, blocking the air.

The diaphragm twitches and pulls flat, pulling air into the lungs.

"Up"

Air leaves.

The vocal cords open again.

The diaphragm relaxes and moves up, pushing air out.

YAWNING

No one knows what purpose yawning serves. Yawns aren't an efficient way of breathing, and although we yawn when we're tired, we also do it when we're nervous. To add to the mystery, yawns are contagious—if you see someone yawn, you'll probably do it too.

LAUGHING

When we laugh, the vocal cords at the top of the trachea open and close repeatedly, chopping our breaths into segments and making a "ha, ha, ha" or "ho, ho, ho" sound. Laughter triggers the release of brain chemicals called endorphins, which make us feel great.

SNORING

The roof of your mouth is hard at the front but soft at the back, where it forms a flap of tissue separating your mouth and nose. In some people, this flap wobbles around during sleep, making a loud noise—snoring. People snore less if they lie on one side.

COUGHING

Coughing gets rid of specks of dirt or germs that have gotten into your airways. First you take a deep breath. Then your lungs squeeze, but the vocal cords stay shut to build up pressure. When they open, air shoots out in a sudden blast.

Making sounds

Many animals make sounds, but humans are the only animals that can communicate using spoken words. Both speech and language are controlled by your brain. It sends out instructions that make your respiratory (breathing) system produce sounds that can be understood by those around you.

WHAT IS SOUND?

Throw a pebble into a pond and circular ripples will move outward from the point of impact. In the same way, if you pluck a guitar string so it vibrates, sound waves will move outward through the air. These sound waves are picked up by your ears.

WOW!

Men have deeper voices than women because their vocal cords are longer and vibrate more slowly.

VOICE BOX

The vocal cords in your voice box (larynx) make the sounds that are shaped into speech. These cords are separated when you are silent and breathing normally. When you speak, your brain sends signals to the voice box muscles to pull the vocal cords together and make them tight. When air pushes between these muscles, they vibrate and create sounds.

The vocal cords stretch across the larynx.

▲ VOCAL CORDS TAUT *Bursts of air passing between the taut vocal cords make them vibrate and produce sounds.*

Sounds are produced by the voice box (larynx).

The trachea carries air to and from the lungs.

▲ VOCAL CORDS OPEN *During normal breathing, the open vocal cords allow air to move to and from the lungs.*

The esophagus is a part of the digestive system.

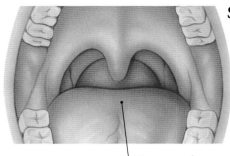

Tongue muscles
help shape sounds.

SHAPING SPEECH

Under orders from your brain, the muscles controlling your tongue, lips, and cheeks shape the sounds coming from your vocal cords. They create a sequence of words, spoken in a recognizable language, which reveals your thoughts and feelings to others.

IN CONTROL

These two scans show which areas of your brain are used when you speak (left) and when you listen to spoken words (right). In the first scan, Wernicke's area finds the correct words to match what the brain has to say and sends signals to Broca's area. This, in turn, sends signals to the voice box and the mouth instructing them to produce speech.

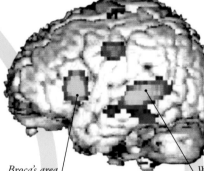
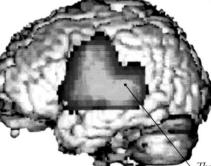
FAST FACTS

■ Around 6,900 languages are spoken in the world today. The top five most spoken languages are Mandarin Chinese, English, Spanish, Hindi, and Russian.
■ The vocal cords of a soprano—a woman with a high singing voice—vibrate at up to 2,000 times a second.
■ The vocal cords of a bass—a man with a low singing voice—vibrate just 60 times a second.

MAKING MUSIC

Some people can use their breathing systems to make sounds much louder than their own voices. Controlled bursts of air from this musician's lungs create buzzing vibrations in her lips. These sound vibrations enter and travel through the long tube-shaped trumpet, which makes the sounds much louder.

▶ HEARING *Sound waves from the speaker's mouth enter the listener's ears. Here they are detected by sound receptors that send signals to the brain.*

117

FUELING THE BODY

Just like a car, your body needs a supply of fuel to keep you going. All your energy comes from food, which your digestive organs break down into simple molecules for your body to absorb.

Food for life

You need to eat food so that your body can get the nutrients it needs to grow, and to repair and maintain itself. Some nutrients are needed in large amounts. These include carbohydrates, which supply energy, and proteins, which are used to build and repair your body's cells. Vitamins and minerals are needed in smaller quantities.

WOW!

Water is an important part of your diet. Some fruit contains a lot of liquid—apples are 84 percent water.

A HEALTHY DIET

The nutrients you need to stay healthy can be found in food. Different types of food provide different nutrients. This platter shows how much you should eat of each type, compared to the others. For example, you should eat a lot of fresh fruits and vegetables, but not very much meat or fat.

Peppers supply minerals and vitamins and are a good source of fiber. This helps speed up digestion.

Carrots contain vitamin A. You need this vitamin to keep the eyes healthy.

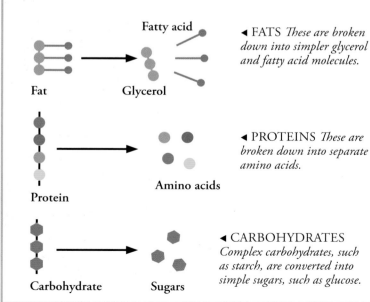

Whole grains are a good source of some B vitamins. These help keep your cells healthy.

BREAKING DOWN FOOD

The nutrients that we need are often "locked" inside food and can't be used by your body right away. Your digestive system breaks down complicated foods into simple sugars, fatty acids, and amino acids—the basic building blocks of protein—that the body can absorb and use.

Fatty acid

Fat → Glycerol

◀ FATS *These are broken down into simpler glycerol and fatty acid molecules.*

Protein → Amino acids

◀ PROTEINS *These are broken down into separate amino acids.*

Carbohydrate → Sugars

◀ CARBOHYDRATES *Complex carbohydrates, such as starch, are converted into simple sugars, such as glucose.*

▶ RICKETS *This X-ray shows the bent leg bones of a child with rickets. Rickets occurs when the body doesn't get enough vitamin D. This vitamin is essential for normal bone growth. It is found in fish and eggs. Your body can also produce it when you get sunlight on your skin.*

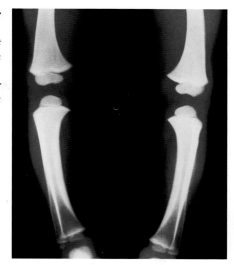

VITAMINS AND MINERALS

Although they are only needed in tiny amounts, vitamins and minerals are essential for good health. A healthy diet should include vitamins A, B group, C, D, and E. Important minerals include calcium, for healthy teeth and bones, and iron, which is needed to make red blood cells.

Citrus fruits, such as lemons, are a good source of vitamin C, which can help you fight infections.

Beans and nuts are a good source of protein, essential for cell growth and repair.

Fish, meat, and eggs are high in protein.

Sweets and fats should be eaten in small amounts.

LIND'S LIMES

Sailors used to develop a deadly disease called scurvy on long sea voyages. In 1747, a navy doctor named James Lind found that feeding them citrus fruits, such as limes, cured them. Later, scurvy was shown to result from a lack of vitamin C.

FEELING HUNGRY

The area of your brain that controls your appetite.

Hunger and fullness are sensations produced by a part of your brain called the hypothalamus. Before a meal, the stomach releases a hormone that makes you feel hungry. After a meal, fat tissue releases another hormone that makes you feel full.

Cheese and other dairy products are a good source of calcium, needed for healthy bones.

Bread and other starchy foods are the body's main source of energy.

Digestion

Food provides the body with nutrients. But releasing those nutrients from food requires a process called digestion. First, the food has to be cut up and churned into small particles. This makes it easier for enzymes to work on the complex chemicals that make up food and split them into substances that can be used by the body. All of this happens inside the digestive system.

DIGESTIVE SYSTEM

The digestive system consists of a long, muscular tube called the digestive tract, which runs from the mouth to the anus. It has several distinct regions, including the esophagus, stomach, small intestine, and large intestine—each with its own tasks. Other organs that help digestion, such as the gall bladder and pancreas, add digestive chemicals at various points along the way.

WOW!

During an average lifetime, a person will eat their way through, and digest, at least 20 tons of food.

Food is moved between the teeth and toward the back of the mouth for swallowing by the tongue.

The throat (pharynx) connects the mouth to the esophagus.

The teeth cut and crush food into small pieces.

The epiglottis stops food from going down the trachea during swallowing.

Salivary glands release saliva into the mouth.

The trachea, part of the respiratory system, carries air to the lungs.

The esophagus transports food from the throat to the stomach.

The stomach stores and partially digests food.

Nutrients are processed by the liver.

Fats are turned into tiny droplets by bile, a green fluid released by the gall bladder.

The pancreas releases digestive enzymes into the small intestine.

Most food is digested in the small intestine. The nutrients that are released are absorbed into the bloodstream.

In the large intestine, water is absorbed from waste to form feces (poo).

The rectum holds and expels feces.

The anus is the opening at the end of the digestive tract.

ENZYMES IN ACTION

Enzymes are proteins that speed up the breakdown of complex molecules into much simpler nutrients that can pass into the bloodstream to be used by cells. Without enzymes, digestion would be so slow that we would starve. Each enzyme acts on a specific food type, such as the enzyme pepsin in stomach juice that breaks down proteins into simpler nutrients. You can see here how an enzyme works.

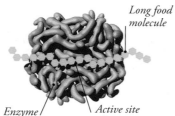

Long food molecule

Enzyme *Active site of enzyme*

▲ ATTACHMENT *Inside the digestive tract, a food molecule attaches itself to a region of its specific enzyme called the active site.*

Long food molecule splits

▲ SPLITTING MOLECULES *The active site breaks some of the chemical bonds in the food molecule, splitting it into smaller nutrient molecules.*

Short, simple nutrient molecules

Enzyme ready for action

▲ NONSTOP ACTIVITY *The enzyme releases the molecule once it has split apart. One enzyme can process hundreds of molecules a second.*

TAKING TIME

It only takes a few seconds for food chewed in the mouth to arrive in the stomach. But, as you can see from this stretched-out view of the digestive tract, the rest of the process takes up to two days longer. This ensures that food is properly digested to release as many nutrients as possible, and that these nutrients are all absorbed into the bloodstream.

00:00:10
Ten seconds after swallowing, food arrives in the stomach.

03:00:00
Food in creamy, liquid form is squirted into the small intestine.

06:00:00
Food is now almost completely digested and its nutrients are being absorbed.

20:00:00
Water is absorbed as waste passes along the large intestine.

08:00:00
Watery, indigestible waste leaves the small intestine.

32:00:00
Feces arrive in the rectum 20 to 44 hours after eating.

Semi-solid feces form as water is removed.

LOOK CLOSER: FOOD POISONING

Most bacteria and other microorganisms in food are destroyed by the harsh, acidic conditions found in the stomach. But some harmful bacteria survive and they, or their poisons (toxins), irritate the stomach and intestines, giving you food poisoning. This causes symptoms such as vomiting (throwing up) and diarrhea (runny poo).

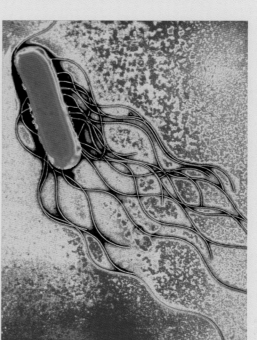

▲ STOMACH BUG *This micrograph shows Salmonella, a bacterium that causes food poisoning. The bacterium is rod-shaped and can move by wiggling its hairlike flagella to push itself forward.*

What a mouthful!

If you tried to swallow a large piece of food without chewing it, you would probably choke. You must first grind it up by repeatedly bringing your teeth together to chop and crush it into smaller pieces. While you chew, the food is moistened with saliva, and moved and mixed up by your tongue. In addition to making food moist, saliva contains an enzyme that starts to digest it.

The parotid gland releases saliva into the mouth.

DOWN THE HATCH

The first part of the digestive system, the mouth, contains the teeth and tongue. Slippery saliva rushes into the mouth from three pairs of salivary glands situated under the tongue and in front of the ears. Saliva lubricates the food as it is chewed into a pulp. A ball of food is then pushed into the throat and travels down the esophagus to the stomach.

The roof of the mouth is called the hard palate.

A duct from the parotid gland carries saliva to the mouth.

The incisor teeth cut up food as it enters the mouth.

The tongue moves food between the teeth, and tastes it.

Two pairs of glands release saliva under the tongue.

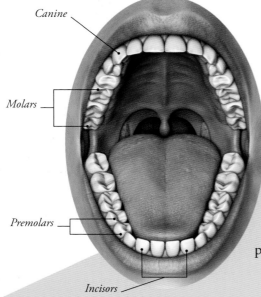

Canine

Molars

Premolars

Incisors

OPEN WIDE

Adults have a full set of 32 teeth, which vary in shape and size according to what they do. Chisel-like incisors cut and slice food, while pointed canines grip and pierce. Farther back are the premolars and molars, which chew and grind food between the pointed tips of their crowns.

Esophagus

Trachea

FUELING THE BODY

124

INSIDE A TOOTH

A tooth has two layers: a smooth enamel crown that provides a hard biting surface, and the dentine beneath, which also forms the root. Inside the dentine is the pulp cavity containing blood vessels that supply tooth cells, and nerve endings that detect pressure, heat, and cold, and also signal pain.

Crown

The gum forms a collar around the base of the crown.

▼ DENTINE *is harder than bone and forms the framework of the tooth. Its honeycomb structure helps it resist the enormous squashing forces that are created during biting.*

Pulp is the soft tissue containing nerve endings and blood vessels.

▲ ENAMEL *is the hardest material in the body and forms the crown of the tooth. It consists of microscopic rods of calcium phosphate.*

The root of the tooth is embedded in a socket in the jawbone.

A band of tough tissue called a ligament anchors the tooth in its socket.

Jawbone

Blood vessels supply the tooth with nutrients.

A nerve provides the tooth with feeling.

FROM MOUTH TO STOMACH

Swallowing, the process that moves food from the mouth to the stomach, has three phases. The first, in the mouth, is under your control, so you decide when to push food into your throat. The other two stages, in the throat and esophagus, are reflex actions that happen automatically.

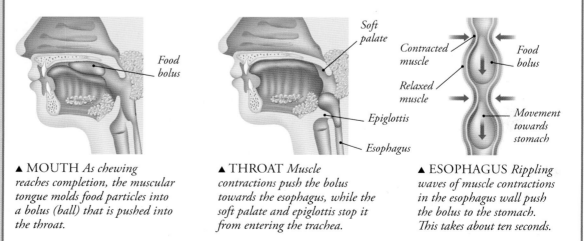

Food bolus

Soft palate

Contracted muscle

Food bolus

Relaxed muscle

Epiglottis

Esophagus

Movement towards stomach

▲ MOUTH *As chewing reaches completion, the muscular tongue molds food particles into a bolus (ball) that is pushed into the throat.*

▲ THROAT *Muscle contractions push the bolus towards the esophagus, while the soft palate and epiglottis stop it from entering the trachea.*

▲ ESOPHAGUS *Rippling waves of muscle contractions in the esophagus wall push the bolus to the stomach. This takes about ten seconds.*

In the stomach

The stomach is a muscular "bag" that sits just below the diaphragm muscle in the middle of the chest. It has two key roles. When you eat, it releases an acidic gastric juice that starts to break down the proteins in food. It also stores food, releasing it at a steady rate so that the small intestine has time to digest it efficiently.

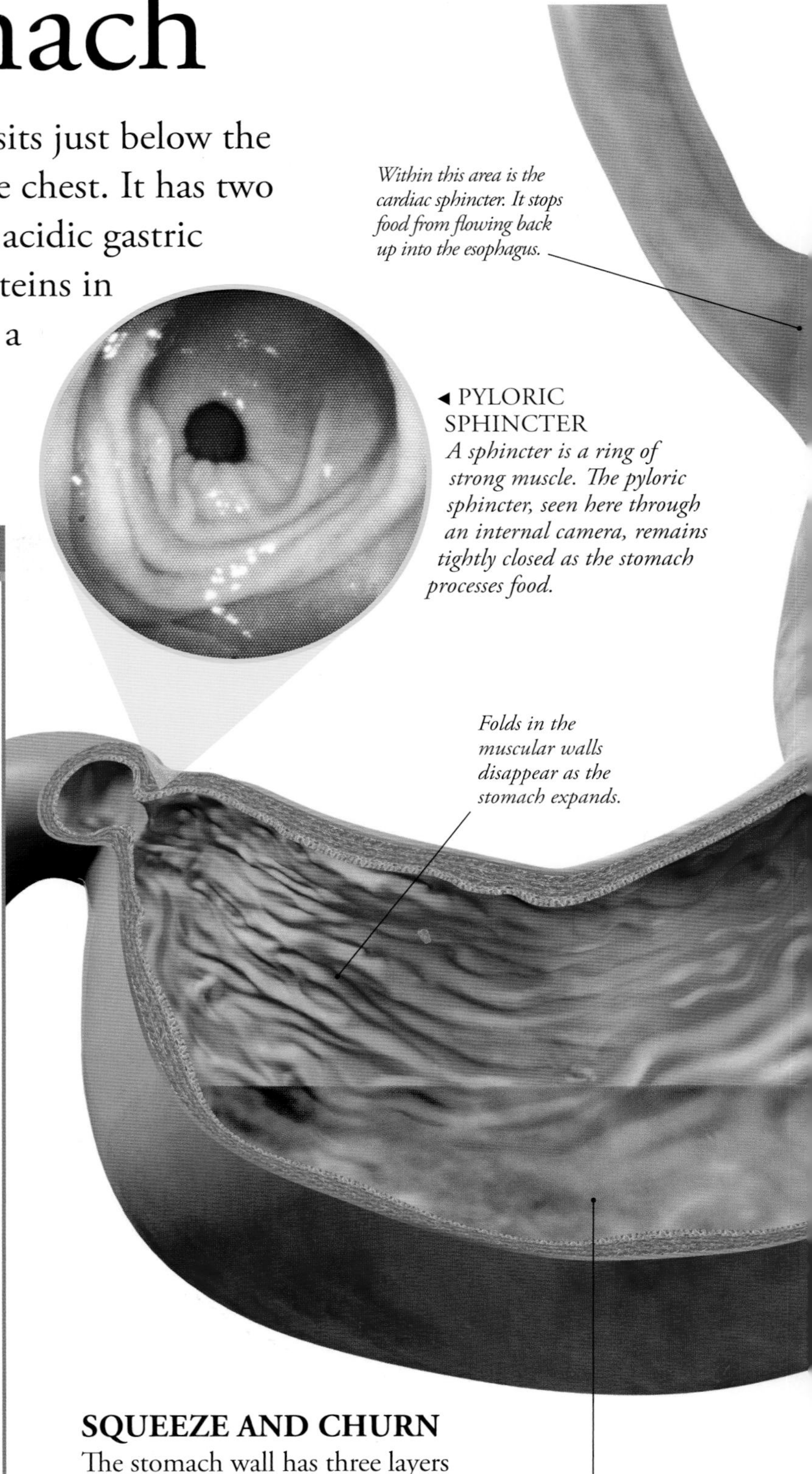

Within this area is the cardiac sphincter. It stops food from flowing back up into the esophagus.

◄ PYLORIC SPHINCTER
A sphincter is a ring of strong muscle. The pyloric sphincter, seen here through an internal camera, remains tightly closed as the stomach processes food.

Folds in the muscular walls disappear as the stomach expands.

FILLING AND EMPTYING

The process of filling and emptying the stomach depends on the type of food eaten, but it takes at least three hours. During this time, food is partially digested and made ready for the main part of digestion in the small intestine. Only when the meal has been turned into liquid form is it released into the duodenum.

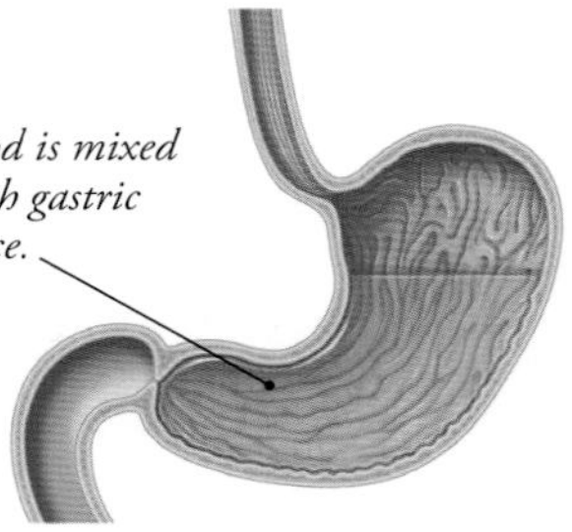

Food is mixed with gastric juice.

◄ DURING A MEAL
As the stomach fills and expands, recently chewed food is mixed with gastric juice by contractions of the stomach's wall.

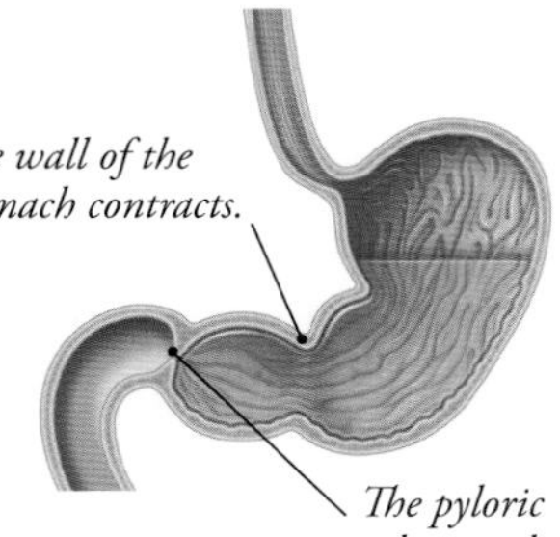

The wall of the stomach contracts.

◄ 1–2 HOURS AFTER EATING
Food is partly digested by gastric juice and churned by powerful muscular contractions into a creamy liquid called chyme.

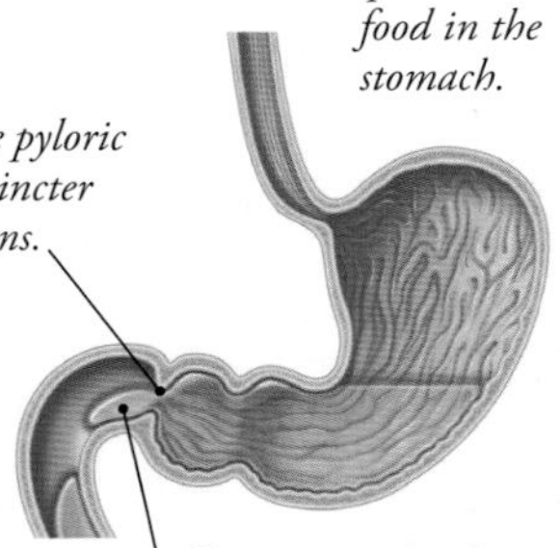

The pyloric sphincter keeps food in the stomach.

The pyloric sphincter opens.

◄ 3–4 HOURS AFTER EATING *The pyloric sphincter opens slightly and the stomach wall contracts to push small quantities of chyme into the duodenum, which is the first part of the small intestine.*

Chyme is squirted into the duodenum.

Chyme (liquid food)

SQUEEZE AND CHURN

The stomach wall has three layers of muscles, arranged at different angles to each other. These produce powerful contractions that squeeze the food and mix it with gastric juice. An enzyme called pepsin gets to work on food proteins, breaking them down into simpler substances.

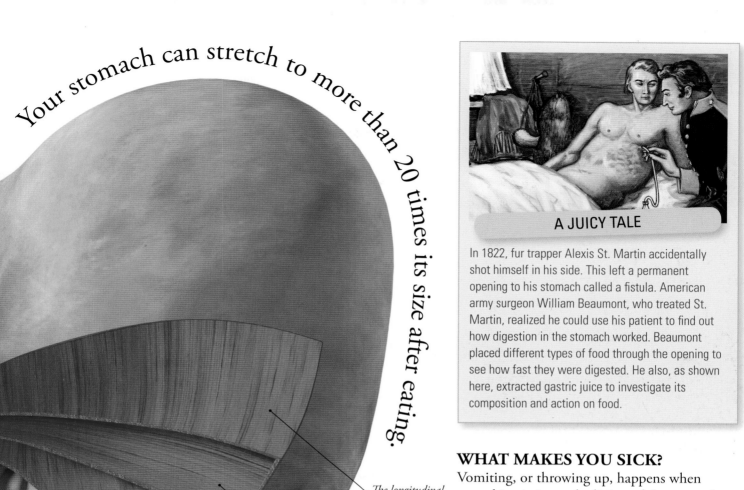

Your stomach can stretch to more than 20 times its size after eating.

The longitudinal muscle layer extends the length of the stomach.

The circular muscle layer wraps around the stomach.

The oblique muscle layer runs diagonally around stomach.

▶ STOMACH LINING
This magnified view of the stomach's lining shows the openings of the glands that release digestive gastric juice into the stomach.

Gastric pit

A JUICY TALE

In 1822, fur trapper Alexis St. Martin accidentally shot himself in his side. This left a permanent opening to his stomach called a fistula. American army surgeon William Beaumont, who treated St. Martin, realized he could use his patient to find out how digestion in the stomach worked. Beaumont placed different types of food through the opening to see how fast they were digested. He also, as shown here, extracted gastric juice to investigate its composition and action on food.

WHAT MAKES YOU SICK?

Vomiting, or throwing up, happens when something irritates the lining of the stomach. This triggers the vomiting reflex. The diaphragm and abdominal muscles contract, squeezing the stomach so that food is forced up the esophagus and out of the mouth.

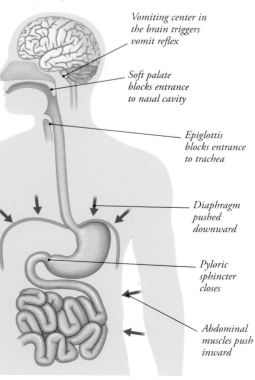

Vomiting center in the brain triggers vomit reflex

Soft palate blocks entrance to nasal cavity

Epiglottis blocks entrance to trachea

Diaphragm pushed downward

Pyloric sphincter closes

Abdominal muscles push inward

Gut reactions

At nearly 23 ft (7 m) in length, the small intestine is the longest and most important part of the digestive system. With the help of the pancreas and gall bladder, the small intestine completes the digestive process. It then absorbs all the released nutrients so that they can be used by your body's cells.

LONG AND WINDING JOURNEY

This long, middle part of the digestive tract is coiled up to fit into the abdomen. The small intestine has three sections. The short duodenum receives chyme from the stomach and digestive juices from the gall bladder and pancreas. The longer jejunum and ileum are where most digestion and absorption of food takes place.

Liver

The pancreas produces enzymes and hormones.

The gall bladder stores and releases bile.

The large intestine lies in front of the duodenum, the first part of the small intestine.

The second part of the small intestine is called the jejunum.

Appendix

The ileum is the final and longest part of the small intestine.

GALL BLADDER AND PANCREAS

The gall bladder and pancreas release fluids through a common duct into the duodenum. This kick-starts digestion in the small intestine. The baglike gall bladder stores bile made by the liver. Bile turns fats into tiny droplets that are much easier to digest. The pancreas makes pancreatic juice. This contains enzymes that break down carbohydrates, proteins, and fats in the food we eat.

Bile duct

Gall bladder

Pancreas

Pancreatic duct

Opening of pancreatic and bile ducts

Duodenum

Muscular wall

◀ INSIDE VIEW *This cross-section of the small intestine reveals its structure. Muscles in its wall create wavelike contractions that both mix food and move it onward. The lining is covered with tiny, fingerlike bumps called villi.*

WOW!

The small intestine is coiled inside the abdomen, but stretched out it would be as long as four adults laid head to toe.

▶ VILLI *These are some of the millions of microscopic villi lining the small intestine. Villi provide a huge surface area for digestion and absorption to take place. If stretched out, the villi in your small intestine would cover an area roughly the size of a tennis court.*

DIGEST AND ABSORB

Inside the small intestine, enzymes attached to the surface of villi complete the process of digestion. They break down food into simple nutrients—glucose, amino acids, and fatty acids.

▶ ABSORPTION *Glucose and amino acids are absorbed into the capillary networks inside villi and are carried in the blood to the liver for processing. Fatty acids enter lymph capillaries (green) for their journey to the liver.*

▲ IN THE MIDDLE *The small intestine, which winds its way from the stomach to the large intestine, takes up much of the space in the abdomen.*

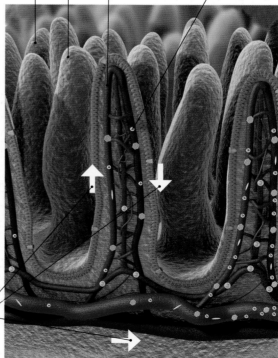

Villi

Capillary network inside a villus

Food molecule in a capillary

Direction of blood flow

BUMPY SURFACE

The inside of your small intestine is lined with thousands of tiny bumps called villi. This magnified view shows the fingerlike extensions on the surface of a villus. These provide a massive surface area to speed up digestion and absorb nutrients.

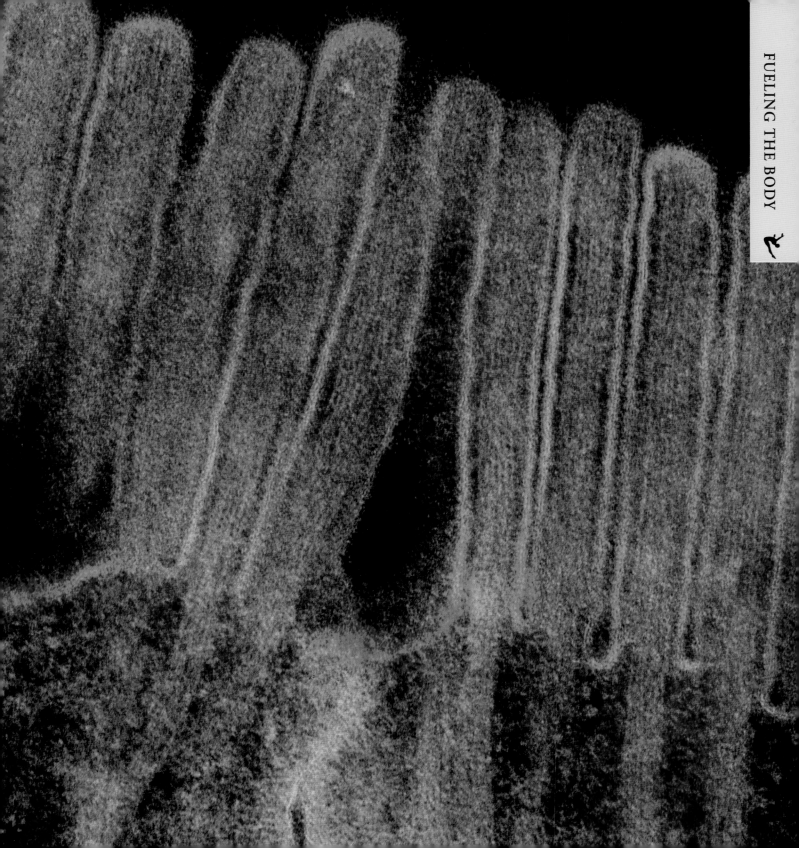

is twice the width of the small intestine but only one quarter of its length. The large intestine receives watery, indigestible waste from your small intestine. Here, it absorbs valuable water from that waste, forming semisolid feces (poo) that are pushed out of your body.

THE BOWELS OF THE BODY

The large intestine has three parts—the cecum, the colon, and the rectum. The longest section, the colon, forms and moves feces, which contain waste food, dead cells, and bacteria. They eventually arrive in the rectum and are expelled when you feel an urge to go to the bathroom.

▶ COLON *This cross-section shows the muscles that produce the movements of the colon. The lining releases slippery mucus to moisten feces and make their passage easier.*

Circular muscle layer

Band of lengthwise muscle

Lining of colon

The ascending colon rises up the right side of the abdomen.

One of three bands of muscle that run along the length of the colon.

The transverse colon passes across the abdomen, just below the stomach.

A valve stops waste from flowing back into the small intestine.

Feces inside the S-shaped sigmoid colon.

The cecum is the first part of the large intestine.

The appendix sticks out from the cecum.

Rectum

The digestive process also produces waste gases, which are expelled through the anus. Flatulence, or "passing gas" as it is known politely, can be noisy and smelly!

Anus

LOOK CLOSER: FRIENDLY BACTERIA

Your colon contains trillions of bacteria, many of which are friendly or helpful to the body. They digest material that human enzymes cannot, releasing useful nutrients, such as vitamin K, which the body absorbs.

▶ COLON BACTERIA *The lining of the colon (brown) is covered by bacteria (purple) that feed on undigested food.*

MOVING THINGS ALONG

As indigestible waste food is mixed and formed into feces, it is propelled along the colon by three types of movements (below). All are produced by contractions of the circular muscles and the three bands of muscle that run the length of the colon. Movement of material along the colon is slower than in other parts of the digestive system. This gives more time for as much water as possible to be absorbed from the waste.

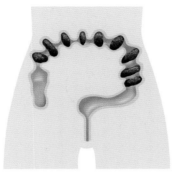

▲ SEGMENTATION *Every 30 minutes, the muscles contract to pinch waste into pellets that are mixed but not moved.*

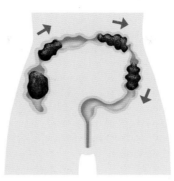

▲ PERISTALSIS *Alternating waves of muscular contraction and relaxation push the pellets towards the rectum.*

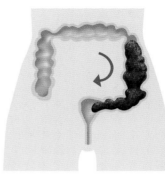

▲ MASS MOVEMENTS *Three times a day, powerful contractions force feces from the descending colon into the rectum.*

The descending colon travels down the left side of the abdomen.

Pouches in the colon are called haustra.

Feces are pushed downward by contractions of the rectum wall

WOW!
Always wash your hands after going to the bathroom. Feces are 50 percent bacteria, and some are harmful.

WHY THE APPENDIX?

The thin, dead-end tube called the appendix was once thought to have no function at all in humans. Scientists now believe that it plays a part in our body's defenses, forming part of the immune system. It also stores friendly bacteria to replace those in the colon, in case they're flushed out during an attack of diarrhea (runny feces).

Bladder

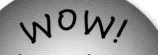

◀ WASTE DISPOSAL
Contractions of the colon push feces into the normally empty rectum. This stretches the rectum wall, triggering an urge to go to the bathroom. Two powerful sphincter muscles, which keep the anus closed, relax. The rectum wall contracts and pushes the feces out through the open anus.

Anal canal links rectum to anus

Anus

Anal sphincter muscles relax to allow feces to pass through

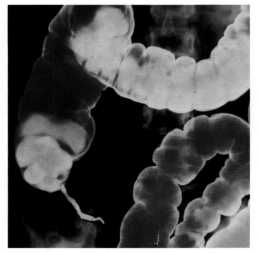

▲ X-RAY OF THE APPENDIX
This colored X-ray image shows the slender, fingerlike appendix located near to where the small intestine (right) joins the large intestine (left).

Chemical factory

The largest internal organ, the liver, is your body's chemical factory. It performs almost 500 different functions, including processing the nutrients released from food. It also makes the bile your digestive system uses to help break down fats.

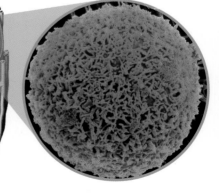

A branch of the hepatic vein carries blood processed by liver cells to the inferior vena cava (a major vein).

The inferior vena cava takes oxygen-poor blood back to the heart.

The hepatic portal vein carries nutrient-rich blood from the stomach and intestines.

The bile duct collects bile from the liver cells.

VITAL ORGAN

The liver is important because it processes, stores, and makes so many substances. For example, it stores and releases energy-rich glucose, processes fats and amino acids, stores vitamins and minerals, breaks down toxins and drugs, and recycles red blood cells. It also releases heat, helping to keep you warm.

LIVER LOBULES

The liver contains around one million sesame seed–sized processing plants called lobules. Inside a lobule, liver cells are arranged in plates that radiate out like spokes from a central vein. The cells filter substances out of the blood as it flows towards the vein and add other substances to it.

Central vein removes processed blood

Surface of lobule

Lobule shown in cross-section

Branch of bile duct

Branch of hepatic artery supplies blood for processing

Branch of hepatic portal vein carries blood rich in nutrients

▶ LOBULE STRUCTURE *Three vessels run along each corner of the lobules. Two supply blood for processing. The third, a bile duct, removes bile made by the liver cells.*

▲ LIVER CELLS *Also called hepatocytes, these cells perform hundreds of tasks, including storing glucose, making proteins, and removing toxins (harmful substances) from the blood.*

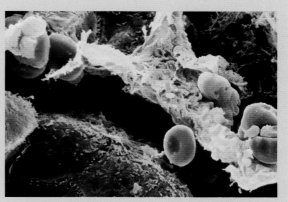

The esophagus carries food from the throat to the stomach.

The hepatic artery carries oxygen-rich blood into the liver.

Left lobe of liver

The stomach lies behind the liver.

LOOK CLOSER: BLOOD CLEANERS

The small blood vessels that pass between liver cells are lined with macrophages (cells that eat other cells) called Kupffer cells. They "clean" blood by removing worn-out red blood cells, along with bacteria and debris. The iron retrieved from red blood cells is recycled.

▲ KUPFFER CELLS *This incredible magnified image shows a Kupffer cell (yellow) trapping and consuming old red blood cells (red).*

WOW!

The liver receives 2½ pints (1.5 liters) of blood every minute.

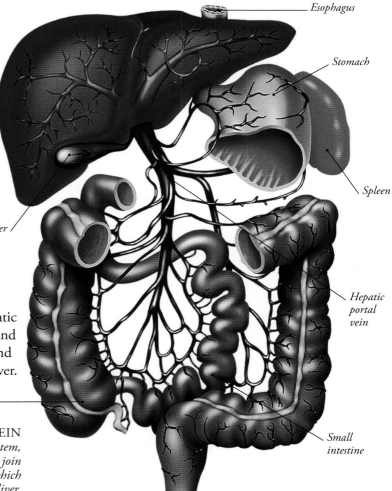

Esophagus

Stomach

Spleen

Gall bladder

Hepatic portal vein

BLOOD SUPPLY

The liver has two blood supplies. The hepatic artery delivers oxygen-rich blood from your heart. The hepatic portal vein carries blood from your digestive organs and supplies 80 percent of the liver's blood. Nutrients and other substances in the blood are processed by the liver.

Large intestine

Small intestine

▶ HEPATIC PORTAL VEIN
Veins from many parts of the digestive system, including the stomach and intestines, join together to form the hepatic portal vein, which takes nutrient-rich blood to the liver.

Balanced diet

Eating the same kind of food every day wouldn't only be boring; it would be bad for your health. To stay healthy and at the right weight for your height you need to eat a balanced diet. This means eating sensible amounts of different foods from five main food groups.

COUNTING CALORIES

The amount of energy contained in different foods is measured in calories. A cheeseburger, packed with energy-rich fat, contains many more calories than, say, an apple. If you regularly eat more calories than you need, the extra energy will be stored by your body as fat and you will become overweight.

FIVE A DAY

You should try to eat at least five portions of fresh fruits and vegetables every day. Scientists have found that a diet including plenty of fruits and vegetables can help reduce the chances of developing serious diseases, such as cancer and heart disease, later in life.

FOOD GROUPS

To stay healthy, you need to eat the right foods in the right quantities, as shown in the chart here. Eat a lot of grains, such as wheat, since they contain starch, which provides fuel—in the form of glucose—to your body. Vegetables and fruit are rich in minerals and vitamins. These help your body cells work normally. Dairy products contain calcium, needed for healthy bones and teeth. Finally, protein-rich foods provide the building blocks for growth and repair.

Grains   Fruit   Proteins

100 calories

360 calories

650 calories

200 calories

30 calories

HOW MUCH ENERGY?

The amount of energy we need each day depends on a number of factors. Teenagers need more energy than adults because they are still growing. Men need more calories than women because, on average, they are bigger and have more energy-burning muscle.

Age	9–11	12–14	15–17	18+
Daily intake of calories (man)	2280	2640	2880	2550
Daily intake of calories (woman)	2050	2150	2150	1940

WOW!

Polar explorers who pull their own sledges need as much as 6,500 calories per day to survive in the cold, icy conditions.

FAST OR SLOW?

Fast foods, such as burgers, contain large amounts of fats and salt. They are often eaten with soft drinks that contain lots of sugar. It is healthier to eat "slow" foods prepared from a balanced mix of fresh ingredients.

Dairy products

Vegetables

137

FOOD MARKET
This colorful food market in Malaysia shows the wide variety of vegetables eaten as part of the Southeast-Asian diet. Eating lots of fresh fruits and vegetables can help keep you healthy and reduce your chances of developing heart disease and cancer later in life.

Vitamins

In addition to providing fuel for your body, food contains the 13 vitamins that are vital to health. You need only tiny amounts, but vitamins keep you looking good and feeling fine—going without them can damage your health and cause nasty diseases.

WOW!

Not all vitamins come from food. Vitamin D is vital for bone growth. One form of it is made by your skin when it is exposed to sunlight.

WHAT ARE VITAMINS?

Each vitamin is a complex natural chemical that has a special job in the body. Vitamins are known by a letter of the alphabet, and sometimes a number. Ascorbic acid, for example, is usually called vitamin C, and riboflavin is vitamin B2. You get vitamins from certain foods in your diet.

CHICKEN FEED

In the past, many people in Southeast Asia died from a wasting disease called beriberi. In the 1890s, Dutch doctor Christiaan Eijkman found that chickens fed only white rice got the same disease, but those given brown rice were healthy. The brown rice contained vitamin B1, which prevented beriberi.

Dairy products, such as milk, are full of vitamin A.

Leafy greens, such as cabbage and spinach, contain vitamin K.

Citrus fruits are a good source of vitamin C.

Eggs are a good source of B vitamins.

Chicken and other meats contain B vitamins.

Wheat germ contains vitamin E.

SICK SCIENCE

Eating food rich in vitamin B12 cures a disease called pernicious anemia. In 1928, Dr. William Castle discovered that a protein made by the stomach helps the body absorb the vitamin. He tested this by giving anemia patients vitamin-rich food mixed with liquid strained from his own vomit! Sure enough, they got better more quickly.

NIGHT VISION

The ancient Romans had a strange cure for people who couldn't see at night. They roasted a goat and rubbed fat from its liver onto the eyes of the patient, who also ate some of the liver. But it worked! Why? Because liver is rich in vitamin A, which helps you see in the dark.

DEADLY VITAMIN

Although vitamin A is vital to health, you can have too much of it. The livers of some animals contain so much vitamin A that they are dangerous to eat. The Arctic Inuit people have long known not to eat the livers of polar bears, seals, or husky dogs. However, several European explorers, desperate for food on long polar expeditions, found out the hard way when they became very ill after eating this meat.

FAST FACTS

■ The best way to make sure you get enough vitamins is to eat a wide variety of foods, and not stick to just a few favorites.
■ Vitamin C is a vital part of the human diet, but most other animals are able to make their own.
■ Some common foods have vitamins added to make them more nutritious.
■ Before they are born, babies need vitamins supplied by their mothers.

CRAZY CORN

In the early 1900s, a strange disease swept across the southern United States. Victims went mad and suffered sores on their skin. In 1915, Dr. Joseph Goldberger found that he could cause the symptoms by feeding people nothing but corn—a staple of the local diet—and cure them with a dose of yeast extract. He realized the disease was related to something missing from corn but found in yeast, later identified as vitamin B3.

WASTE DISPOSAL

Every day your kidneys clean hundreds of pints of blood and filter out harmful waste chemicals. The wastes are flushed out of your body in urine, along with water your body doesn't need.

Urinary system

Your body's cells release poisonous waste products. Many are flushed out of the body by the urinary system. Two kidneys process your body's blood and remove excess water and waste. This waste liquid, called urine (pee), is carried to the bladder, and released from the body via the urethra when you go to the bathroom.

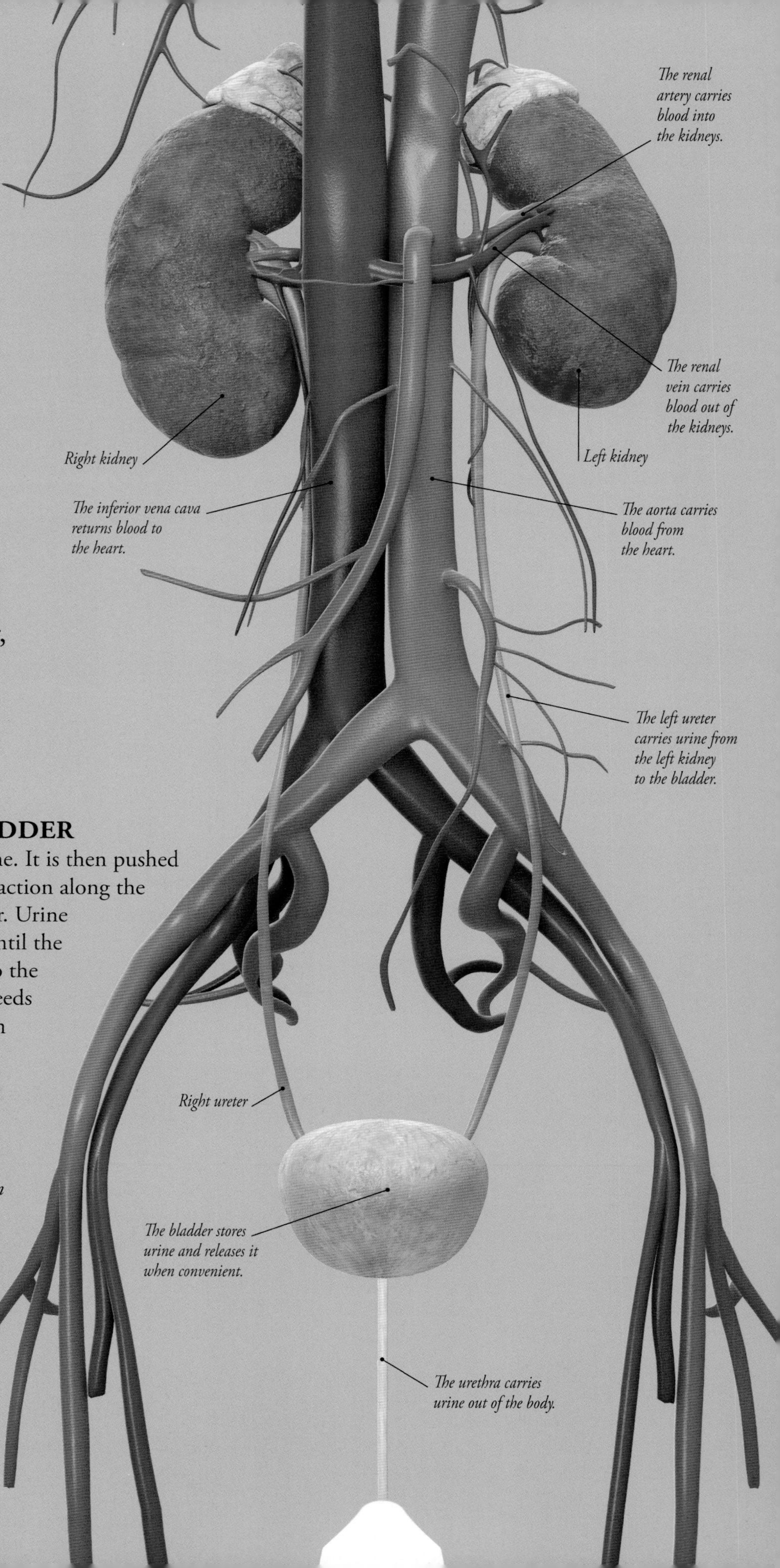

FILLING THE BLADDER

The kidneys produce urine. It is then pushed by waves of muscle contraction along the two ureters to the bladder. Urine is stored in the bladder until the bladder sends messages to the brain indicating that it needs to be emptied. Urine then flows out of the body along the urethra.

▶ LONG AND SHORT
In the female system (shown here), urine is expelled out of the body through a short urethra. The male system is the same except that the urethra is longer and passes along the penis.

The renal artery carries blood into the kidneys.

The renal vein carries blood out of the kidneys.

Right kidney

Left kidney

The inferior vena cava returns blood to the heart.

The aorta carries blood from the heart.

The left ureter carries urine from the left kidney to the bladder.

Right ureter

The bladder stores urine and releases it when convenient.

The urethra carries urine out of the body.

卫生间
Toilets

DAILY BREAKS

We make up to 2½ pints (1.5 liters) of urine every day—enough to fill half a dozen coffee cups. When your bladder is full, nerve endings in the bladder's muscle wall signal to the brain that it is time for a bathroom break. A sphincter muscle keeps your bladder shut until you are ready to pee. The sphincter muscle relaxes and the bladder contracts to help push the urine out.

WOW!

Your hardworking kidneys make up just 1 percent of your weight, but they consume 25 percent of your body's oxygen.

OTHER JOBS

Your kidneys don't just filter and clean blood to make urine. They help control your blood pressure to make sure it stays within safe limits. Your kidneys also release a hormone (chemical messenger) that increases the production of red blood cells in your bones. What's more, they activate vitamin D made by the action of sunlight on the skin. Active vitamin D is needed in the body to make sure that bone-building calcium is absorbed from the small intestine.

FAST FACTS

- Every minute of the day, about a quart (liter) of blood passes through your kidneys to be filtered and cleaned.
- It takes less than an hour to clean your entire blood supply.
- Each kidney contains around one million tiny filtration and urine-making units called nephrons.
- In an average lifetime, the kidneys process 12 million gallons (45 million liters) of blood, enough to fill 18 Olympic-size swimming pools.

KIDNEY MACHINE

Sometimes the kidneys stop working properly due to disease. One solution is to transplant a healthy kidney into the body of a person with failing kidneys. But this isn't always possible. Kidney dialysis is an alternative treatment, which cleans a patient's blood by passing it through a machine that acts like an artificial kidney.

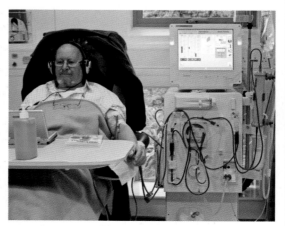

TESTING THE WATER

In the past, doctors used uroscopy—or urine gazing—to help them diagnose diseases, as shown in this 15th-century woodcut. They would examine the color, smell, and cloudiness of a patient's urine. Sometimes doctors would also taste it!

Waterworks

For your body to work at its best, the substances that make up your blood have to be carefully controlled. Your kidneys play a key role in this. All through the day and night, they remove excess water, salts, and poisonous wastes from your blood to make urine. The cleaned blood is then returned to your body's blood supply.

INSIDE A KIDNEY

A network of blood vessels delivers blood to and from the cortex (outer part) and the medulla (inner part) of your bean-shaped kidneys. These areas are where urine is made. Urine then drains into the renal pelvis, a flattened, funnel-like tube, which empties it into the ureters for the next part of its journey out of the body.

The cortex is the outer part of the kidney.

The hollow renal pelvis collects urine.

The renal artery delivers the blood that has to be cleaned.

The renal vein removes the cleaned blood.

▲ BLOOD FILTERS
A microscopic view of the kidney reveals the tiny nephrons that loop between the kidney's cortex and medulla. They produce urine by filtering blood.

The ureter carries urine away from the kidney.

The medulla is the inner part of the kidney.

148

HOW URINE IS MADE

The capsule forms a protective coat around the kidney.

Each urine-making nephron consists of a cluster of blood capillaries surrounded by a capsule that leads to a long, winding tubule (tiny tube). Fluid, without blood cells, passes from blood flowing through the bundle of capillaries into the capsule and tubule. As the filtered fluid travels down and up the tubule, most of the water and other useful substances that the body needs, such as glucose (a sugar that gives us energy), are taken back into the bloodstream. What remains—excess water and salt, and waste substances—forms urine.

As blood flows through a cluster of capillaries, fluid passes out of it into a tubule (yellow).

The tubule twists and turns as it travels downward and then upward to join the collecting duct.

► FILTRATION UNIT *The capillaries and the tubule form a filtration unit that separates waste matter and returns water and other essential substances to the bloodstream.*

The collecting duct (tube) drains urine from many nephrons into the hollow pelvis of the kidney.

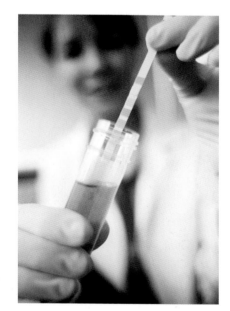

WHAT'S IN URINE?

Your urine is made up of water and dissolved substances that the body needs to get rid of. Urine usually has a yellow tint due to a chemical from worn-out blood cells, which the kidneys filter out of the bloodstream. It is the same chemical that makes bruises yellow.

Water makes up 94 percent of urine.

Urea is produced in the liver when proteins are broken down into amino acids.

Sodium (excess salt) is also disposed of in urine.

Urine also contains small amounts of other dissolved substances.

TESTING URINE

A doctor may test urine to help find out what is wrong with a patient. A dipstick with several colored bands is dipped in a sample of the patient's urine. The bands change color when they react with certain chemicals in urine. These are then matched against a color chart to detect abnormal levels of any substance in the urine sample.

Filling and emptying

Urine is produced by the kidneys in a steady trickle, 24 hours a day. If it was released from the body in the same way, the constant dribble of urine would make life very unpleasant. Fortunately, we have a stretchy, muscular bag called the bladder, which stores urine until we feel the need to release it.

The ureters carry urine to the bladder.

▼ BLADDER LINING *This photograph shows the folds in the bladder's lining when it is empty. These disappear as the bladder fills and expands.*

Urine fills up the bladder.

Ureter

The external sphincter is closed.

The internal sphincter is closed.

► BLADDER FILLS *As urine flows into the bladder from the ureters, its muscular wall relaxes. Both the sphincters are closed.*

STORE AND RELEASE

The exit from the bladder is normally closed by two rings of muscle, the internal (inside) and external (outside) sphincters. As your bladder fills, you feel the need to urinate. When you are ready to go to the bathroom, the bladder's muscular wall squeezes, the sphincters relax, and urine gushes out of your body.

The internal sphincter relaxes.

The muscular wall squeezes urine out.

The external sphincter relaxes.

◄ BLADDER EMPTIES *Both the sphincters relax, and the bladder contracts and shrinks to squeeze urine out of the body.*

Urine flows out along the urethra.

NO CONTROL

Babies can't control the bladder's external sphincter muscle, which remains open. As the bladder fills up, the internal sphincter automatically relaxes and urine flows out. Most babies can control their bladder by the age of two. Until that time, they wear diapers to soak up the urine.

HOW MUCH?

The amount of urine made each day, and how concentrated it is, depends on how much you drink and whether or not your body is sweating. The hypothalamus in your brain has overall control, monitoring water levels in your blood. If there's too little, it tells the pituitary gland to release a hormone into the blood. This hormone tells the kidneys to absorb more water into the bloodstream and make smaller amounts of stronger urine.

The hypothalamus monitors the concentration of water in the blood.

The pituitary gland releases hormones into the blood.

▲ WATER CONTROL
The hypothalamus and pituitary gland together make sure that the body's water content stays the same, no matter how much you drink.

WOW!

Globally, humans release 1.7 trillion gallons (6.4 trillion liters) of urine each year, enough to fill a lake.

FULL STRETCH

The wall of the bladder is extremely stretchy. This means that it can expand as it fills with urine. When it is empty, the bladder is about the size of a plum. As it fills, it reaches the size of an orange, or even a grapefruit. By this stage, you will really feel the need to go to the bathroom!

Grapefruit

Orange

Plum

Wonderful water

Water is vital to life. It is an essential part of every tissue in your body, including your bones, and makes up more than half your body weight. If your water content falls by just 10 percent you can get seriously ill. But your body is always losing water, so it has a special system that makes you drink when you need to.

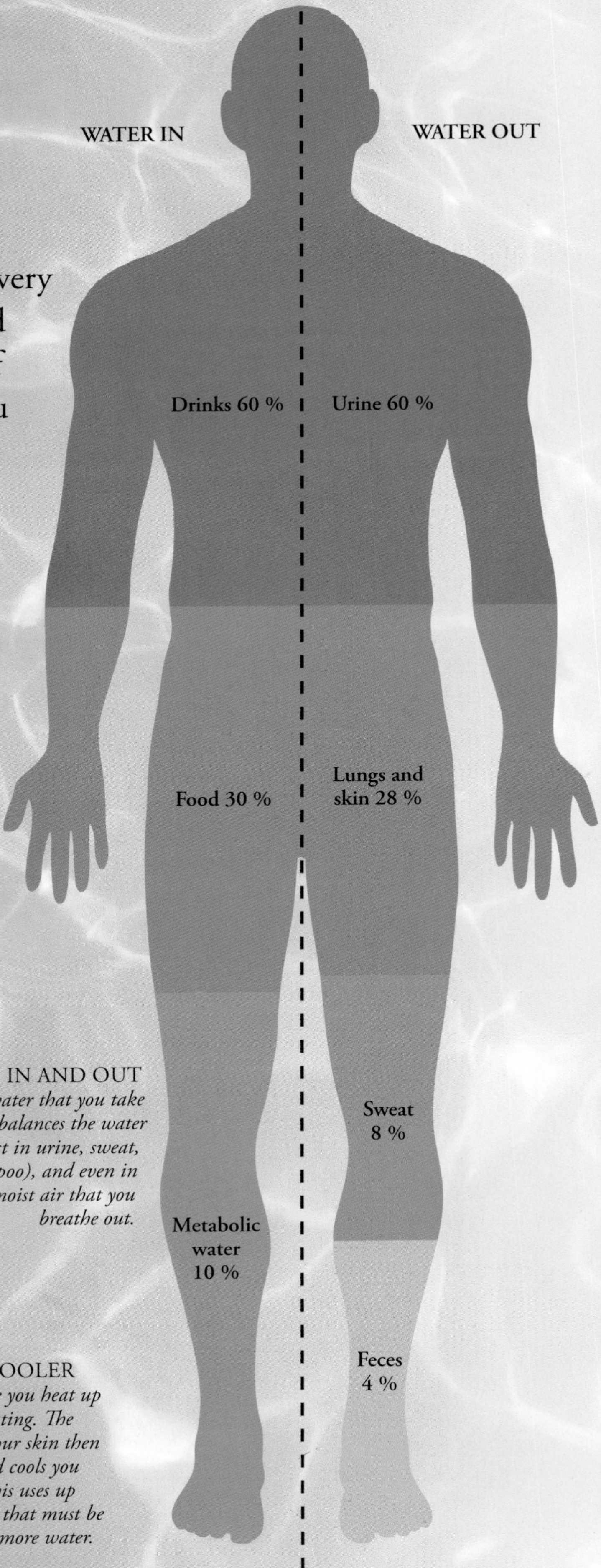

FEELING THIRSTY?

You can go without food for a long time, but your body needs a regular supply of water to replace all the moisture that it loses. Some is made by chemical reactions in body cells that produce metabolic water, but the rest is in your food and drink. Part of your brain called the hypothalamus monitors the water in your blood, and if the level is too low it triggers the thirsty feeling that makes you take a drink.

WATER IN   **WATER OUT**

Drinks 60 %   Urine 60 %

Food 30 %   Lungs and skin 28 %

▶ IN AND OUT
The water that you take in balances the water lost in urine, sweat, feces (poo), and even in the moist air that you breathe out.

Sweat 8 %

Metabolic water 10 %

Feces 4 %

◀ WATER COOLER
As you exercise you heat up and start sweating. The moisture on your skin then evaporates and cools you down—but this uses up body moisture that must be replaced with more water.

WOW!

Every day your body loses at least 3½ pints (2 liters) of water—enough to fill a big soda bottle!

WATER CONTENT

Up to 74 percent of a baby's body weight is water. As he or she gets older the water content gradually goes down. A young man's body is around 60 percent water, because if he is in good shape he has plenty of water-rich muscle tissue. A young woman's body is less muscular, so it contains less water—about 50 percent. Older people have even less muscle, so water may account for only 40 percent of their total body weight.

60 %

50 %

DESERT SURVIVAL

Deserts are places where water is incredibly scarce. Any water on the surface soon dries out, so finding a drink is very difficult. Desert people survive by carrying water with them, but the bodies of desert animals are adapted to cut down their water loss. For example, a camel's body temperature can rise by 11 °F (6 °C) before its starts losing moisture by sweating. This would almost certainly kill a human.

ESSENTIAL FOR LIFE

All the chemical reactions that power life take place in the water contained in each of your 100 trillion body cells. Without water, there would be no body chemistry and no life. But some of your body tissues contain more water than others. Muscle has three times as much water as fatty tissue, and vital body fluids, such as your blood, are mostly made up of water.

Blood cells
83% water

Muscle
75% water

Fat
25% water

Bone
22% water

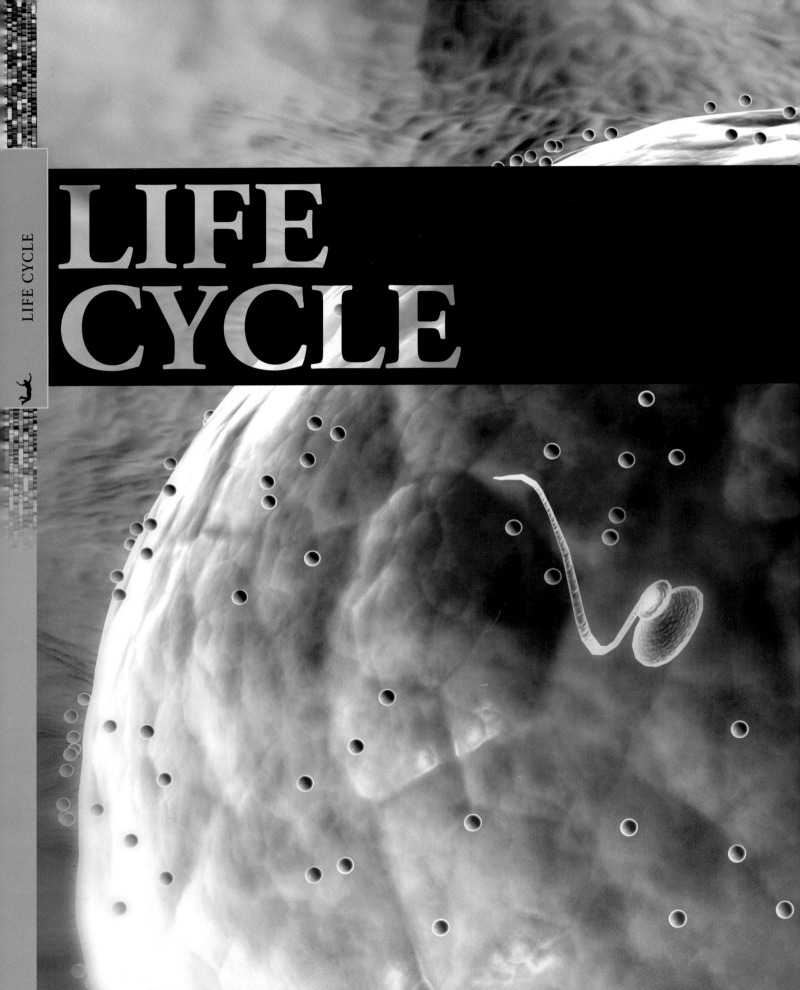

LIFE
CYCLE

Your life began as a single cell—no bigger than a pinprick—inside your mother's body. Over time, that cell grew and developed into your complex body containing trillions of cells.

Starting out

The reproductive system is the body system that differs most between males and females. You need a mother and a father to make a baby. Each produces sex cells—the male sperm and female egg—which join to produce a fertilized egg that eventually becomes a baby. Your reproductive system doesn't start working fully until your teenage years.

FERTILIZATION AND AFTER

When sperm meet an egg, they surround it and try to push their way through its tough, jellylike outer layer. Eventually a single sperm succeeds and loses its tail as it enters the egg. The sperm's head and egg's nucleus join together, creating a store of 46 chromosomes that contain the instructions needed to build a new human being. Now fertilized, the egg cells divide repeatedly, eventually forming a tiny embryo.

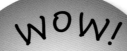

WOW! A man's testes make around 3,000 sperm every second. That's 250 million sperm every day.

The fertilized egg splits into two cells.

The egg divides again into 16 cells, as it travels along the tube.

The egg is fertilized just after it's released from the ovary.

MALE SYSTEM

The male sex organs—the two testes and the penis—dangle outside the body. The organs are connected to each other by various tubes and glands. In teenagers and adults, millions of sperm are made in the testes. Sperm are carried along the tubes and released through the penis.

▶ SPERM MEETS EGG *Once a month an egg is released from an ovary. If a sperm meets the egg within 24 hours of its release then fertilization will happen.*

🔍 LOOK CLOSER: SWIMMING SPERM

With a streamlined shape that allows it to swim easily, each sperm is ideally suited to its job. The lollipop-shaped head contains gene instructions. Its long, thin tail whips from side to side to push the sperm toward its destination—the female egg.

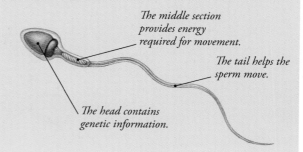

The middle section provides energy required for movement.

The tail helps the sperm move.

The head contains genetic information.

The glands release fluids that activate the sperm.

The penis releases sperm into a female vagina.

The testes produce sperm.

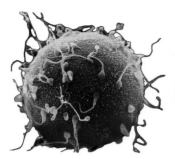

▲ FERTILIZATION *Sperm mass around an egg cell. One succeeds in entering and fertilizing the egg.*

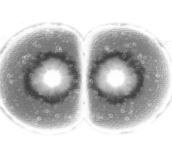

▲ TWO CELLS *Around 36 hours after fertilization, the egg divides into two linked cells.*

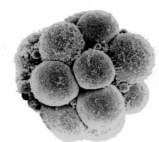

▲ CELL DIVISION *Three days after fertilization, cell division creates a berrylike morula made of 16 cells.*

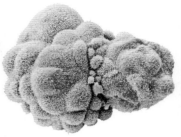

▲ CLUSTER OF CELLS *A hollow blastocyst forms six days after fertilization. Its inner cells will develop into the embryo.*

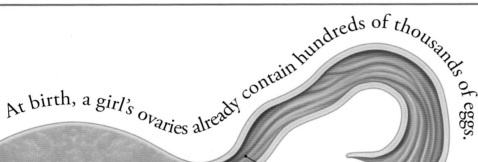

At birth, a girl's ovaries already contain hundreds of thousands of eggs.

Fallopian tube

Ovary

The cell cluster implants in the lining of the womb (uterus).

HOW LIFE BEGINS

Millions of sperm from the father's penis are released into the mother's vagina, but only a few reach the tunnel of the fallopian tubes, and just one fertilizes an egg. The fertilized egg is then pushed along the fallopian tube toward the womb, a journey that takes around six days. During this time it divides again and again.

The vagina is the entrance to the uterus.

FEMALE SYSTEM

The main female sex organs are inside the pelvis. Each month an egg is released from one of two ovaries. If fertilized, the egg travels along a fallopian tube and settles in the lining of the womb, where it develops into a baby.

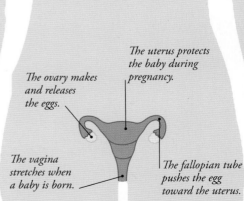

The ovary makes and releases the eggs.

The uterus protects the baby during pregnancy.

The vagina stretches when a baby is born.

The fallopian tube pushes the egg toward the uterus.

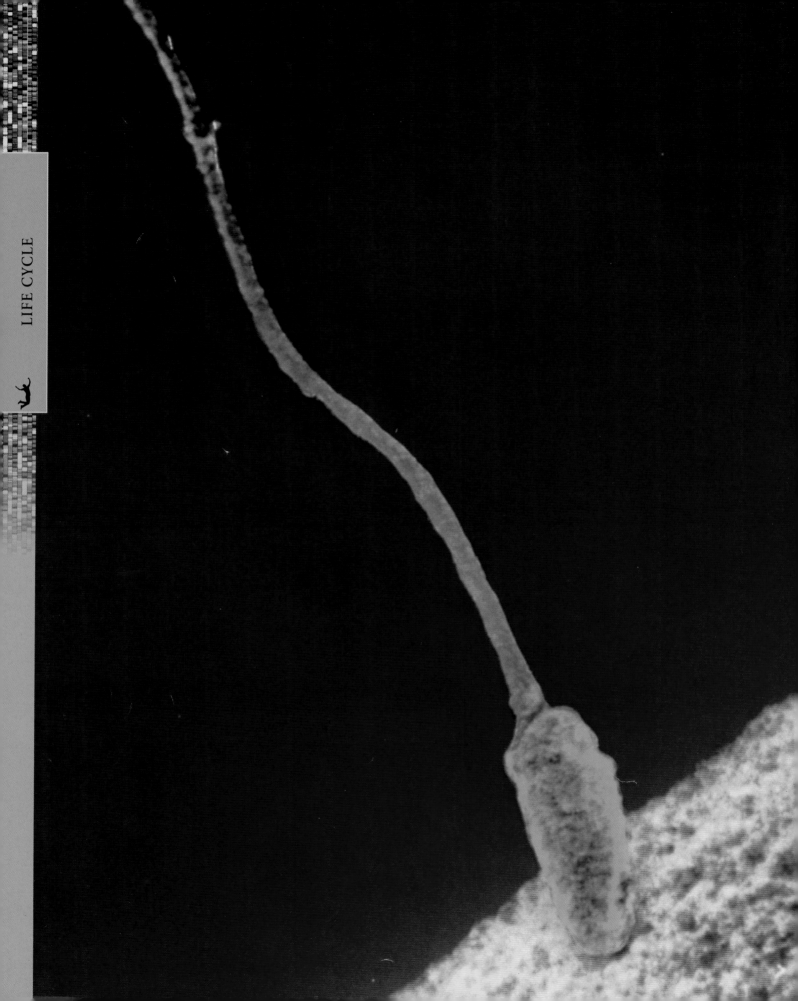

FERTILIZATION

A single male sperm (blue) releases chemicals from its head in order to get through the tough outer covering of a female egg (pink). If it can break through the egg's protective layer, then fertilization—the joining together of sperm and egg—may happen.

Pregnancy and birth

During pregnancy—the nine months that follow fertilization of an egg—a remarkable sequence of events takes place inside a mother's womb. A tiny ball of cells develops into a baby that can move and sense its environment, and breathe for itself once it is born.

The baby floats in a liquid called amniotic fluid.

The placenta links the mother's blood supply to that of the baby.

The baby is upside down and ready for birth.

The umbilical cord links the baby to its mother.

The muscular wall of the womb squeezes to push the baby out during birth.

The birth canal widens to allow the baby to be pushed out of the body.

PROTECTED AND NURTURED

Inside its mother's expanding womb (uterus), the growing baby has its own life support system—the placenta. Food and oxygen pass through the placenta from the mother's blood and are carried to the baby by the umbilical cord. Wastes travel in the opposite direction.

GROWING BABY

Within weeks of arriving in the womb after fertilization, the tiny ball of cells becomes an embryo. It has a beating heart and most of its organs are in place. By 11 weeks after fertilization, the growing baby, now called a fetus, looks human. During the remaining period of pregnancy, the fetus grows rapidly and becomes stronger and more active. It finally develops into a baby and is pushed out into the world.

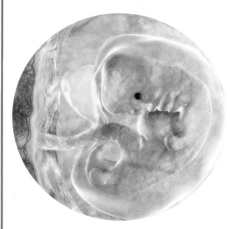

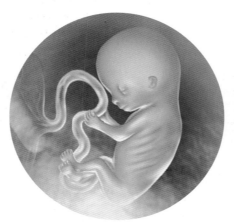

▲ EMBRYO AT 5 WEEKS *The bean-sized embryo's organs are developing and it has "buds" from which arms and legs grow.*

▲ FETUS AT 11 WEEKS *The lemon-sized fetus can move, and has fingers, toes, a large head, and a growing brain.*

▲ FETUS AT 26 WEEKS *The fetus has eyelashes and eyebrows, and can blink. The mother can feel it moving inside her.*

TWO OF A KIND

Women usually have only one baby at a time, but sometimes twins—or even more babies—are born together. Twins can either be identical (they look the same) or nonidentical. Identical twins occur when a single egg splits into two separate embryos after fertilization. Nonidentical (fraternal) twins happen when two eggs are released at the same time and both are fertilized by different sperm.

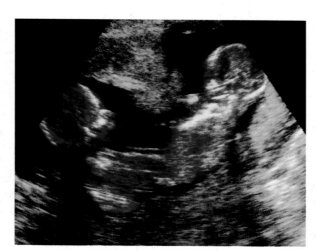

◄ TWINS *An ultrasound scan shows twins growing and developing inside their mother's womb at about four months old. Since the babies are still very small, there is plenty of space for them to move around.*

You first started to dream while you were still in your mother's womb—around 20 weeks before you were born!

NEW ARRIVAL

After around 40 weeks of pregnancy, a mother gives birth. The muscular wall of the womb contracts to push out the fully grown baby. The umbilical cord, which is no longer needed, is cut and the baby starts to breathe using her lungs.

Life story

Our bodies change and develop over the course of a lifetime. From birth to old age, we go through several distinct stages of life. During infancy and continuing through childhood, we grow rapidly and pick up life skills. In our teenage years we mature into adults. As grown women and men we may have children of our own. Finally, in old age, our bodies start to wear out.

CHILDHOOD

Between the ages of one and 10, children grow and change proportion. As limbs grow longer, the head looks smaller compared to the body. The brain develops rapidly and makes lots of new connections, enabling children to acquire new skills, including speaking, reading, and writing. They also learn to walk, run, and ride a bike.

WOW!

Frenchwoman Jeanne Calment had the longest-known lifespan. She was 122 years and 164 days old when she died in 1997.

INFANCY

In the first year of life, a baby is completely dependent on his or her parents. However, babies grow rapidly and gradually gain more control of their muscles, moving from sitting to crawling, standing up, and then walking. Infants develop a basic understanding of language and interact with their parents using eye contact, sounds, and facial expressions.

ADOLESCENCE

The change from being a child to an adult, which happens during the teenage years, is called adolescence. It includes puberty, a period of rapid growth as the body changes shape and the reproductive system develops. During this stage, behavior alters as teenagers learn to live with less help from their parents and do things for themselves.

CHANGES DURING PUBERTY

Puberty is a time when rapid change sets in, between the ages of 10 and 12 in girls, and 12 and 14 in boys. Both girls and boys show a "growth spurt" as their bodies mature and their reproductive systems start working. By the age of 14 or 15, the average boy is taller, heavier, and stronger than the average girl.

▶TEENAGE YEARS *Surging hormones make boys' voices deepen and facial hair appear, so they have to start shaving.*

OLD AGE

As you grow older, your body takes longer to repair itself and replace worn-out cells. This causes aging, the signs of which are more obvious over the age of 60. Hair thins and turns gray, the skin wrinkles, and sight and hearing become less efficient. Muscles become weaker, joints stiffer and less mobile, and bones may become brittle and more likely to break. However, a good diet and regular exercise during adulthood can reduce the effects of aging.

ADULTHOOD

Between the ages of 18 and 20, the body stops growing. This is the beginning of adulthood. In early adulthood, we reach the peak of fitness and fertility (the ability to have children). Adulthood is also a time of great responsibility when we focus on work and family.

Code of life

Inside every one of your cells is a unique set of instructions needed to build and maintain your body. Except for identical twins, no one in the world has exactly the same set of instructions. This genetic information is carried by a substance called DNA found inside the nucleus of each cell.

One of the two strands that make up DNA.

SUPER SPIRAL

Within a cell's nucleus are X-shaped structures called chromosomes. Each chromosome is made of tightly coiled-up DNA. Unraveled, DNA can be seen to be made of two long, linked strands that spiral around each other, resembling a twisted ladder. Together the DNA strands that make up a cell's 46 chromosomes carry about 23,000 gene instructions.

The rungs hold the two strands together.

Cell

The coiled-up DNA forms one of the cell's chromosomes.

The nucleus is the cell's control center.

A jellylike fluid called cytoplasm surrounds the nucleus.

The spiral structure is known as a double helix.

Stretched out, the DNA in one cell alone would reach 6 ft (1.8 m).

CODED MESSAGES

The rungs of the DNA ladder consist of four chemicals called bases. They form the coded instructions for making proteins. These vital substances are essential for making sure that your body works—your hair, skin, and muscles are all made from proteins.

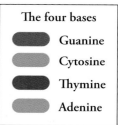

The four bases

- Guanine
- Cytosine
- Thymine
- Adenine

WOW!

If the DNA in all your cells was put end-to-end, it would reach to the Sun and back around 600 times.

Thymine always pairs with adenine.

Cytosine always pairs with guanine.

CLOSE RELATIVES

Our closest living relative is the chimpanzee. It's perhaps not surprising then that chimps share around 96 percent of their DNA with humans. Both belong to a group of mammals called primates that also includes gorillas and monkeys.

CHROMOSOMES

Inside the nucleus of a body cell there are two sets of 23 chromosomes, one inherited from Mom and one from Dad. Each chromosome is made up of one long, coiled-up strand of DNA. When a cell divides (see page 13) its chromosomes appear X-shaped, like this one. The bands show the position of genes on the chromosome.

IDENTICAL TWINS

These twins look very similar because they share identical DNA and genes. However, each twin is also affected by different life experiences, so each has their own individual character. Scientists investigate identical twins to see whether or not, for example, the chance of developing a particular disease is due to genes or upbringing.

▲ IDENTICAL TWINS FESTIVAL *In addition to being fun, gatherings like this one give scientists the chance to study similarities and differences between identical twins.*

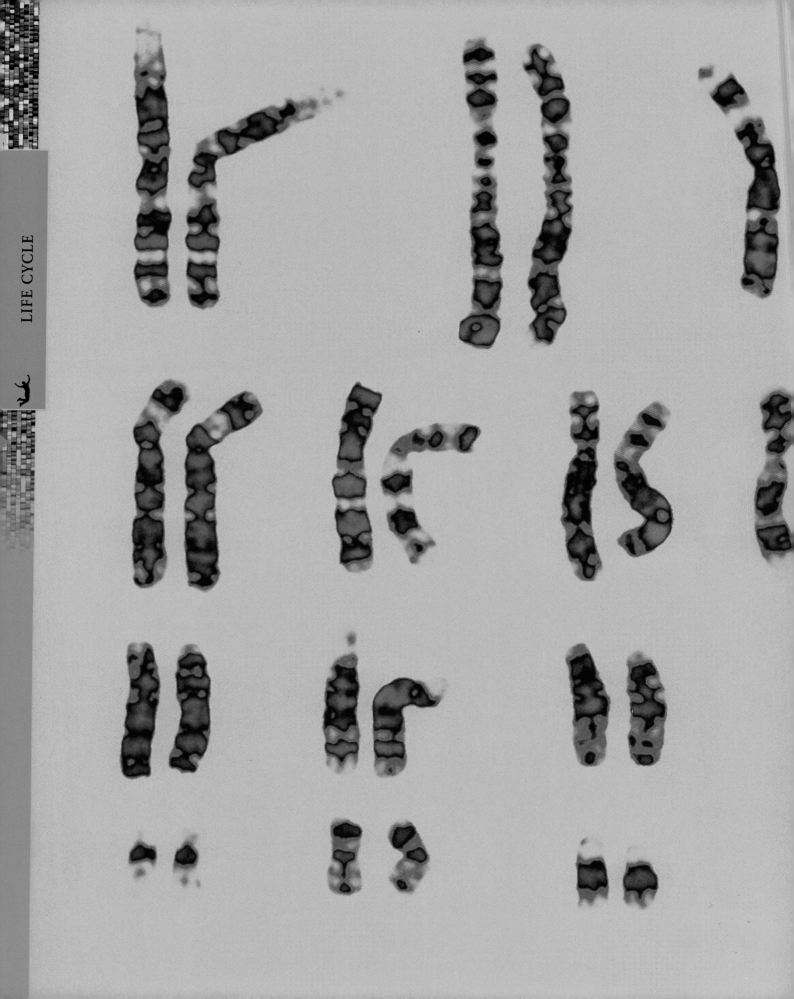

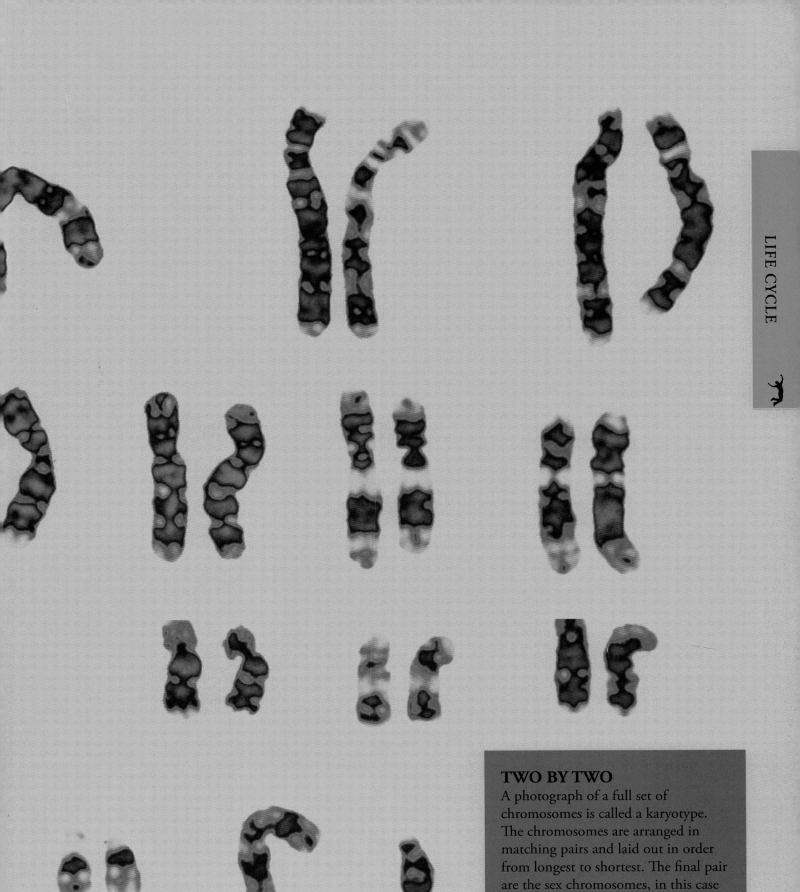

TWO BY TWO
A photograph of a full set of chromosomes is called a karyotype. The chromosomes are arranged in matching pairs and laid out in order from longest to shortest. The final pair are the sex chromosomes, in this case one X and one Y—meaning this karyotype belongs to a male.

In the genes

We inherit 23 gene-carrying chromosomes from each of our parents. When a sperm fertilizes an egg, a full set of 46 chromosomes—containing thousands of genes—begins building a new human body. Our genes help make each of us a unique individual.

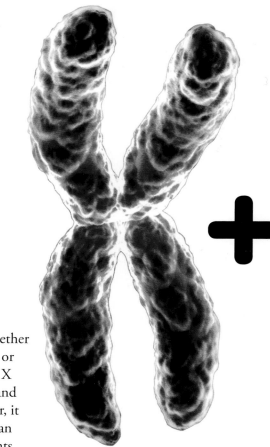

X chromosome

WOW!

A human body cell contains around 23,000 genes, which is not many more than those found in a mouse!

GIRL OR BOY

Two of the 46 chromosomes are special. Called the X and Y chromosomes, they control whether an embryo develops into a boy or a girl. If the embryo receives an X chromosome from the mother and a Y chromosome from the father, it will become a boy. If it receives an X chromosome from both parents, it will become a girl.

DIFFERENT FEATURES

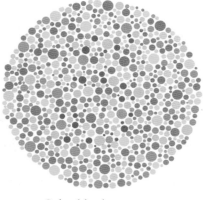

The way you look depends on your genes. You may inherit slightly different versions of genes from your parents. Some genes are dominant and their effects are felt regardless of the other version you inherited. Others are recessive and only take effect if no dominant gene is present. If you can bend your thumb back like this, you have two recessive thumb-bending genes.

COLOR BLINDNESS

If you can't see the number 5 in this circle, you have red-green color blindness. A color-blind person cannot tell the difference between two colors. This problem is caused by a gene inherited from the mother, but it mainly affects males.

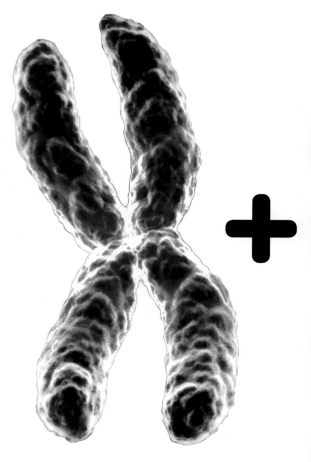

Color-blindness test

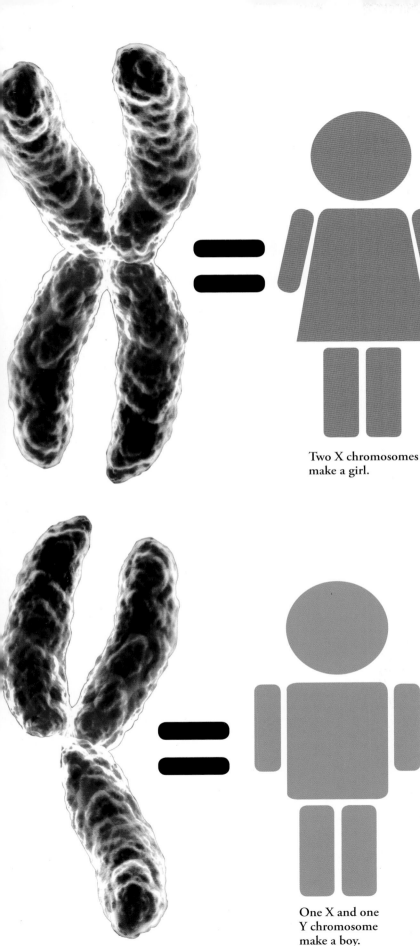

Two X chromosomes make a girl.

Y chromosome

PASSING ON GENES

Eye color is an example of how genes are passed on. If the father has two recessive blue-eye genes and the mother has two dominant brown-eye genes, then their child will have brown eyes because she has inherited a dominant brown-eye gene.

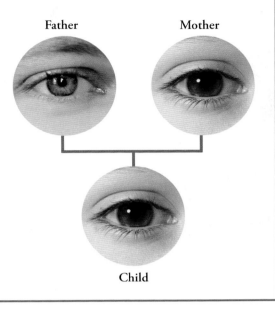

Father

Mother

Child

One X and one Y chromosome make a boy.

NATURE OR NURTURE

It's not just our genes that determine the way we look and behave. Our upbringing, surroundings, and lifestyle all play a part as well. Sumo wrestlers don't have "fat" genes. They put on weight by following a special lifestyle, which includes plenty of exercise and sleep, and eating large amounts of a protein-rich stew called chanko.

The human genome

You started life as a cluster of cells containing the genetic instructions needed for you to grow into a unique person. Each of the 100 trillion cells in your body contains a copy of your genome—the coded information found in the two sets of 23 chromosomes inherited from your parents. Throughout life, this controls the way your body develops.

THE HUMAN GENOME PROJECT

Each DNA molecule that makes up the genome is like a twisted ladder linked by rungs called bases (see page 164). There are four different types of bases, and the sequence in which they occur in DNA provides the coded instructions—or genes—that make us human. In 1990, scientists began the Human Genome Project to determine the sequence, a goal that they reached in 2003.

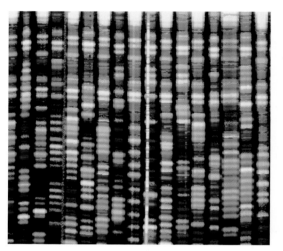

SEQUENCING DNA

Decoding the entire human genome means working it out letter by letter—a process known as sequencing. Scientists do this by chopping up the DNA into shorter strands and then separating these out by size to form a series of bands (a banding pattern). The base (A, T, C, or G) at the end of each strand is color-coded by chemicals, and the colored bands are then read by a computer and turned into a sequence of letters.

◄ GROWING DNA *This robotic arm is holding a tray containing colonies of bacteria, which are used to grow human DNA. Tiny pieces of DNA are cloned by the bacteria to make amounts large enough for scientists to analyze.*

GENE CHIPS

Doctors can now scan your DNA for thousands of different genes—the pieces of DNA that control how the body works—by using a biochip. These chips contain thousands of DNA sensors and may help predict your chances of developing a range of diseases.

◀ BIOCHIP SCAN
A sample of DNA from one person is dropped onto a biochip containing thousands of sensors. It's then scanned for any matches.

WOW!

Only three percent of your DNA forms the genes that make you what you are.

DNA FINGERPRINTS

Everyone, except for identical twins, has a slightly different genome. This means that a criminal who leaves a speck of blood, saliva, or a hair at a crime scene can be identified from the DNA it contains. Scientists extract the DNA in the sample and use it to generate a "DNA fingerprint" with its own unique pattern. They then compare this with the DNA fingerprints of any criminal suspects. Can you see a DNA match for the sample shown here?

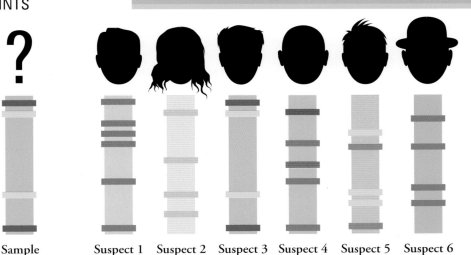

Sample   Suspect 1   Suspect 2   Suspect 3   Suspect 4   Suspect 5   Suspect 6

GENETIC IDENTITY

One day, we may all have to carry an identity card like this one featuring our genetic information. It has a fingerprint, personal data in the form of a bar code, a coded pattern of the holder's iris, and information about her genome encoded in a special electronic chip. Such genetic information would be difficult to fake or deny, meaning that people could be identified more quickly and accurately.

IDENTITY CARD

GEMMA PEARSON

IN CONTROL

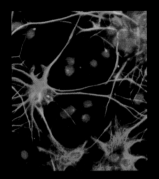  

Your brain and nervous system control your body. Electrical signals whizz along your nerve network to every organ and muscle, carrying commands and bringing back information.

Control network

The human body is controlled by a special network of cells known as the nervous system. The nerve cells that make up this system transmit electrical signals, which dart throughout your body all the time, carrying information from your sense organs to your brain and controlling your organs and muscles.

NERVOUS SYSTEM

All parts of the body are connected to the nervous system. The system's control center is the brain—an incredibly complicated mass of nerve cells that work together like a living computer to process information. Electrical signals from the brain are carried to the rest of the body by nerve cells, which are bundled together to form cables called nerves.

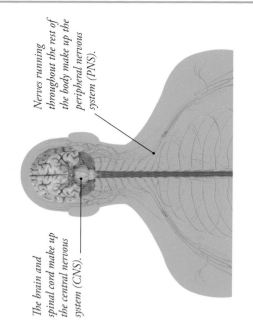

The brain controls the nervous system.

The cranial nerves run between your brain and your face and ears.

The spinal cord links the brain to the rest of the body.

Thirty-one pairs of nerves branch off the spinal cord.

WOW!

A nerve signal travels all the way from the brain to the big toe in just 1/100 of a second.

The ulnar nerve runs under a bone called the humerus. If you bump your elbow, the nerve tingles, which is why the humerus is also called the funny bone.

PARTS OF THE NERVOUS SYSTEM

Your nervous system has two main parts. The central nervous system (CNS) is your body's control center and consists of the brain and spinal cord. The peripheral nervous system (PNS) carries signals everywhere else in the body, using cables called nerves. These nerves link the CNS to your sense organs, muscles, and internal organs.

Nerves running throughout the rest of the body make up the peripheral nervous system (PNS).

The brain and spinal cord make up the central nervous system (CNS).

Where nerves lead

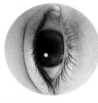

▲ SENSES
Nerves carry incoming signals from sense organs, such as your eyes, to your brain. Your brain then figures out how to respond.

▲ MUSCLES
Nerves also carry outgoing signals from your brain to your muscles to make them move. You control most of your muscles voluntarily.

▲ ORGANS
Internal organs such as your heart are also controlled by nerves. This happens automatically, without your voluntary control.

HIGH-SPEED COMMUNICATION

Your nerves transmit signals to and from the brain with great speed. This ping-pong player is able to hit a ball hurtling toward him because signals are traveling along his nerves at up to 220 mph (350 kph). In a split second, signals zoom from his eyes to his brain to warn that the ball is on its way. His brain then sends signals to his arm muscles, controlling his return shot with amazing precision.

FAST FACTS

■ An average adult human brain weighs 2½–3 lb (1.3–1.4 kg).

■ A sperm whale's brain—the world's biggest animal brain—weighs 18 lb (8 kg).

■ The longest human nerves are more than 3 ft (1 m) long and stretch from the lower part of the spinal cord to the toes.

■ A giraffe has nerves more than 10 ft (3 m) long running down its neck.

The femoral nerve activates muscles that straighten the leg.

The sciatic nerve is the longest in the body, running from the spine to the foot.

The tibial nerve flexes the calf and foot and provides the push that allows you to walk.

The peroneal nerve moves the toes up and down.

The median nerve carries signals from touch sensors in your hand to your brain.

Your ulnar nerve carries signals to muscles in your hand.

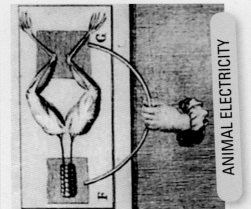

ANIMAL ELECTRICITY

The first person to realize that the human body uses electricity was an Italian doctor named Luigi Galvani. In the 1780s, Galvani discovered that he could make a frog's leg twitch by jolting the muscle with electricity. He concluded that animal muscles are activated by electrical signals, which he called "animal electricity."

Sending signals

The nervous system is made up of billions of cells called neurons (nerve cells). These are connected to each other by thin, wirelike threads that carry electrical signals and can extend for more than a meter. Neurons form the body's living wiring system and make up most of the cells in your brain.

MAKING ELECTRICITY
Neurons generate the electrical signals that dart around your nervous system. When a cell is resting (switched off), it builds up a charge. When a signal arrives and switches it on, this charge rushes through the cell to the next neuron.

A LIVING COMPUTER

You may not realize it, but your brain has more processing power than the most advanced computer on Earth. Brain cells work like the tiny transistors that make up a computer chip. But while a computer chip has around a billion transistors with three to four connections each, your brain contains 100 billion neurons, each with up to 10,000 connections to other neurons. The vast number of connections and circuits allows the brain to process millions of pieces of information at the same time.

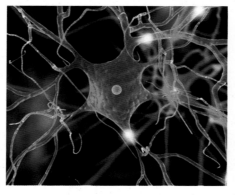

▲ BRAIN CIRCUIT *Unlike a computer, a living brain can grow new connections and continually rewires itself throughout life.*

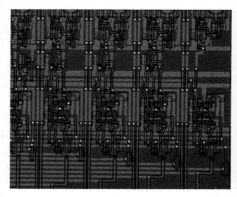

▲ COMPUTER CHIP *The circuits on a computer chip are printed in a factory and cannot change afterward.*

Dendrite

Nucleus

Axon

Synapse

Neuron
cell body

NERVE CELLS

Neurons are odd-looking cells, with many finely branched fibers extending from the main cell body. A typical neuron has one large fiber (an axon) that carries outgoing electrical signals, and a large number of smaller fibers (dendrites) that carry incoming signals. Neurons connect with each other at junctions called synapses, but there's a tiny gap in the synapse that signals cannot jump across. Instead, chemicals called neurotransmitters flood into the gap and trigger a new signal in the next neuron.

▲ CHEMICAL TRIGGER *When the electrical signal reaches the end of a neuron, the cell releases chemicals that cross the gap (synapse) and switch on the next cell.*

▼ NERVES
Nerves are the body's main electric cables. A nerve is made up of bundles of long axons, each of which carries a separate electric signal. Tough casings protect the axons from damage.

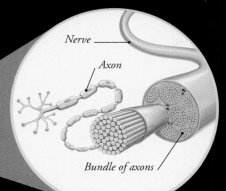

Nerve

Axon

Bundle of axons

BRANCHING OUT

Your body is riddled with nerves. Most nerves branch out from your spinal cord, which runs down the spine from the base of your brain. The nerves divide into finer and finer branches as they reach out into the body, eventually connecting with every single muscle cell and sensory cell.

The brain

Locked safely within your skull is your brain, the headquarters of the nervous system and the control center of your body. Inside the brain, billions of nerve cells sort and store incoming messages, and send out the instructions that keep your body working normally. These cells are also responsible for the way that you think and remember things, and your imagination.

This band of nerve fibers connects the left and right sides of the cerebrum.

GROOVES AND WRINKLES
The largest part of the brain is the cerebrum. It is divided into left and right halves by a long, deep groove. Smaller grooves and folds cover the cerebrum's surface. The wrinkles created by these folds increase the cerebrum's surface—allowing more thinking power to be packed inside the skull.

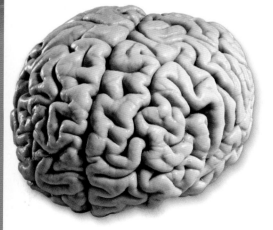

INSIDE THE BRAIN
Slicing down the center of the brain reveals its three main parts: the cerebrum, the cerebellum, and the brain stem. The cerebrum is the most powerful part of your brain, responsible for all your conscious actions, speech, and feelings. The smaller cerebellum coordinates your movements and balance. The brain stem connects the brain to the spinal cord and controls your reflexes and basic functions, such as heart rate and blood flow.

BIG BRAINS
The human brain is four times heavier than a chimp's (our closest relative). The human skull is also much larger, but it is still a very tight squeeze—the cerebrum takes up 85 percent of the space. A chimp's brain is less wrinkly, but shares many of the same structures.

Human skull

Chimp skull

178

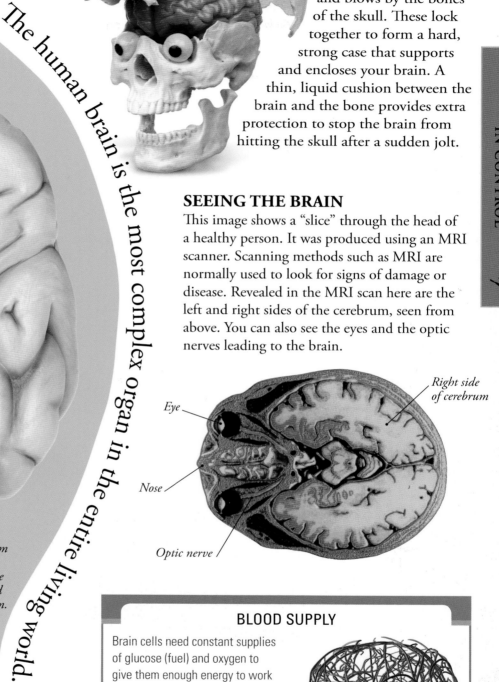

The grooves in the brain are called sulci and the bulges are called gyri.

The human brain is the most complex organ in the entire living world.

The cerebellum is situated at the base of the brain, behind the brain stem.

The brain stem controls functions you don't have to think about, such as breathing and digestion.

The spinal cord relays signals between the brain and every part of the body.

BRAIN PROTECTION

Your soft, delicate brain is protected from knocks and blows by the bones of the skull. These lock together to form a hard, strong case that supports and encloses your brain. A thin, liquid cushion between the brain and the bone provides extra protection to stop the brain from hitting the skull after a sudden jolt.

SEEING THE BRAIN

This image shows a "slice" through the head of a healthy person. It was produced using an MRI scanner. Scanning methods such as MRI are normally used to look for signs of damage or disease. Revealed in the MRI scan here are the left and right sides of the cerebrum, seen from above. You can also see the eyes and the optic nerves leading to the brain.

Right side of cerebrum

Eye

Nose

Optic nerve

BLOOD SUPPLY

Brain cells need constant supplies of glucose (fuel) and oxygen to give them enough energy to work properly. These essentials are delivered by the many blood vessels (arteries in red, veins in blue) that supply the head. In fact, one-fifth of the body's entire quota of blood goes to the brain. If the blood supply is interrupted, the brain will die or be severely damaged within minutes.

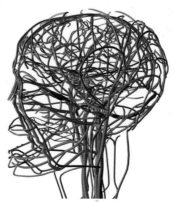

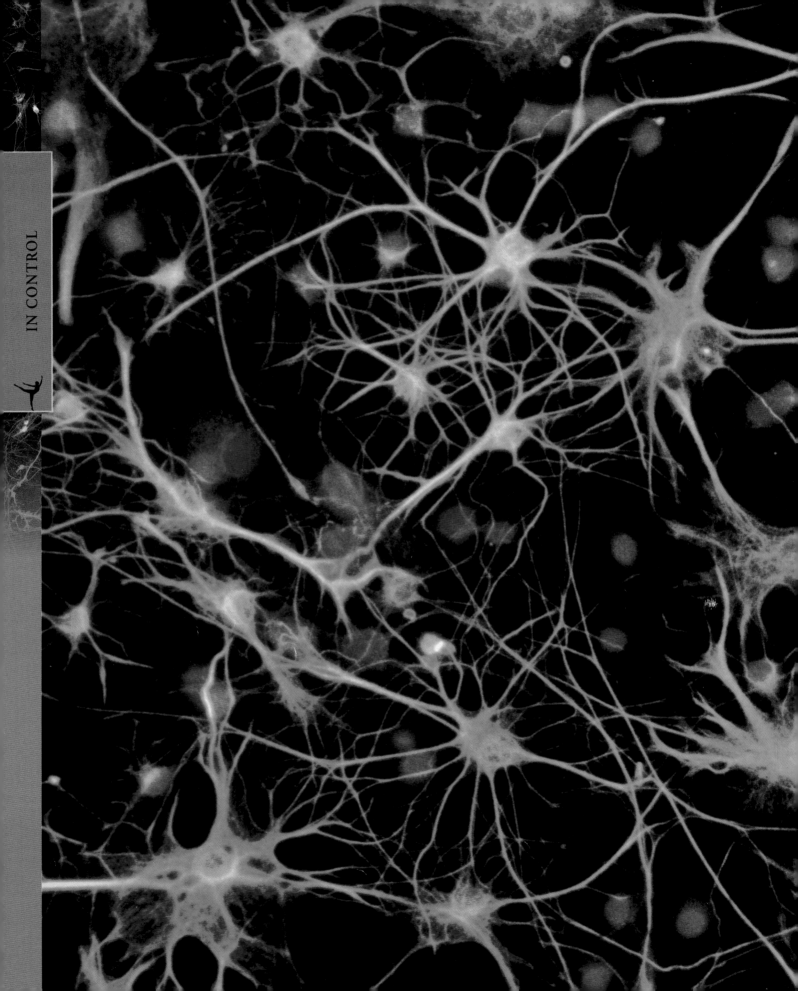

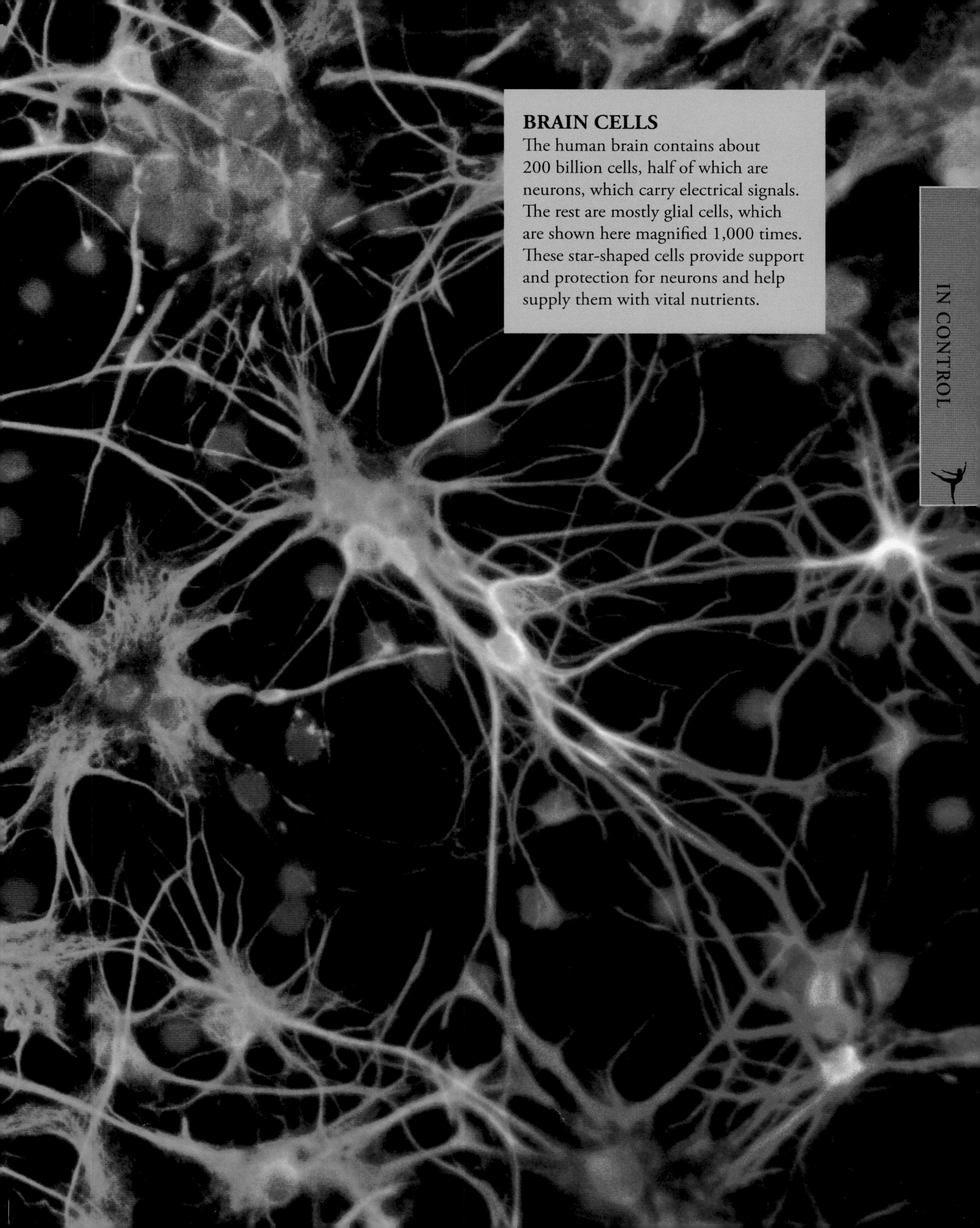

BRAIN CELLS

The human brain contains about 200 billion cells, half of which are neurons, which carry electrical signals. The rest are mostly glial cells, which are shown here magnified 1,000 times. These star-shaped cells provide support and protection for neurons and help supply them with vital nutrients.

Gray matter

The largest part of your brain is called the cerebrum. Its wrinkly outer surface is made up of a thin layer of nerve cells known as gray matter, or the cerebral cortex. This layer is vital, because it is where you feel, see, hear, think, imagine, and remember. It also controls all your body movements.

WHITE MATTER
Beneath the thin outer layer of gray matter lies the paler white matter. This is packed with nerve fibers that carry signals between different parts of the brain, and between the brain and the rest of the body.

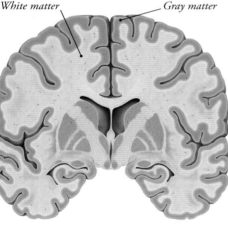

White matter　　*Gray matter*

> FAST FACTS
> - There are more than 125 trillion (125,000,000,000,000) connections between your brain cells.
> - Your brain is only 2 percent of your weight, but it uses around 20 percent of your body's energy.
> - The cerebrum takes up two-thirds of the space in your skull.

If your wrinkly cerebral cortex was spread out flat, it would cover the same area as a pillowcase.

This area is associated with thinking, imagination, and personality.

Known as Broca's area, this region controls speech.

This area controls complex movements.

Signals received from the ears are turned into sounds here.

Sounds, and where they come from, are identified here.

MAPPING THE MIND
Different parts of the cerebral cortex specialize in different jobs. Scientists discovered this by studying people with brain damage in particular parts of the cortex. People with damage in a part of the brain called Broca's area, for example, lose the ability to speak, so Broca's area must be important in controlling language.

This area tells muscles to move various body parts.

Touch receptors in the skin send signals here.

Skin sensations are identified here as pressure, pain, cold, or heat.

Here, visual signals are turned into pictures of the world we see.

A HOLE IN THE HEAD

In September 1848, Phineas Gage, an American construction worker, met with a freak accident. An explosion propelled an iron rod through his head, damaging the front part of his brain. Incredibly, Gage survived—but his behavior changed from polite and responsible to rude and reckless. This led scientists to conclude that the front part of the brain controls personality.

◄ GAGE'S BRAIN
This computer image of Gage's skull and brain shows how he was injured. The rod went in under his left eye and came out through his brain and skull.

This visual area interprets signals from the eyes.

This region figures out the meanings of words.

BRAIN IN ACTION

Modern scientists can use scanners to see which parts of the cerebral cortex "light up" when someone is asked to do something. For example, this scan shows several areas lighting up when a person moves a finger. Such studies show that many mental tasks can't be mapped to one site since they involve several parts of the cortex working together.

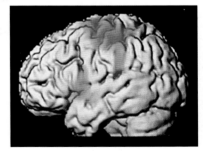

MUSCLE MAN

The top of the cerebral cortex controls muscles, but some parts of the body have a lot more cortex devoted to them than others. This strange-looking model shows how much of the brain is involved in controlling different muscles. A large area of the cortex is devoted to moving the hands, but a much smaller area controls the arms and legs.

Sleep

Everybody needs sleep. We can't survive without it, and we spend about a third of our lives sleeping. Our eyes close, breathing and heart rate slow down, and we become much less aware of the outside world. No one understands the exact purpose of sleep, but it may give the brain the chance to process the day's information.

SCN (Suprachiasmatic nucleus)

Hypothalamus

CONTROL CENTER

The daily cycle of sleeping and wakefulness is controlled by a part of the brain called the hypothalamus, which sends signals to many other parts of the brain and body to control their activity. The timing of these signals is set by a part of the hypothalamus called the SCN, which picks up signals from the eyes to determine when day becomes night.

THE SLEEP CYCLE

There are five different stages of sleep, and we pass through these several times a night. Dreams occur during a stage called rapid-eye-movement (REM) sleep, when our brains are highly active. The other four stages of sleep are called non-REM sleep. Stage 4 is the deepest and the most difficult to wake up from. If you wake someone in stage 4 sleep, they are likely to feel groggy and confused.

ALERT

STAGES OF SLEEP

HOURS OF SLEEP

1   2   3   4   5

▲ AWAKE
You are alert and aware of your surroundings when awake. It is the opposite of being asleep.

▲ STAGE 1 SLEEP
This is the lightest stage of the sleep cycle, when you feel drowsy rather than fast asleep.

▲ STAGE 2 SLEEP
As you enter this stage of light sleep, body temperature falls and heart rate slows down.

▲ STAGE 3 SLEEP
In this stage between light and deep sleep, delta brain waves (see right) first appear.

IN CONTROL

184

HOW MUCH SLEEP?

The older you are, the less sleep you need. Babies need as much as 16 hours a day to develop normally. Schoolchildren need between eight and 10 hours of sleep each day. Adults can manage on only seven hours.

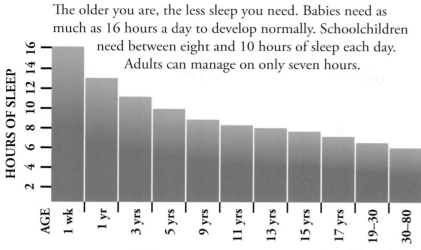

DREAMS

No one knows why we dream, and dreams often throw up crazy, mixed-up images of people and impossible events, such as flying unaided. During dreams, the brain stops body muscles from moving, preventing us from acting out the dream, but our eyes can still move.

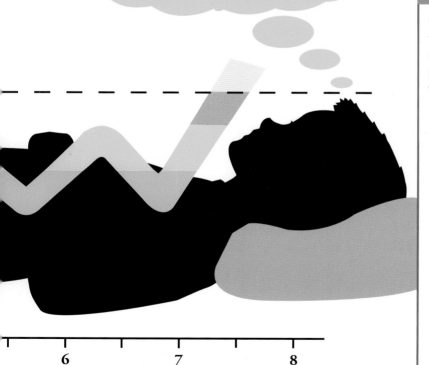

6   7   8

▲ STAGE 4 SLEEP
This is the deepest stage of sleep and each episode lasts for about 30 minutes.

▲ REM SLEEP
In rapid-eye-movement (REM) sleep, your eyes move under the eyelids and you have dreams.

SLEEPWALKING

Some people get out of bed while asleep and walk around in a trancelike state with their eyes open. This is called sleepwalking. Sleepwalkers have been known to cook meals, drive cars, and even send emails, though they have no memory of doing so later. Sleepwalking takes place during deep sleep and is not connected with dreams.

BRAIN WAVES

Scientists can monitor how active our brains are by measuring the electric field generated by millions of brain cells firing at once. The electrical activity goes up and down in a wavelike pattern, and our brains generate distinctive patterns, or "brain waves," when we're active, relaxed, or asleep.

Alpha waves occur when you're awake but relaxed.

Beta waves are produced when you're alert.

Theta waves occur when you feel drowsy.

Delta waves occur during deep sleep (stages 3 and 4).

Spinal cord

Stretching all the way down your back from your brain is your spinal cord—a large bundle of nerve tissues containing billions of nerve cells. The spinal cord carries information between the brain and most of the body. It also controls reflexes—automatic actions that happen without us having to think.

INFORMATION HIGHWAY

Your spinal cord is like a highway with smaller roads, in the form of spinal nerves, branching off it. Not all messages from the body travel to the brain. Some only get as far as the spinal cord, which activates a muscle or gland in response to a stimulus, such as making you pull your hand away from something hot. This is called a reflex action.

Signals travel to and from the brain along the spinal cord.

The spinal cord extends 18 in (45 cm) down an adult's back.

Nerves branch out from the spinal cord in pairs.

Nerves from the base of the spinal cord run to the legs.

PROTECTION

The spinal cord is well protected. It runs through a tunnel formed by interlocking bones called vertebrae, which make up the spine. This protection is vital because damage to the spinal cord can have very serious effects. If the spinal cord gets broken by an injury, a person can become paralyzed (unable to move or feel their body).

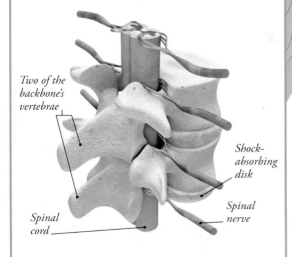

Two of the backbone's vertebrae

Shock-absorbing disk

Spinal cord

Spinal nerve

WOW!

The spinal cord is no wider than a finger for most of its length yet it contains billions of nerve cell fibers.

REFLEX ACTIONS

Most of the signals from your sense organs are processed by your brain before your body reacts. A reflex action, however, happens much more quickly since it takes a shortcut through your spinal cord, bypassing your brain. For example, if your hand gets too close to something hot, a reflex action immediately causes the muscle in your arm to pull your hand out of harm's way. This happens before your brain even has time to feel heat or pain.

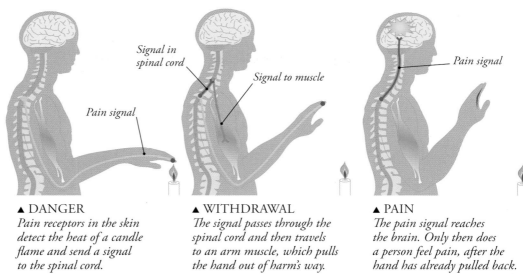

Signal in spinal cord

Signal to muscle

Pain signal

Pain signal

▲ DANGER
Pain receptors in the skin detect the heat of a candle flame and send a signal to the spinal cord.

▲ WITHDRAWAL
The signal passes through the spinal cord and then travels to an arm muscle, which pulls the hand out of harm's way.

▲ PAIN
The pain signal reaches the brain. Only then does a person feel pain, after the hand has already pulled back.

PINS AND NEEDLES

If you lean on your elbow for a while, your arm might feel numb. This happens because the pressure cuts off the blood supply to your nerves, preventing them from sending touch messages to your brain. Stop leaning, and as the blood supply returns to your arm, you'll feel a tingling sensation called "pins and needles."

BABY REFLEXES

Babies are born with some built-in reflexes that fade during their first year. For example, a baby can swim underwater because a reflex stops water from getting into the lungs. Other baby reflexes include gripping when the hand is touched, and sucking to get milk when a nipple is put in the mouth.

GAG REFLEX

If something other than food touches the back of your throat, it triggers the gag reflex. This automatic squeezing of your throat stops unwanted objects from going any farther and prevents choking. Sword swallowers learn to overcome the gag reflex so they can push a sword down their throat. About one-third of people have a weak gag reflex or no gag reflex.

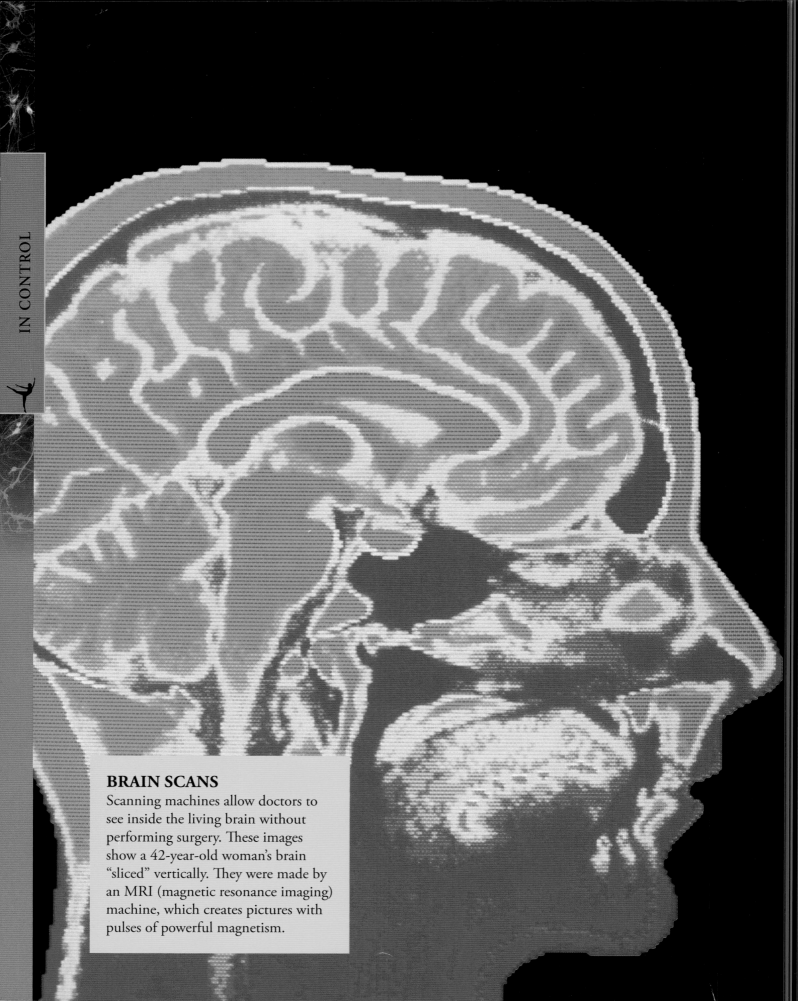

BRAIN SCANS

Scanning machines allow doctors to see inside the living brain without performing surgery. These images show a 42-year-old woman's brain "sliced" vertically. They were made by an MRI (magnetic resonance imaging) machine, which creates pictures with pulses of powerful magnetism.

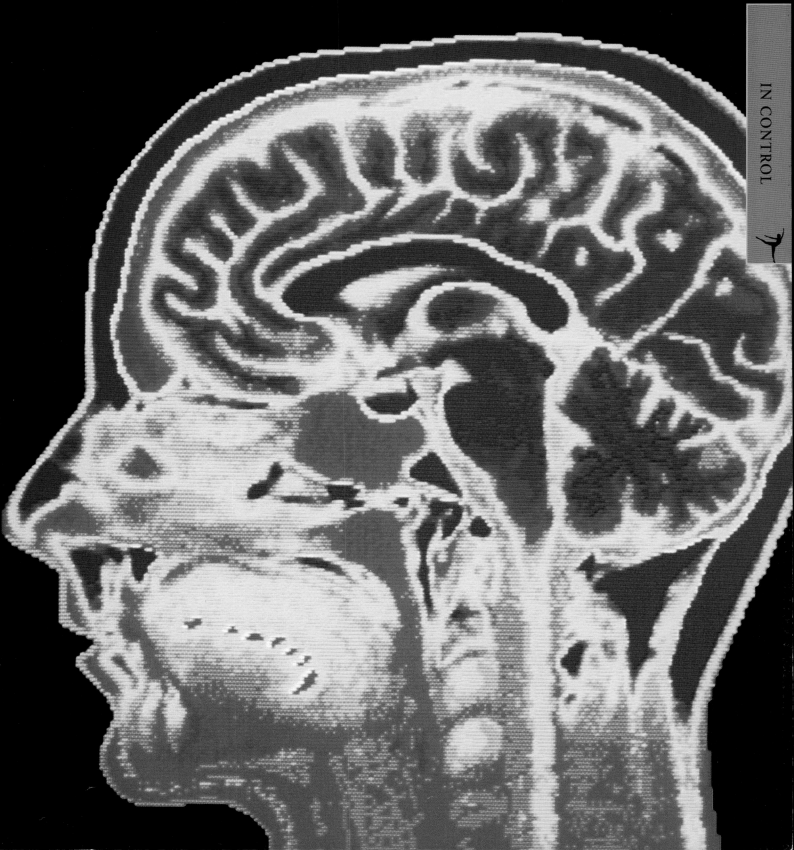

On autopilot

In addition to controlling parts of the body that you use deliberately, such as the muscles you need to walk and talk, your nervous system controls involuntary processes that happen without thinking, such as the beat of your heart. These involuntary processes are controlled by your autonomic nervous system (ANS).

AUTONOMIC NERVOUS SYSTEM

The nerve cells of the ANS run to all the main internal organs, as well as the skin, eyes, and mouth. The ANS is usually divided into two parts: one that makes the body more active, ready for action, and another that makes the body more relaxed, ready for resting.

▶ EYES
The ANS controls the tear glands and makes your eyes' pupils widen and constrict automatically.

TAKE A DEEP BREATH

You can control your breathing voluntarily, but your ANS normally does the job automatically. During exercise, when your body needs extra oxygen, your breathing rate rises and your breaths get deeper and more forceful. The sudden gasp that people make when something scares or surprises them is caused by the ANS telling the lungs to work harder.

▲ HEARTBEAT *The ANS makes your heart beat faster and more powerfully when you're physically active, excited, or frightened.*

◀ SWEATY PALMS *When you're frightened or nervous, the ANS opens sweat pores in your palms and makes them damp.*

◀ HAIRS ON END *Cold weather and fear both cause your ANS to send signals to tiny muscles under the hairs in your skin. These muscles make your hairs stand on end and raise goosebumps in your skin.*

◀ RUMBLING TUMMY *The rumbling sound that your belly makes is caused by muscles churning food in your stomach or pushing it through your intestines. These muscles are controlled by your ANS.*

BLADDER CONTROL

To let urine pass out of your bladder, you need to open two tight rings of muscle that normally keep the bladder's exit closed. The first one is controlled automatically by your ANS, and the second is under your voluntary control.
However, controlling these muscles is a skill that can take years to fully acquire, which is why children sometimes empty their bladders without meaning to.

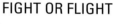

FIGHT OR FLIGHT

When something scares, angers, or excites you, your ANS prepares your body for sudden action. It triggers the release of a hormone called adrenaline, which works with the ANS to speed up your heart and breathing, divert blood to your muscles (making your skin pale), and heighten your senses. This reaction is called the "fight or flight" response.

MOUTHWATERING FOOD

The sight or smell of delicious food makes your mouth release saliva automatically, thanks to your ANS. Your salivary glands produce saliva all the time to keep your mouth and throat moist. However, the sight of food triggers the release of a more runny, watery saliva, ideal for starting the digestive process.

191

Hormones

The electrical signals that zoom along nerves are not the only kinds of messages that travel around the body. Hormones are chemicals that carry messages. They are released into the blood by glands and have powerful effects elsewhere, acting more slowly than nerve signals. Hormones control growth, reproduction, and many other processes.

The pituitary gland makes seven hormones, including growth hormone, which causes bones to grow longer.

The thyroid gland produces thyroxine, which affects the speed of chemical reactions inside cells.

The adrenal glands release the hormone adrenaline, which prepares the whole body for sudden action.

THE ENDOCRINE SYSTEM

The glands and tissues that produce hormones make up the endocrine system. The main endocrine glands are found in the brain, neck, belly, and groin. Many other organs release hormones too, including the heart, stomach, intestines, and even the skin and bone.

The pancreas makes the hormones insulin and glucagon, which control blood sugar levels.

SEX HORMONES

The development of male and female characteristics as we grow up is controlled by sex hormones. The male sex hormone testosterone is made by the testes. It causes muscles to get larger and makes facial hair grow. The female sex hormone estrogen is made in the ovaries. It makes breasts develop and controls the reproductive cycle.

In males, the two testes make the sex hormone testosterone.

192

MASTER GLAND

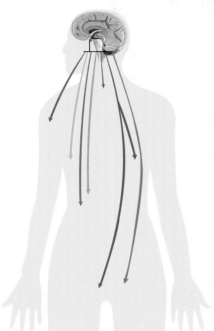

The pituitary gland is about the size of a pea and dangles by a stalk from the base of the brain. Seven different hormones are made in this tiny gland, four of which control endocrine glands elsewhere in the body. For this reason, the pituitary is sometimes called the master gland. Hormones released by the pituitary affect growth, blood pressure, stress, body chemistry, water balance, the production of breast milk in mothers, and the female reproductive cycle.

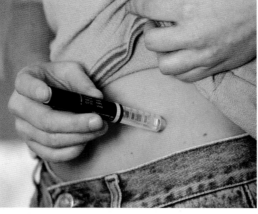

▲ INSULIN INJECTOR *People with diabetes use insulin pens to inject themselves with insulin.*

DRUGS IN SPORTS

The hormone testosterone makes muscles grow larger and stronger. Some athletes try to cheat by taking man-made versions of testosterone before a competition to improve their performance. These drugs are outlawed by most sports organizations, including the International Olympic Committee. Athletes are routinely tested for drugs and disqualified if traces are found in their blood.

SUGAR CONTROL

The pancreas releases two hormones that control the level of sugar in the blood. The hormone insulin lowers the level of blood sugar, and the hormone glucagon raises it. In people with the disease diabetes, the pancreas makes too little insulin and the blood sugar level can get dangerously high, making insulin injections necessary.

LOVE POTION

Oxytocin is a hormone made by brain cells and stored in the pituitary gland. One of its effects is to help create loving bonds between people, including mothers and their babies, couples, and close friends. For this reason it's sometimes called the love hormone. Oxytocin increases trust, reduces fear, and makes you feel happy in the company of people you love.

WOW!

There are more than 50 known hormones made by the human body and scientists are still discovering new ones.

Growth hormone

The speed at which your body grows during childhood and the teenage years is controlled by a chemical called growth hormone. Released into the blood by the pituitary gland in the brain, growth hormone affects every part of the body. It makes organs larger, muscles stronger, and bones longer, slowly transforming your body.

IN CONTROL

HOW GROWTH HORMONE WORKS

Growth hormone makes body cells divide, causing organs to grow larger and muscles to become bulkier. In the liver, it triggers the release of another hormone, IGF-1, which makes bones extend. During the early teenage years, sex hormones cause the pituitary gland to release extra growth hormone, leading to a spurt in growth. Afterward, growth hormone levels fall steeply as you reach adulthood and stop growing.

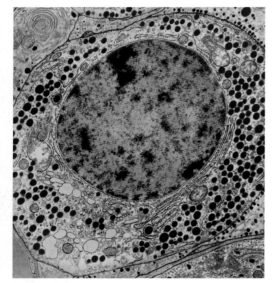

HORMONE CELL

Growth hormone is made by specialized cells in the pituitary gland. The image above, taken by an electron microscope, shows one such cell. In the middle of the cell is its control center, the nucleus (purple). Outside this are numerous granules (brown) that store newly made growth hormone, ready to be released.

Growth hormone also boosts your body's immune system.

Growth hormone

Pituitary gland

Muscles become bulkier.

IGF-1

The liver, stimulated by growth hormone, releases the hormone IGF-1.

IGF-1 causes bones to grow longer and wider.

194

GROWING BONES

Growth hormone makes you taller by making your bones grow longer. Your bones are too hard to simply stretch in length, but they contain areas of soft tissue near the ends where new bone cells are laid down. Called growth plates, these look like gaps on X-rays. When you reach adulthood and your bones stop growing, they fill up with solid bone and disappear.

— Growth plates

▶ CHILD'S HAND
In this 10-year-old's hand, the long bones are still growing at the growth plates, which look like gaps in the X-ray.

▶ ADULT'S HAND *In this 20-year-old's hand, the bones have stopped growing and the growth plates have filled with bone.*

Growth hormone molecule

GROWTH DRUG

Some children don't produce enough growth hormone and so are shorter than usual. They can be treated with artificial growth hormone (left), which is produced by genetically engineered bacteria. In the past, natural growth hormone taken from the brains of corpses was used, but this treatment carried a risk of disease and was stopped in 1985.

WOW!

Growth hormone makes every organ in the body grow larger except for the brain.

DWARFISM AND GIGANTISM

Problems with the pituitary gland in childhood can have dramatic effects on growth. A lack of growth hormone slows down bone growth, resulting in dwarfism, a condition in which someone is shorter than usual. Too much growth hormone, which can be caused by an overactive pituitary gland, results in gigantism, a condition in which someone grows very tall. This is what happened to Robert Wadlow, an American man who grew to 8 ft 11 in (2.72 m) by age 22, making him the tallest person ever.

▶ ROBERT WADLOW
At age 13, Robert Wadlow was 7 ft 4 in (2.2 m) tall, making him far taller than his father and nearly twice the height of his 9-year-old brother.

195

SUPER
SENSES

Sight, hearing, touch, smell, and taste are your main senses. Sense organs such as your eyes monitor the world around you and send signals to your brain to keep you aware.

In touch

Most of your senses involve individual organs such as your eyes and ears, but your sense of touch works all over your body. The touch sensors in your skin tell you what things feel like and warn you when you might get hurt. Some parts of your body are far more touch sensitive than others.

WOW!

Some people cannot feel pain. This may sound nice, but it actually makes them much more likely to injure themselves.

SKIN SENSORS

Your skin is much more than just a flexible cover for your body. It is packed with touch sensors, which detect sensations ranging from the lightest pressure to the sharpest pain. There are at least six types of sensors. Some are free nerve endings, which detect temperature. Others are tiny disks or capsules (corpuscles), which sense pressure, stretching, and touch.

Free nerve endings sense pain, heat, and cold.

Light pressure is detected by Meissner's corpuscle.

Faint touch is felt by Merkel's disks.

The top layer of the skin is called the epidermis.

Ruffini's corpuscle feels stretching.

Blood vessels

The large, oval Pacinian corpuscle detects deep pressure.

▶ LIGHT TOUCH
Small receptors close to the skin's surface pick up the sensation of light touch. Larger receptors deep in the dermis detect pressure.

TYPES OF TOUCH

Why do you need so many different types of touch receptors in your skin? Although they do a similar job, each receptor responds most strongly to a particular type of touch, from feeling the temperature of freezing cold snow, or the faint tickle of a feather, to the pull of skin as it is pinched. Here are five pictures of different types of touch.

TOUCH SENSATIONS

The shape of this model has been distorted to show how different parts of the body react to touch. The size of each part reflects how sensitive it is. The highly sensitive hands and lips are shown large and the less sensitive feet are small.

FEELING PAIN

Some nerves in your skin (and in other parts of your body) react to physical injury by generating pain. This is unpleasant, but a useful warning. For example, if you prick your finger on a thorn, the pain makes you pull it away before you do more damage. Touching a tender bruise causes pain, which teaches you to leave the injury alone and allow it to heal.

COLD COMFORT

Have you ever hurt yourself and not noticed, because you were enjoying yourself too much? This shows how your mind can affect your sense of pain. Doctors have been able to help people with severe burns take their minds off the pain by getting them to play virtual reality games set in cold, snowy places!

TRACING THE DOTS

Your sensitive fingertips can pick up the slightest differences in the feel of an object. A blind person can use touch to read, by feeling the patterns of raised dots on paper. Each pattern stands for a specific letter of the alphabet. The system is called Braille, which is named after its inventor, Louis Braille.

Light pressure

Heat and cold

Deep pressure

Faint touch

Stretching

Smell and taste

The senses of smell and taste allow you to experience a whole range of aromas and flavors. They work as close partners. Smell sensors in your nose detect odors in the air you breathe while taste sensors in your mouth pick out tastes in the food you eat.

NOSE AND MOUTH

There are millions of special cells at the top of the nasal cavity inside your nose that can detect different scents. In your mouth, your tongue contains thousands of taste buds that recognize different tastes. Nerves (yellow) carry signals from these receptor cells to the brain to be analyzed.

◀ SENSING SMELL *In your nose there are millions of smell receptors like this one (blue). Tiny hairlike structures on the receptors detect more than 20,000 different smells.*

Taste hole (pore) in papilla

▶ TASTE BUD *Food dissolved in saliva enters through a hole at the top of the taste bud and is tasted by tiny hairs.*

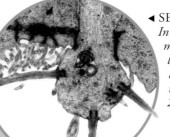

Taste hairs detect tastes

Receptor cell sends signals

Nerve fiber carries signals to the brain

◀ TINY BUMPS *Your tongue is covered with pimplelike bumps called papillae. Pointy ones help the tongue grip food during chewing. Round ones contain taste buds.*

FIVE BASIC TASTES

There are more than 10,000 taste buds in your tongue. Together, they sense just five tastes—sweet, sour, salty, bitter, and umami (savory). This combination doesn't account for all the tastes you experience because your sense of smell also plays an important role in "tasting" food.

◄ SWEET *We are attracted to sweet foods because they are packed with energy. Foods tasting sweet include sugary treats, as well as fruits and honey.*

► SOUR *This acid taste can be so sharp that it makes the lips pucker. Sour-tasting foods include lemons and vinegar.*

◄ SALTY *Adding salt to food, such as fries, can make them more tasty. Other salty foods include soy sauce, pretzels, and bacon.*

► BITTER *Many children find bitter tastes unpleasant, but adults learn to enjoy bitter flavors such as coffee.*

◄ UMAMI *This mouthwatering savory or meaty taste is found in foods such as grilled meat, cheese, mushrooms, soy sauce, and seafood.*

►DISGUST *A really nasty taste or particularly unpleasant smell produces a grimace of disgust—your nose wrinkles and your lips curl.*

SCENT SIGNALS

Our human sense of smell is far less powerful than that of many other animals. These coyote pups are using scent signals to communicate. They use smells to identify each other and mark territory. Humans also respond to scent signals, but more weakly—babies can tell their mother's scent from that of other women.

WOW!

Peppers taste "hot" because they contain capsaicin, a substance that triggers the tongue's pain detectors.

SENSING DANGER

Our senses of taste and smell help us survive by warning us about threats in two very different ways. Bitter or sour tastes warn us that foods may be poisonous to eat, and smells, such as smoke, alert us to danger. However, both senses also encourage us to eat by enabling us to experience the delicious flavors of food.

►DELIGHT *The pleasure we get from eating sweet foods, such as ice cream, encourages us to eat more. Sweet foods are often high in energy.*

Sound detectors

When you make a noise you send sound waves through the air. These are collected by your outer ears, which funnel the vibrations inward. Signals are sent from your ears to your brain that let you hear sounds and communicate using speech.

WAVES OF SOUND

Sounds are created by something vibrating and travel through the air as waves. How does this happen? Imagine pushing one end of a spring. Coils at the pushed end get squeezed then push apart, squeezing coils farther along, creating a wave of compression. With sounds, vibrations press air molecules together, causing waves to ripple away from the source.

The ear flap (pinna) helps direct sound waves into the outer ear canal.

▶ SPRING WAVES
A wave of compression, or squeezing, passes along a spring, mimicking the way sound travels as waves through the air toward your ears.

Cartilage provides springy support for the flexible earflap.

The ear lobe is filled with fatty tissue.

HOW YOUR EARS WORK

Sound waves enter your ear along its outer canal and hit the thin, skinlike eardrum, making it vibrate. These vibrations are passed to three tiny bones, called ossicles, that cross the middle ear. They move back and forth, pushing and pulling at the oval window, a membrane at the entrance to your inner ear. This sends ripples through fluid in the coiled tubes of the snail-shaped cochlea. Tiny hairlike receptors in the cochlea turn the ripples into nerve signals that are sent to the brain.

▲ INSIDE YOUR EAR
Each ear has three sections—the outer, middle, and inner ear. The outer ear canal is separated from the air-filled middle ear by the eardrum. The fluid-filled inner ear is entered through the oval window and contains the spiral cochlea.

WOW!

Many mammals, including porpoises, bats, and cats, can hear very high-pitched sounds, which humans cannot detect.

HEARING PROBLEMS

There are many reasons why people may have impaired hearing. Most commonly it is because the inner ear, or cochlea, is not working properly. It may, for example, lack enough hair cells to pick up vibrations caused by sounds. This type of problem may be helped by wearing a hearing aid that makes noises louder and easier to detect.

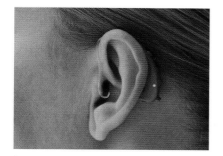

▼ HAIR CELLS *V-shaped groups of between 40 and 100 tiny hairs top each hair cell. Incoming vibrations bend the hairs and this causes the cells to send signals to your brain.*

Three tiny linked bones (ossicles) transmit sound vibrations.

The entrance to the cochlea is a thin, skinlike membrane, called the oval window.

The cochlea is made up of three fluid-filled tubes or canals.

Incoming vibrations (blue) ripple through fluid in the cochlea.

Sound waves (blue) travel along the outer ear canal to the eardrum.

The eardrum is a thin membrane that vibrates when hit by sound waves.

Outgoing vibrations (red) travel to the round window and leave the ear.

The Eustachian tube connects the ear and throat.

Tiny hair cells inside the organ of Corti, in the cochlea, detect incoming vibrations.

▲ ORGAN OF SOUND *This cutaway view of the cochlea shows the spiral organ of Corti, located in the middle tube of the cochlea. It contains sound-detecting hair cells.*

HOW LOUD?

Our amazingly sensitive ears can hear everything from the rustling of leaves to the roar of a jet plane taking off. Sound intensity, which determines loudness, is measured in decibels. A really loud sound, such as a jackhammer, can damage the ears and lead to deafness.

**Jet taking off
140 decibels**

**Normal conversation
60 decibels**

**Leaves rustling
10 decibels**

**Jackhammer
100 decibels**

Keeping balance

Your ears allow you to hear sounds but they also give you your sense of balance. Special sensors in each inner ear keep your brain updated about how upright you are, so it can tell your body how to balance. Without your ears, you'd fall off your bike!

SIXTH SENSE

Your body has a sixth sense that keeps you on your feet automatically. The balance sensors in your ears send signals to your brain. These are supported by information from your eyes, and from position and pressure sensors in your muscles, joints, and skin. Your brain processes all this data, and sends a stream of instructions to your muscles to help you balance.

These loops deep inside the ear help monitor balance.

◄ INSIDE YOUR EAR *Most of the organs in your ear are used for hearing, but some parts of your inner ear do the work of keeping you balanced and upright.*

IN BALANCE

Inside your ears are three hollow, fluid-filled loops at right angles to each other, called semicircular canals. These are your main organs of balance. When you move your head, the fluid in these canals moves too. This movement is detected by sensory hair cells, which are wired to your brain by connecting nerves. The signals update your brain about your body's position and keep you on your feet.

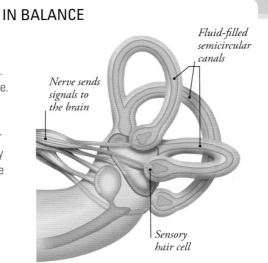

Fluid-filled semicircular canals

Nerve sends signals to the brain

Sensory hair cell

FEELING DIZZY

The balance sensors in your ears depend on a system of fluid-filled tubes. This works perfectly most of the time, but if you are spinning around on a carnival ride, the fluid in the tubes sloshes around, and takes time to settle down again after you stop moving. As a result, the sensors in the tubes send a lot of puzzling information to your brain, which gets confused about which way around you are. This is what makes you feel dizzy.

WOW!

Ear problems can give you vertigo—a nasty feeling that you are off-balance all the time.

LOSING BALANCE

Your sense of balance involves several body systems all working together. If you remove parts of it, such as vision, solid ground underfoot, or two legs to support the body, staying upright becomes much more difficult—you may lose your sense of balance and fall over. Try putting a blindfold over your eyes and standing on one leg to test this yourself.

MOTION SICKNESS

Normally, your sense of balance is backed up by the evidence of your eyes. But if you are inside a boat, for example, and your eyes can't see the movement that you feel, your brain gets confused and you may start feeling sick. This is known as motion sickness. Watching the horizon can stop this from happening, because the information gathered by your eyes then matches the movement detected by your balance sensors.

BALANCING ACT

It takes incredible balance to walk along a slackline (a thin rope slung between two points) 2,000 ft (610 m) above the ground in Yosemite National Park. To keep you balanced, your brain takes in information from your eyes, muscles, and the balance organs in your ears, and monitors your position.

Eyes and seeing

Sight is the most important sense because it provides you with pictures of the world and what is happening around you. You don't see only with your eyes but also with your brain. Your eyes detect light and send signals to your brain, which puts them together to create the moving, color, 3-D images that you see.

HOW YOUR EYES WORK

Light bouncing off objects enters your eyes through a transparent window at the front, called the cornea. It then passes through an opening, the pupil, and the flexible lens, which focuses the light on the retina at the back of your eye. From here, signals are sent to your brain along the optic nerve.

Muscles adjust the lens shape so it can focus light from any distance.

The iris controls how much light enters the eye.

The pupil is the opening that allows light into the inside of the eye.

Just one-sixth of the eyeball can be seen from the outside.

The cornea is a clear layer that helps focus light.

The lens changes shape to fine-focus light on the retina.

The white of the eye, or sclera, is the tough outer layer of the eyeball.

Muscles on the outside of the eye move the eyeball in its socket.

IMAGE MAKING

When light rays from an object hit your eye, they are bent by the cornea and lens. The rays cross inside your eye to make a clear but upside-down image on the retina. This information is sent along the optic nerve to your brain, which flips the image right side up.

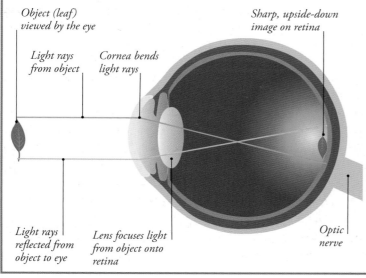

Object (leaf) viewed by the eye

Sharp, upside-down image on retina

Light rays from object

Cornea bends light rays

Light rays reflected from object to eye

Lens focuses light from object onto retina

Optic nerve

208

The retina contains millions of cells that detect light.

LIGHT CONTROL

Muscles in the colored part of the eye, the iris, control how much light enters your eye by changing the size of the pupil. In bright light (left) the iris makes the pupil smaller, allowing in less light so you are not dazzled. In dim light, the iris widens the pupil (right), letting in extra light to help you see.

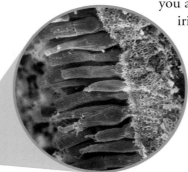

◄ LIGHT DETECTORS
Cells shaped like rods (green) and cones (blue) detect light. Rods work best in dim light; cones detect color and detail.

The blind spot is the area where nerve fibers leave the eye.

The optic nerve carries signals from the retina to the brain.

▲ INSIDE THE EYE *The eyeball is formed of two fluid-filled cavities. The space in front of the lens holds watery fluid and the space behind it is filled with a jellylike substance.*

BLIND SPOT TEST

Your eye's blind spot has no light-detecting rod or cone cells. To test this, hold the book at arm's length, close your right eye and stare at the cross. Move the book towards you and the center of the wheel will disappear when light from it falls on your blind spot.

TRACK AND SCAN

Six small muscles control the movements of each eye. They are attached to the eyeball at one end and the skull at the other. Between them they move the eyeball very precisely up or down, outward or inward. Bigger movements allow the eyes to track moving objects. Smaller movements enable the eyes to scan stationary objects such as faces.

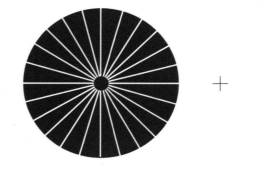

Moves eye upward

Pulls eye inward

Moves eye out to the side

Pulls eye downward and inward

Very visual

Your eyes detect patterns of light and turn them into electrical nerve signals. These pass down the optic nerves to your brain, which converts the signals into a mental image. This means that you "see" with your brain, not just your eyes. The visual processing areas of your brain enable you to see in color and three dimensions (3-D), and your memory lets you recognize what you see.

SEEING IN 3-D

You can see in 3-D because you have two forward-facing eyes with overlapping fields of view. Both eyes see this row of bowling pins, but since each eye sees it from a slightly different angle, they form different images. The eyes turn these images into electronic code, which your brain can combine to create a 3-D view.

Image formed by left eye

Left field of vision

Combined image formed by the brain

Right field of vision

Optic nerve carries data from eye

Optic tract carries data to the visual areas of the brain

Image data is processed in visual areas on both sides of the brain

FAST FACTS

■ The colored iris of your eye has patterns that are unique to you, just like your fingerprints.
■ Humans and apes are among the very few mammals that can see red.
■ The cone cells that detect color don't work in low light. That's why all color seems to fade out at night.
■ Adult human eyes are all the same size. If someone's eyes look big, it's because he or she has a small face.

IN FOCUS

Eyes work much like cameras—they have to focus light with a lens to create a sharp image. Camera lenses do this by moving forward and back, but the lens in a human eye focuses by automatically changing its shape. When you want to focus on something near your eye, special muscles squeeze the lens into a more rounded shape. If you want to look at something in the distance, the muscles relax so the lens flattens and focuses farther away.

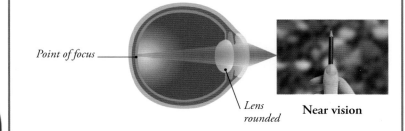

Point of focus

Lens rounded

Near vision

Lens flattened

Distant vision

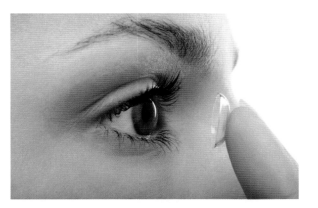

Image formed by right eye

SEEING IN COLOR

The cone cells in the retina of each eye allow you to see in color. Different cells respond to various levels of red, blue, and green light. They send signals to your brain, which combines the data and lets you distinguish thousands of different colors. Some people are not able to see the difference between colors such as red and green. This is known as color blindness.

NEAR- AND FARSIGHTED

Many people are nearsighted—they cannot focus on things in the distance. Older people often develop the opposite problem, and cannot focus close up enough to read. Both problems can be corrected by wearing glasses or contact lenses, which are placed directly on the eyes.

FILLING IN THE GAPS

Sometimes you recognize something you are looking at, even though you don't get a clear view of it. This is because your brain fills in the gaps between the visual clues. There is a spotted dog in this picture, but it is very difficult to see because so much visual information is missing. Can you see it? If so, it's because your brain is using memory to complete the picture.

WOW!

The farthest object that the human eye can see without a telescope is the Andromeda Galaxy, which is an amazing 2.25 million light-years away.

Visual tricks

Sometimes you can't believe your eyes—or more accurately, you can't believe what your brain thinks it is seeing. Optical illusions can jangle your nerves, creating strange visual effects such as flashing spots. Or they can make your brain come up with impossible solutions as it tries to make sense of confusing visual information.

WALKING TALL
Your brain uses visual "rules" to analyze what you are looking at. One of these rules is that same-sized objects always look smaller in the distance. This makes the more distant figures in this picture seem taller, even though they are all the same height. Try measuring them to prove it.

MOVING TARGET
As you scan across this pattern, parts of it seem to be moving. This effect is caused by the light-sensitive cells in your eyes rapidly switching on and off as they react to different parts of the pattern. This sends messages to your brain that fool it into seeing movement.

CLOUDED VISION
Can you see a pig shape in this cloud? That's because your brain is programmed to recognize things that are useful or dangerous. To our ancestors, an animal might be vital food or a threat, so any hint of an animal shape—even in a cloud—triggers a response in your brain.

SEEING SPOTS

When you look at this grid, dark spots seem to flash within the white spots at the corner of each square. Scientists still don't know why this happens, although it probably has something to do with the optical cells in your eyes switching on and off. Oddly, tilting your head to one side seems to reduce the effect of the illusion.

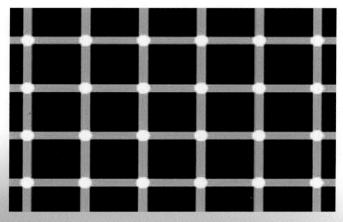

IMPOSSIBLE OBJECT

This triangle looks like a solid, three-dimensional (3-D) object, even though such an object could not exist. The illusion works because each corner of the triangle follows the optical rules that your brain uses to identify 3-D shapes, so it insists on making the pattern represent a 3-D object. The shape is called the Penrose triangle after its creator, mathematician Roger Penrose.

DOUBLE IMAGE

What does this picture look like to you? Some people see a white vase against a darker background, while others see two people facing each other. Now that you've read this, you can probably see both images. Your brain uses information stored in your memory to interpret confusing images, and sometimes it comes up with two conflicting solutions at once.

MIND AND PERSONALITY

In addition to controlling your nervous system and senses, your brain creates your feelings, thoughts, memories, talents, and personality. All these mental processes make up what we call the mind.

Left or right?

The wrinkly outer part of your brain is divided into two halves. The left half controls the right side of your body, and the right half controls your left side. For most tasks, one side of your brain is dominant, making you right- or left-handed, right- or left-footed, and even right- or left-eyed and eared.

DIFFERENT SIDES

In addition to controlling different sides of the body, the two sides of the brain specialize in different mental tasks. In most people, for instance, the left side of the brain processes the meaning of words. However, if one side of the brain gets damaged, the other side can sometimes learn to do its job.

WOW!

Enjoying music is strongly linked to the right brain, but creating music that other people enjoy uses the skills of the left brain.

WHICH HAND?

If you're right-handed, the part of your left brain that controls your right hand is dominant over the corresponding part of your right brain. About 90 percent of people are right-handed and 10 percent are left-handed, including President Barack Obama and former presidents Bill Clinton and George H.W. Bush. A few people are ambidextrous: they can use both hands equally well.

Left brain

USING WORDS

Being able to use words fluently is a skill controlled by the left brain. This includes both talking and writing, since both involve using words.

ROUTINE TASKS

The left side of your brain often takes charge of routine tasks such as brushing your teeth—things that you do every day without thinking.

THINKING LOGICALLY

The left brain is usually better than the right brain at dealing with numbers and thinking logically. It gives you the ability to analyze a problem and work out an exact answer, rather than make a guess.

Right brain

TONE OF VOICE

Although the left brain processes words, the right brain controls your accent, tone of voice, and the rhythm of speech.

SPATIAL SKILLS

Your ability to think in 3-D is a right-brain skill. It allows you to imagine what an object or structure will be like when it is changed or turned around.

RECOGNIZING OBJECTS

How do you know that this is a kitten and not a puppy? You are able to recognize familiar objects instantly, thanks to the workings of the right side of your brain.

HAPPY OR SAD?

In most people, the left half of their field of vision is dominant. Look at these two portraits and focus on the girl's nose. Does she look happier in one of them? Most people find that she looks happier in the image on the right. That's because the smile is in the left half of their field of vision.

WHICH EYE?

One of your eyes is stronger than the other. Hold up one finger and line it up with something in the distance, using both eyes. Then cover one eye at a time. When you cover your stronger eye, your finger seems to move sideways, but covering your weaker eye has less effect.

BEST FOOT FORWARD

If you kick a ball without thinking, you naturally use your dominant foot. If you are right-handed you would expect to be right-footed, too. But strangely, it's not always so. Some right-handed people prefer to use their left foot, and plenty of left-handers favor their right foot.

217

How memory works

The human brain is always gathering information and storing it for future use, but not everything we learn or experience is easy to remember. Some memories last only seconds and are meant to be forgotten. Others leave a permanent stamp on our brains.

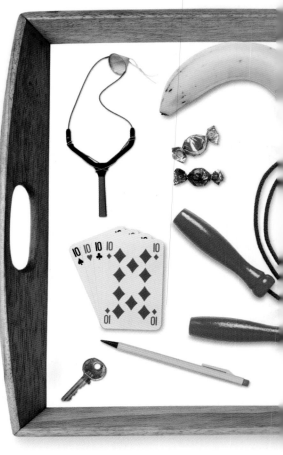

The hippocampus helps us store long-term memories.

The frontal lobes hold short-term memories.

The amygdala helps us form powerful emotional memories.

The temporal lobe helps us remember words and facts.

WHERE ARE MEMORIES STORED?

Memories aren't stored in one place in the brain. Instead, they're spread out across the whole brain, and a single memory can involve several parts of the brain. The areas most important in storing memories are the temporal lobe and the hippocampus.

MAKING MEMORIES

Your brain stores memories and other kinds of information as networks of connections between brain cells. Every experience you have causes your brain cells to fire (send electrical signals) in a specific pattern. When you remember something, you trigger the same network of neurons that originally fired. Each time you use the memory, the connections are strengthened and the memory becomes easier to recall.

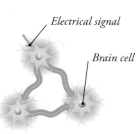

Electrical signal

Brain cell

1. LINKS FORM
An experience causes a brain cell to send signals to other cells, forming a network of connections.

New connection

2. MEMORY WEB
Each time the circuit is used, the connections grow stronger. The cluster of cells also grows larger, making the memory easier to access.

More cells join the circuit

218

MEMORY GAME

How good is your memory? Study the objects on the tray for 45 seconds and try to memorize them. Then close the book, wait one minute, and write down as many objects as you can remember. If you can remember half of the 15 objects, you've done very well. Most people can hold only about seven chunks of information in their short-term memory at a time.

LONG-TERM MEMORIES

Some memories can last for years. We call these long-term memories, and they are stored in various parts of the brain, depending on whether they're events, skills, or facts. Some of our clearest long-term memories are those linked to powerful emotions, such as the shock of hearing someone has died or the excitement of going on an exotic vacation.

◄ EVENTS *Exciting experiences such as a trip to a theme park have a filmlike, photographic quality, though details are blurred. These memories are stored by the hippocampus and various parts of the outer brain (cortex).*

▶ SKILLS *Physical skills such as playing the piano or riding a bicycle are learned by practice and stored in a part of the brain called the cerebellum. Once learned, such skills stay with us for life.*

▶ FACTS *Words and facts that we learn are stored in the temporal lobe on the side of the brain. Committing new facts to long-term memory can be difficult. The trick is to keep using them—each time you recall the information, it gets easier to remember.*

SHORT-TERM MEMORIES

Some memories last only seconds. These short-term memories are made to be forgotten quickly, so they don't clutter your brain. They are held in a kind of mental notepad for a few seconds, in case you need to use them. If the information isn't used, the brain discards it and you forget about it.

Are you a genius?

People who know a lot often strike us as smart, but there's far more to intelligence than memorizing facts and figures. Being intelligent means being quick to grasp complex ideas, solve problems, and learn skills. Some psychologists think there are many different types of intelligence, from how good you are at math to how well you interact with people. To find out what you might be best at, try the brainteaser tests on pages 238–241.

WOW!

Korean scientist Kim Ung-yong has an IQ of 210—the world's highest. A child genius, he could read in four languages at the age of two.

SPATIAL INTELLIGENCE

Thinking spatially means seeing an object in your mind's eye and turning it around or changing it. High spatial intelligence makes people good at building or repairing mechanisms made of many parts. It also helps with reading maps and navigating.

MATHEMATICAL INTELLIGENCE

People with high mathematical intelligence have logical, scientific minds. They are not only good at math but also tend to be good at figuring out how computers and other complicated gadgets work. They enjoy the challenge of solving puzzles that require logical, step-by-step thinking.

VERBAL INTELLIGENCE

This is a measure of reading and writing ability. People with high verbal intelligence tend to read a lot and are quick to absorb information from books. They tend to be good at writing and at communicating complex ideas in words.

WHAT IS A GENIUS?

A genius is someone who is exceptionally brilliant at a particular skill. Albert Einstein is called a genius because his work in physics led to amazing discoveries. To become a genius you need to have a natural talent in a subject, as well as an obsessive interest that lasts for many years.

► FATHER OF PHYSICS
Einstein made incredible discoveries about the nature of time, light, and gravity.

IQ TESTS

IQ (intelligence quotient) tests are designed to predict how well children are likely to do at school. They focus on mathematical, verbal, and spatial intelligence and often include puzzles like the one below. Can you spot the odd one out?

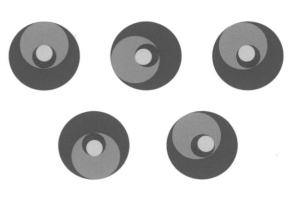

EMOTIONAL INTELLIGENCE

If you're good at figuring out what other people feel and think, you have high emotional intelligence (emotional IQ). People with high emotional IQ make good team leaders and managers. They can be very successful in life, even if they have low scores for other types of intelligence.

PHYSICAL INTELLIGENCE

While some people are clumsy and awkward, others are agile and quick to master physical skills like cycling, skiing, and gymnastics. People with high physical intelligence do well in sports. They are also good with their hands and enjoy practical activities and making things.

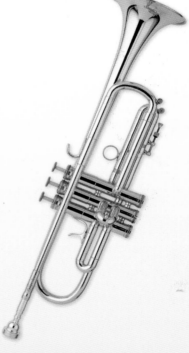

MUSICAL INTELLIGENCE

This form of intelligence makes people good at picking up a tune or a rhythm. People with high musical intelligence are often good singers or dancers. They learn how to play musical instruments quickly and may even start to compose their own music.

What's your personality?

What kind of person are you—a party animal or a quiet bookworm? Are you friendly and good-natured or argumentative and bad-tempered? Everyone has a unique personality. Your personality is molded by your genes and your upbringing, and it has a big influence on your life and the career you might choose.

◀ CONSCIENTIOUSNESS
A person with a high score for conscientiousness is reliable, hardworking, and punctual (on time). Conscientious people strive to do their best and are usually neat and tidy, though they can be a little fussy.

▶ EXTROVERSION *Extroverts thrive best in the company of others and are confident and talkative. Introverts are the opposite and tend to be shy and wary of strangers.*

FIVE DIMENSIONS

When we get to know someone, we instinctively form our own personal opinion about their personality. Psychologists try to measure personality in a more scientific way. They focus on five or more different "dimensions" of personality, such as extroversion and agreeableness, each of which is measured separately by answering questions. You can measure the five dimensions of your own personality by taking the quiz on page 236.

◀ NEUROTICISM
People with a high score for neuroticism get upset, worried, or excited more easily than other people. They might be regarded as sensitive or high-strung. The opposite is someone who's always calm, even in stressful situations.

▶ AGREEABLENESS
This is a measure of how easy you are to get along with. If you score highly, people find you cooperative and good-natured. If you have a low score, you might be argumentative. People tend to become more agreeable as they get older.

FAST FACTS

■ The male sex hormone testosterone affects personality, making boys more competitive and aggressive than girls.

■ Men have slightly bigger brains than women, but the average IQ of men and women is the same.

■ Some people think you can use a person's handwriting to study their personality, but there's no scientific evidence that this works.

◀ OPENNESS *If you're very open, you like new experiences and change. You make decisions on the spur of the moment rather than following plans, and you tend to dip into things rather than immersing yourself in one hobby.*

Understanding your own personality can help you choose a career that will suit you.

WHAT SEX IS YOUR BRAIN?

Psychologists think male and female brains tend to have different skills. On average, male brains are better at systemizing skills, such as understanding how machines work. And female brains, on average, tend to be better at empathizing skills, such as understanding people's feelings. Most people's brains have a mixture of typically male and female skills, with just a leaning to one side or the other. Some girls are perfectly at home fixing bikes or computers, for instance, and some boys have good social skills.

▲ BIKE TEST *A fun way to find out how male someone's brain might be is to get them to draw a bicycle. Men tend to draw more accurate bikes. Women draw less accurate bikes but might include a rider!*

▶ FINGER TEST *If your ring finger is longer than your index finger, you're likely to have a male brain. The difference is caused by the level of the male sex hormone testosterone in the body very early in life, when we're still developing inside the womb.*

Index finger | Ring finger

DOES PERSONALITY CHANGE?

If you think you have a bad personality, don't panic—personality changes during life, even during adulthood. In your 20s and 30s, your levels of agreeableness and conscientiousness will probably go up. In women, neuroticism and extroversion levels go down with age. In men they stay the same, but start off lower.

WOW!

People with "multiple personality disorder" claim to have up to 16 distinct personalities that take turns occupying their body.

IN THE GENES?

Is personality encoded in our genes or molded by our experiences as we grow up? Scientists think that both are important. Studies of identical twins (who have the same genes) adopted into different families reveal that their personalities are very similar, though not exactly the same.

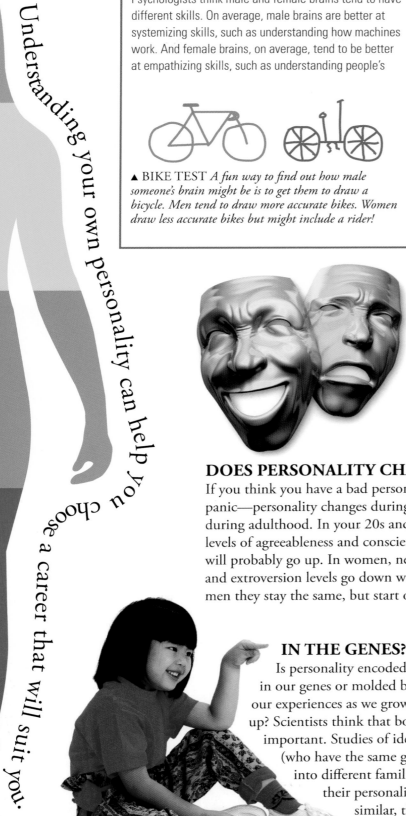

The feeling mind

In addition to creating thoughts and memories, the brain conjures up powerful feelings called emotions. Our most basic emotions, such as fear, anger, and disgust, are survival instincts that protect us from danger. Emotions don't just affect the mind—they affect the whole body, causing physical reactions as well as mental ones.

EMOTIONS

Our emotions are produced by parts of the brain that we don't voluntarily control. They seem to well up from nowhere, and they are difficult to hide since we show them with our faces and our body language. But they can also be enjoyable—the best movies are those that succeed in triggering genuine feelings of fear, surprise, sadness, and joy.

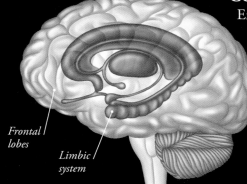

Frontal
lobes

Limbic
system

CONTROL CENTER

Emotions are generated in a part of the brain called the limbic system. This structure is found in animal brains too, which is why some scientists call it primitive. Unlike animals, we can resist the urge to act on strong emotions because more advanced parts of the human brain—the frontal lobes—act like policemen, enabling us to think before we act.

PRIMARY EMOTIONS

Psychologists think there are six primary emotions, each of which causes a characteristic facial expression. These expressions are the same in all the world's people—a smile means the same thing whether you live in the Sahara desert or the Amazon rain forest. Secondary emotions are more complex and include guilt, shame, pride, and envy.

Fear

Disgust

Surprise

Joy

Anger

Sadness

EMOTIONAL MEMORY

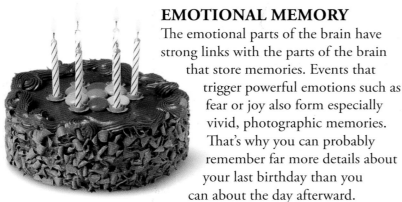

The emotional parts of the brain have strong links with the parts of the brain that store memories. Events that trigger powerful emotions such as fear or joy also form especially vivid, photographic memories. That's why you can probably remember far more details about your last birthday than you can about the day afterward.

PHOBIAS

Some people experience a feeling of terror in reaction to something harmless, such as the sight of a spider. Before they have time to think, their brain has put the body on red alert, causing a racing heart, queasy stomach, and feeling of dread. This kind of overreaction is called a phobia. Most phobias are caused by animals, but other triggers include heights, flying, and the sight of blood.

HOW FEAR WORKS

Fear is the most powerful emotion of all. Lightning reactions are vital in times of danger, so the fear signal takes a shortcut from your brain to your body.

1 Signals from your eyes pass through part of the brain called the limbic system. This makes a quick visual analysis, and if it spots anything that looks scary, it puts the body on red alert. The hormone adrenaline is released, making you feel fear.

2 A slower signal from your eyes reaches the visual cortex at the back of the brain. This makes a detailed analysis of what you've seen. The front of your brain then uses thought and memory to decide whether the threat really is dangerous.

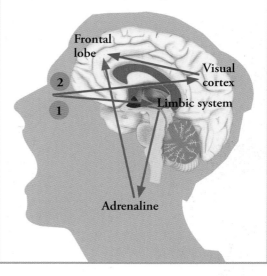

Frontal lobe

Visual cortex

2

1

Limbic system

Adrenaline

LIE DETECTORS

Your emotions tend to trigger certain physical reactions if you're lying. Your heart speeds up, and the skin on your hand becomes slightly damp with sweat. Lie detector machines monitor these physical reactions, but good liars can stay calm and fool the system.

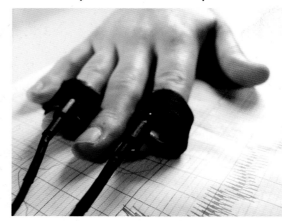

THRILL-SEEKERS

Some people become anxious in risky situations, but others get a buzz of excitement when doing anything new or dangerous, such as extreme skiing. Thrill-seekers are thought to have a higher level of a brain chemical called dopamine, which produces a sensation of pleasure and excitement.

The body clock

Deep inside your brain is a kind of inner clock that controls your daily rhythms, telling you when to wake, sleep, rest, and play. Some people have a body clock that makes them most active in the mornings, but others prefer staying up late. To find out which you have, take the test on the opposite page.

AROUND THE CLOCK

Your body clock sends signals to other parts of the brain and to the body, controlling how active various functions are throughout the day. Your bowels are most active in the early morning, for instance, but your brain doesn't reach peak alertness until about three hours later. The best time to compete in sports is late afternoon, when your heart and lungs are at their most efficient.

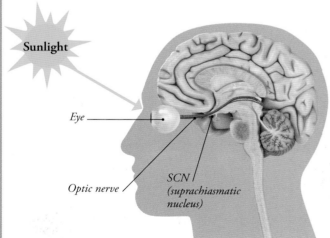

Sunlight

Eye

Optic nerve

SCN (suprachiasmatic nucleus)

TIMEKEEPER

About the size of a grain or rice, the body's main clock is called the SCN (suprachiasmatic nucleus). It is located in the base of the brain next to the optic nerve, which carries signals into the brain from the eyes. Special clock genes in the SCN switch on and off regularly, keeping time. They are reset every 24 hours by the rise and fall of the Sun, detected by the eyes.

12 p.m.
Noon

11:00 a.m.
Brain fully alert
and active

9–10 a.m.
Highest risk of
heart attack

8:30 a.m.
Bowel movement
most likely

8:00 a.m.
Rapidly rising
alertness

6.45 a.m.
Sharpest blood
pressure rise

4:00 a.m.
Most likely to give birth

3:00 a.m.
Lowest body
temperature

2.00 a.m.
Deepest sleep

12:00 a.m.
Midnight

The clock labels (outer dial):

1 — 1–2 p.m. Dip in wakefulness
2 — 2:30 p.m. Best coordination
3 — 3:30 p.m. Fastest reaction time
4 — 4:00 p.m. Best time for sporting performance
5 — 5:00 p.m. Heart and lungs at peak efficiency
6 — 6:30 p.m. Highest blood pressure
7 — 7:00 p.m. Eyes detect fading light, causing energy levels to fall
8 — 8:00 p.m. Body temperature and blood pressure fall
9 — 9–10 p.m. Increasing feeling of tiredness
10 — 10:30 p.m. Bowels least active
11 — Bowels least active

LIGHT THERAPY

The cycle of day and night, detected by our eyes, governs not just the body clock but other brain functions too. In countries with long, dark winters, lack of daylight can cause a kind of depression called seasonal affective disorder (SAD). People with this problem sometimes use bright light to try and relieve symptoms.

WOW!

The average person has a body clock of 24 hours and 11 minutes.

JET LAG

If you fly to a distant country in a different time zone, your body clock will be out of sync with the local time and you'll experience jet lag. This condition makes it hard to sleep at night and hard to stay awake during the day. After a few days in the new time zone, your body clock resets automatically and jet lag disappears.

ARE YOU AN OWL OR A LARK?

1. When your alarm clock wakes you up, do you:
a. Get right out of bed?
b. Switch it off and get up slowly?
c. Put the alarm clock on snooze?
d. Switch it off and go back to sleep?

2. What time do you go to bed on Friday evenings?
a. 8:00–9:00 p.m.
b. 9:00–10:00 p.m.
c. 10:00–11:00 p.m.
d. After 11:00 p.m.

3. What time do you get up on Saturday mornings?
a. Before 9:00 a.m.
b. 9:00–10:00 a.m.
c. 10:00–11:00 a.m.
d. After 11:00 a.m.

4. How hungry are you when you eat breakfast?
a. Very hungry
b. Only slightly hungry
c. Not really hungry but you make an effort to eat
d. Disgusted by the thought of food

5. At what time of day do you feel most energetic?
a. Morning
b. Afternoon
c. Evening
d. Late at night

6. How long does it take you to fall asleep?
a. Under 10 minutes
b. 10–20 minutes
c. 20–30 minutes
d. More than 30 minutes

RESULTS
Add up your points for each question to work out your score: **a** = 4 points, **b** = 3 points, **c** = 2 points, **d** = 1 point.
6–11 points: You're an owl and you love staying up late. But you might be sleep-deprived, which could make you bad-tempered during the day and hurt your studies. Try going to bed a little earlier on weekdays if you think you need more sleep.
12–18 points: You're neither an owl nor a lark, and you probably have sensible sleeping habits.
19–24 points: You're a lark and you love the mornings. Consider yourself lucky—most people hate getting up early.

Teenage brain

During the teenage years, the brain goes through dramatic changes. Circuits that aren't needed are pruned away, while others strengthen and mature. This period of change affects how you feel and behave, causing mood swings, risky behavior, and sometimes physical and social clumsiness.

USE IT OR LOSE IT

In early life, millions of connections form between brain cells, making your brain quick to learn. During the teenage years, however, circuits that haven't been used are pruned away, making your brain faster but less adaptable.

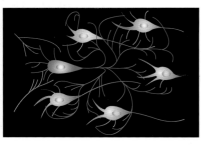

▲ EARLY CHILDHOOD
Connections form between brain cells, creating millions of potential circuits.

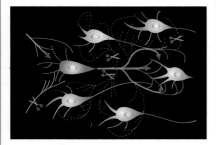

▲ TEENAGE YEARS
Unused connections are pruned away, while others become stronger.

Learning skills such as skiing or surfing becomes harder after you reach the teenage years because your brain becomes less flexible.

INSIDE THE TEENAGE BRAIN

The human brain keeps on changing and developing well into our twenties. Changes happen in many parts of the brain, including the gray matter on the surface and deeper structures in the heart of the brain. The maturing process starts at the back and works forward, with the frontal lobes—the areas responsible for thinking and problem solving—maturing last.

The corpus callosum is a bundle of nerves joining the left and right sides of the brain. It thickens during our teens.

In charge of planning and decision-making, the frontal lobes enable us to think ahead before acting rashly. They are the last parts of the brain to mature.

SLOW RISER

Teenagers find it much harder than adults to get up in the morning. The teenage brain not only needs about two hours more sleep, but also has a different cycle of daily activity, being most active late in the day and sluggish in the mornings.

THE MATURING BRAIN

These scans show how the brain's surface tissue (gray matter) changes during the teenage years. Red and yellow areas have a large amount of gray matter, whereas blue areas have less. As unused brain circuits are pruned away, the amount of gray matter falls. Although the remaining gray matter has less potential to learn new skills, it becomes much more efficient in the skills it has acquired.

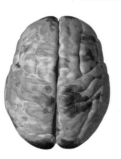

13 years old

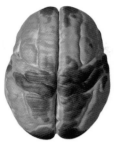

15 years old

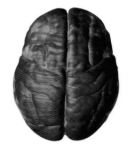

18 years old

The basal ganglia region includes the brain's reward pathway. It generates the "buzz" we feel during pleasure and excitement.

The amygdala is the emotional hub of the brain. It creates powerful feelings such as fear and anger. It is one of the areas of the brain that makes teenagers moody.

The cerebellum helps coordinate the body's movements. During the teenage years, when the body grows rapidly, the cerebellum has to relearn how to control our movements.

RECKLESS YOUTH

People take the most risks at the age of 14. At this age, the basal ganglia—the parts of the brain that generate the thrill of excitement—are fully formed. But the thinking frontal lobes are not, so the brakes are missing. Lacking sound judgment, some teenagers take crazy risks, especially when trying to impress friends.

MOODY PHASE

Tantrums and mood swings are common among teenagers. One reason is that the parts of the brain that create emotions develop faster than the parts that help us control emotions. Adults are good at suppressing or hiding their feelings and staying polite, but teenagers are more likely to act first and think later.

231

Body language

Although words and facial expressions are important ways of communicating, body language can also reveal a lot about what we think and feel. This language is made up of a mixture of gestures and movements that we make all the time, often without thinking.

BODY TALK

Most of our "body talk" happens unconsciously, which means that we express what we think or how we feel without being aware that we're doing it. We also read body language unconsciously. For example, we may get the feeling that someone likes or dislikes us, without really knowing why.

Public zone

Social zone

Personal zone

Intimate zone

PERSONAL SPACE

How close we allow people to come depends on how well we know them. Normally only best friends and family enter our intimate zone. Other people we know well and trust can enter our personal zone, while people we know less well stay in the social zone. If someone comes too close, it makes us feel uncomfortable and we move away.

▶ FRIENDLY
When two people copy each other's posture and gestures, it shows they are getting along well.

▶ DISHONEST
When lying, people may try to suppress their body language, making them appear stiff or uncomfortable. They are likely to touch the face and fidget.

POINTING WITH THE BODY

When people meet up and chat, the directions their bodies point can send out powerful signals. If two people face or turn toward each other while chatting, they can make a third person feel unwelcome. This message stays the same even if they occasionally glance at the third person to be polite. Sometimes, a person in a group may unconsciously point a part of their body at someone they are thinking about.

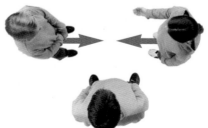

▲ LEFT OUT *With their bodies facing each other as they talk, the two girls make the boy feel left out.*

▲ POINTING *The boy also feels left out when the girls point toward each other with their feet.*

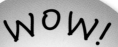

WOW!
Psychologists claim that up to two-thirds of communication between people is nonverbal.

SPOT THE FAKE SMILE

A real, emotional smile happens automatically and sends out a message of happiness and welcome. It spreads across the face and makes the mouth widen and the skin around the eyes wrinkle. A fake smile appears and ends quickly, widening the mouth without any real feeling. See if you can tell which of these six smiles are real.

1, 2, and 4 are fake smiles; 3, 5, and 6 are real.

◄ DEFENSIVE
A cautious or anxious person feels defensive and may instinctively protect themselves with folded arms and crossed legs.

► DOMINANT
Dominant means being in charge. A dominant person feels powerful or superior and shows it with a relaxed, confident posture.

► SUBMISSIVE
Hiding the hands, standing still, and looking down are ways of showing you're submissive (not in charge). Submissive is the opposite of dominant.

▲ SECRET FEELINGS? *Although the girls are facing, one of them is pointing her foot at the boy. Does she secretly like him?*

GESTURES

Some types of body language, such as a smile, have exactly the same meaning all over over the world and in every culture. But other signs, from nods and winks to bows and hand gestures, vary in meaning from place to place. For example, two fingers in a V-shape means "victory" in some places but "peace" in others. In England, showing a V with the back of the hand is a rude gesture meaning "get lost!"

REFERENCE SECTION

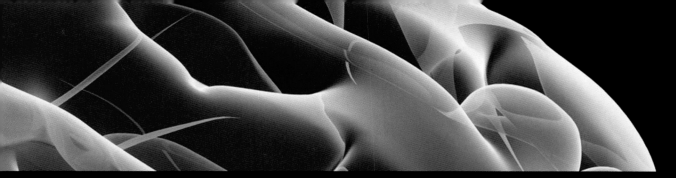

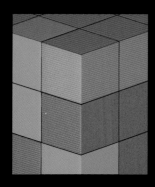
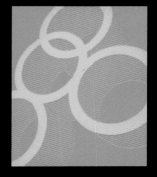

Are you shy or self-confident? Are you good with numbers or words? Find out more about your personality and some of the people who have helped us understand what makes us tick.

Test your personality

Take this simple quiz to find out more about your personality. Write the answers "yes," "no," or "not sure" on a piece of paper and use the box opposite to work out your scores. There are no right or wrong answers—just choose the answers that best describe you. See page 222 to find out what the results mean.

6 Are you very sensitive to criticism?

7 Do you get bored easily with new hobbies, and keep starting new ones?

8 Do you enjoy meeting new people?

1 Do you like doing things that are a little dangerous?

2 Are you afraid to tell someone when you don't like them?

3 Do you enjoy having long phone conversations?

4 Are you good at remembering birthdays?

5 Would you rather hang out in a large group than with one or two good friends?

9 Do you usually do your homework on time?

10 Do you feel sorry for people who are unhappy?

11 Do you usually manage to stay calm under pressure?

12 Do you usually "forgive and forget" when someone upsets you?

13 Do you think others would describe you as shy?

14 Do you usually have a plan for what you will do over the weekend?

15 Do you make sure your room is neat and tidy?

16 Do you rarely have arguments with other people?

17 Do you like exploring unfamiliar places?

18 Are you scared of what other people might think about you?

19 Do you ever offer to help with the laundry?

20 Do you consider yourself to be a bit of a rebel?

21 Do you usually do things to the best of your abilities?

22 Would you like to try bungee jumping, skydiving, or white-water rafting?

23 Do you find that you often get angry over small things?

WORK OUT YOUR SCORE

Openness: Score 2 points if you answered "yes" to questions 7, 17, 20, 24, and 26. Score 2 points if you answered "no" to question 14, and 1 point if you answered "not sure" to 7, 14, 17, 20, 24, and 26.

Conscientiousness: Score 2 points if you answered "yes," and 1 point if you answered "not sure," to questions 4, 9, 15, 19, 21, and 29.

Extroversion: Score 2 points if you answered "yes" to questions 1, 3, 5, 8, and 22. Score 2 points if you answered "no" to question 13. Score 1 point if you answered "not sure" to questions 1, 3, 5, 8, 13, and 22.

Agreeableness: Score 2 points if you answered "yes," and 1 point if you answered "not sure," to questions 2, 10, 12, 16, 25, and 27.

Neuroticism: Score 2 points if you answered "yes" to 6, 18, 23, and 30. Score 2 points if you answered "no" to questions 11 or 28. Score 1 point if you answered "not sure" to 6, 11, 18, 23, 28, and 30.

Add up your scores for each personality trait: 3 or less = low, 4 to 8 = medium, and 9 or more = high. Now read about the different personality traits by turning to page 222.

24 Does your music and fashion taste change often?

25 Do you trust people easily?

26 Do you enjoy any artistic or creative hobbies?

27 Would you speak up if you disagreed with someone?

28 Do you think you are carefree and relaxed?

29 When you start a book, do you usually finish it?

30 Do you feel anxious easily?

Thinking logically

Try these puzzles to find out if you're good at numerical and logical thinking. Allow about 30 minutes for the number puzzles (watch out for the trick questions) and take as long as you want on the logic puzzles. See pages 220–221 to find out more about different types of intelligence.

Number puzzles

1 A man has 14 camels and all but three die. How many are left?

2 The sum of all numbers from 1 to 7 is

a) 8   b) 15   c) 22   d) 25   e) 28

3 The day after tomorrow is two days before Tuesday. What day is it today?

a) Friday
b) Saturday
c) Sunday
d) Monday
e) Tuesday

4 What number comes next in the following sequence?

1, 2, 3, 5, 8, 13…

a) 15   b) 17   c) 19   d) 21   e) 23

5 If two cooks can peel two potatoes in one minute, how many cooks will it take to peel 20 potatoes in 10 minutes?

a) 1   b) 2   c) 3   d) 4   e) 5

6 How many birthdays does the average man have?

7 A man lives next to a circular park. It takes him 80 minutes to walk around it in a clockwise direction but 1 hour 20 minutes to walk the other direction. Why?

8 Brian and Graham collect 30 snails in a garden. Brian found five times more snails than Graham. How many snails did Graham find?

a) 6   b) 8   c) 3   d) 0   e) 5

9 You're running a race and you overtake the person in second place. What place are you in now?

a) last   b) 4th   c) 3rd   d) 2nd   e) 1st

10 Janet is taller than Penny, and Claire is shorter than Janet. Which of the following statements is correct?

a) Claire is taller than Penny.
b) Claire is shorter than Penny.
c) Claire is as tall as Penny.
d) It's impossible to tell.
e) Claire is Penny's sister.

11 A group of ducks are walking in a line. There are two ducks in front of a duck, two ducks behind a duck, and a duck in the middle. How many ducks are there?

a) 1   b) 2   c) 3   d) 4   e) 5

12 What number is one half of one quarter of one tenth of 800?

a) 2   b) 5   c) 8   d) 10   e) 40

13 There are 30 crows in a field. The farmer shoots four. How many crows are in the field now?

14 Brad is four years old and his sister Celine is three times older. When Brad is 12 years old, how old will Celine be?

a) 16   b) 20   c) 24   d) 28   e) 36

15 What number comes next in the following sequence?

144, 121, 100, 81, 64…

a) 55   b) 49   c) 36   d) 16   e) 9

16 How many animals of each sex did Moses take on the Ark?

17 If there are three pizzas and you take away two, how many pizzas do you have?

18 If you have three sweets and you eat one every half hour, how long will they last?

Logic puzzles

THE FRUSTRATED FARMER

A farmer is trying to use a small boat to row a fox, a chicken, and a bag of corn across a river. However, he can only take one thing at a time in the boat. If he leaves the fox with the chicken, the fox will eat the chicken. If he leaves the chicken with the corn, the chicken will eat the corn. How can the farmer get across the river without anything eating anything else?

THE RIGHT DOOR?

A prisoner is given a chance to win his freedom. In his cell are two doors—behind one is a hungry lion and behind the other is the exit to the prison. In front of each door stands a guard—one guard always speaks the truth, and the other always lies. The prisoner is allowed to ask one of the guards just one question. So what question should he ask to gain his freedom?

TWO AT A TIME

A group of four men—made up of two brothers plus their father and grandfather—is walking to a railway station in the dark. They come to an old, narrow bridge that leads to the station. The bridge can support just two people at a time and they have only one flashlight between them, so after one pair has crossed, one of the men will have to bring the flashlight back for the next pair. The four men take different times to cross the bridge.

- Brother one takes 1 minute
- Brother two takes 2 minutes
- The father takes 5 minutes
- The grandfather takes 10 minutes

Each pair can walk across the bridge only as fast as the slowest man, and the next train arrives at the station in 17 minutes. How can all the men cross the bridge to the station on time?

239

Thinking creatively

Try these puzzles to find out if you're good at spatial thinking (a sign of high IQ) and lateral thinking (a sign of creativity). See pages 220–221 to find out more about different types of intelligence.

Spatial thinking

MISSING PIECES

Putting a jigsaw puzzle together is a good example of pattern recognition. Your brain has to figure out how each small piece fits together to make the big picture. To do this you need to study both the contents of the pieces and their shapes. Four pieces from this puzzle are mixed up with pieces from a different puzzle. Can you complete the puzzle?

FIND THE SHAPE

This cube is made up of 27 smaller cubes. It has been split into three colored sections. When the blue and orange areas are removed, only the pink section is left. But which of the 3-D shapes below matches the remaining pink section?

Both these shapes are removed from the cube

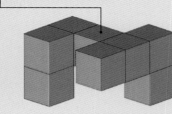

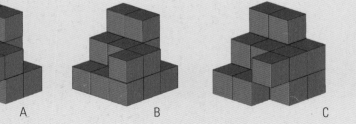

A   B   C   D   E

DIFFERENT ANGLES

Although these nine 3-D shapes all look very different, two of them are identical—they're just being shown from different angles. See if you can find the two matching shapes. You will need to visualize each shape at different angles.

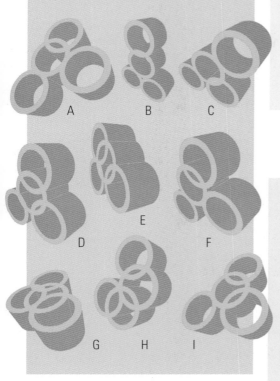

BOTTOMS UP

Here you can see three different views of the same cube. Each side of the cube is a different color. Can you figure out what color the face-down side is in the third picture?

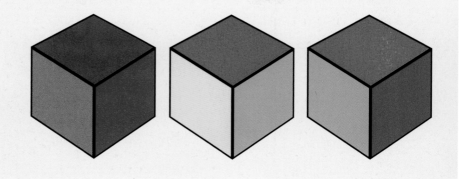

Lateral thinking

1 I live alone in a small home with no doors or windows, and when I leave I must break through the walls. What am I?

2 It's spring. You see a carrot and two pieces of coal together in somebody's front yard. How did they get there?

3 A man is lying dead in a field next to a backpack. How did he get there?

4 Two babies are born at the same time on the same day in the same month in the same year at the same hospital from the same biological mother. Why are they not twins?

5 A man went to a party and drank some of the punch. He then left early. Everyone else at the party who drank the punch subsequently died of poisoning. Why did the man not die?

6 Why is it better for manhole covers to be round and not square?
Clue: Think about turning them.

7 What's more powerful than God? The rich need it, the poor have it, and if you eat it you'll die.
Clue: The answer is a word.

8 Three switches in the basement are wired to three lights in a room upstairs. How can you determine which switch turns on which light with just one trip from the basement to the room?
Clue: There are light bulbs in the lights.

9 A man lives on the tenth floor of a building. Every day he takes the elevator to the ground floor to go to work. When he returns, he takes the elevator to the seventh floor and walks the rest of the way. If it's raining, he takes the elevator all the way up. Why?
Clue: The man owns an umbrella.

241

Medical discoveries

Your body is a fantastic, complex, living machine and, for thousands of years, people have been making groundbreaking discoveries that have enabled us to understand how it is assembled. Even today, scientists continue with their medical research, hoping to complete the missing pieces of our knowledge.

▼ **c. 1750 BCE** *Babylonian king Hammurabi produces a set of written laws, some of which regulate the work of doctors, including cutting the arms off surgeons who make mistakes during surgery.*

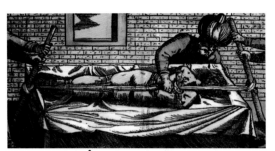

c. 350 BCE *Greek philosopher Aristotle states that the heart is the origin of feeling and intelligence.*

▲ **1000** *Arab doctor Ibn Sina (also known as Avicenna) publishes important medical information, which influences medicine for the next 500 years.*

▼ **1545** *Ambroise Paré, a French surgeon, publishes* Method of Treating Wounds, *in which he describes his less painful, more successful techniques for treating wounds, such as using egg yolk and rose petals on injuries rather than boiling oil.*

1800 BCE	800 CE	1400	1600

890–932 *Persian doctor Abu Bakr ar-Razi produces a number of important medical publications, and accurately describes measles and smallpox.*

▼ **c. 130–210 CE** *Roman-Greek doctor Claudius Galen describes how the body works. Although many of his ideas are wrong, they remain unchallenged for nearly 1,500 years.*

▲ **Late 1400s to early 1500s** *From his own dissections, Italian artist Leonardo da Vinci produces accurate anatomical drawings of the human body.*

1628 *English doctor William Harvey publishes* On the Movement of the Heart and Blood, *describing how blood circulates around the body pumped by the heart.*

▼ **1543** *Flemish doctor Andreas Vesalius publishes* On the Structure of the Human Body, *the first accurate description of the human body, including the brain.*

▲ **c. 420 BCE** *Greek doctor Hippocrates is one of the first people to realize that diseases have natural causes and cures.*

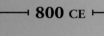

▼ **1663** *Italian doctor Marcello Malpighi discovers blood capillaries, helping to confirm that blood circulates around the body.*

▲ **1674–77** *Dutchman Antonie van Leeuwenhoek discovers microscopic red blood cells, sperm, and bacteria.*

▼ **1775** *French chemist Antoine Lavoisier discovers oxygen, and later shows that cell respiration is, like burning, a chemical process that consumes oxygen.*

▲ **1800** *French doctor Marie François Bichat publishes a book in which he shows that organs are made of different groups of cells called tissues.*

1691 *English doctor Clopton Havers describes the structure of bones.*

► **1816** *The stethoscope, a device used to listen to a patient's heart and breathing sounds, is invented by French doctor René Laënnec.*

1650 ——————— **1700** ——————— **1800** ——— **1835**

1667 *English doctor Richard Lower carries out a blood transfusion from a sheep to the student Arthur Coga. Amazingly, Coga survives.*

1833 *American surgeon William Beaumont records the results of his researches into the mechanism of digestion.*

▼ **1665** *English scientist Robert Hooke publishes* Micrographia, *in which he uses the new term "cell."*

▲ **1780** *Italian doctor Luigi Galvani experiments with nerves, muscles, and electricity.*

▼ **1796** *The first vaccination against smallpox is carried out on an eight-year-old boy by English doctor Edward Jenner.*

MICROGRAPHIA:
OR SOME
Physiological Descriptions
OF
MINUTE BODIES
MADE BY
MAGNIFYING GLASSES
WITH
Observations and Inquiries thereupon.

By R. HOOKE, Fellow of the ROYAL SOCIETY.

LONDON, Printed for *John Martyn*, Printer to the ROYAL SOCIETY, and are to be sold at the Shop at the Bell a little without Temple Bar. MDCLXVII.

▲ **1747** *British naval doctor James Lind discovers that citrus fruits prevent the vitamin C deficiency disease scurvy during long sea voyages.*

1672 *Regnier de Graaf, a Dutch doctor, describes the structure and workings of the female reproductive system.*

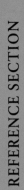

▼ **1901** *Austrian scientist Karl Landsteiner identifies blood types—later called A, B, AB, and O—enabling safe blood transfusions to take place.*

▲ **1860** *Pioneering French scientist Louis Pasteur (and later, German doctor Robert Koch) proves that bacteria and other microorganisms cause infectious disease.*

▲ **1849** *English-born Elizabeth Blackwell graduates from medical school in the United States and becomes the first woman doctor.*

▲ **1844** *Irish doctor Francis Rynd invents a syringe.*

1835	1850	1900

▼ **1895** *X-rays are discovered by scientist Wilhelm Roentgen. The first X-ray image is of his wife's hand.*

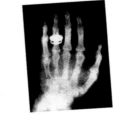

▲ **1853–56** *The work of Florence Nightingale and Mary Seacole during the Crimean War changes how wounded soldiers are nursed and leads to the establishment of modern nursing practices.*

1838 *German scientists Theodor Schwann and Jakob Schleiden state that all living things are made from cells.*

▼ **1865** *To reduce wound infection by bacteria, British surgeon Joseph Lister introduces antiseptic (germ-killing) sprays into his operating theater, dramatically reducing the death rate.*

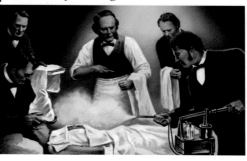

▲ **1928** *Scottish scientist Alexander Fleming discovers penicillin, the first antibiotic drug.*

1972 *CT scanning is used for the first time to produce images of organs and tissues inside the body.*

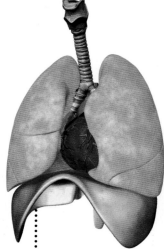

▼ **1955** *Doctors start using ultrasound scanners to examine developing babies inside the womb.*

▲ **1931** *German engineers Max Knoll and Ernst Ruska invent the electron microscope, which can magnify objects up to an incredible 1 million times.*

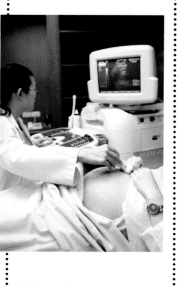

▲ **1978** *On July 26, Louise Brown—the world's first test tube baby—is born in Britain. She was conceived by IVF nine months earlier in a laboratory.*

▲ **2008** *A Colombian woman has her damaged windpipe replaced by one custom-made using her own cells, reducing the risk of rejection by her body's defenses.*

1930 ——————————————————— 1970 ——————————— 2000 ———————— PRESENT

1954 *The first successful kidney transplant—the transfer of a healthy kidney to a person with a diseased kidney—is performed in Boston.*

▼ **1967** *Surgeon Christiaan Barnard carries out the first heart transplant, in an operation lasting nine hours and involving a team of 30 people.*

▼ **1980** *Surgeons start using minimally invasive surgery to look inside the body and perform operations through tiny openings rather than large incisions.*

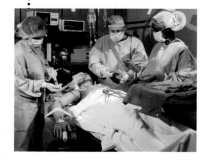

▼ **2003** *Started in 1990, the Human Genome Project completes its goal of identifying the DNA sequence of a full set of human chromosomes, and shows that humans have about 23,000 genes.*

▲ **1953** *Scientists Francis Crick and James Watson discover the structure of DNA, the body chemical that carries genes.*

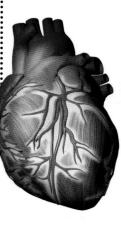

1977 *The killer infection smallpox becomes the first disease to be eradicated by a coordinated program of vaccination.*

Glossary

Abdomen The lower part of the main body (the torso), below your chest.

Absorption The process by which nutrients from digested food are taken in through the wall of your small intestine and passed into your blood.

Adrenaline A hormone that prepares your body for sudden action in times of danger or excitement. Adrenaline is produced by glands on top of the kidneys.

Allergy An illness caused by overreaction of the body's immune system to a normally harmless substance.

Amino acid A simple molecule used by the body to build proteins. Proteins in food are broken down into amino acids by the digestive system.

Antibody A substance made by the body that sticks to germs and marks them for destruction by white blood cells.

Antigen A foreign substance, usually found on the surface of pathogens such as bacteria, which triggers the immune system to respond.

Artery A blood vessel that carries blood away from your heart to your body's tissues and organs.

Autonomic nervous system (ANS) The part of the nervous system that controls unconscious functions such as your heart rate and the size of the pupil in your eyes.

Axon A long fiber that extends from a nerve cell (neuron). It carries electrical signals away from the cell.

Bacterium (plural **Bacteria**) A small type of microorganism. Bacteria live everywhere. Some types cause disease in humans, but some are beneficial and help keep your body functioning properly.

Blood A liquid tissue containing several types of cells. Blood carries oxygen, salts, nutrients, minerals, and hormones around your body. It also collects waste for disposal, such as carbon dioxide that is breathed out by your lungs.

Blood vessel Any tube that carries blood through your body.

Bone A strong, hard body part made chiefly of calcium minerals. There are 206 bones in an adult skeleton.

Brain stem The part of the base of your brain that connects to your spinal cord.

Calcium A mineral used by your body to build bones and teeth. Calcium also helps muscles move.

Capillary The smallest type of blood vessel. Your body contains thousands of miles of capillaries.

Carbohydrate A food group that includes sugars and starches that provide your body's main energy supply.

Cartilage A tough, flexible type of connective tissue that helps support your body and covers the ends of bones in joints.

Cell The smallest living unit of your body.

Central nervous system Your brain and spinal cord together make up your central nervous system. One of the two main parts of the nervous system.

Cerebellum A small, cauliflower-shaped structure at the base of the back of your brain that helps coordinate body movements and balance.

Cerebral cortex The deeply folded, outer layer of your brain. It is used for thinking, memory, movement, language, attention, and processing sensory information.

Cerebral hemisphere One of the two symmetrical halves into which the main part of your brain (the cerebrum) is split.

Cerebrum The largest part of the brain, which is involved in conscious thought, feelings, and movement.

▶ SPIRAL SHAPE
DNA has a double-helix structure that looks like a twisted ladder.

Chromosome One of 46 threadlike packages of DNA found in the nucleus of body cells.

Computed Tomography (CT) scanning An imaging technique that uses X-rays to produce 2-D and 3-D images of body organs.

Conception The time between fertilization of an egg cell by a sperm and settling of an embryo in the lining of the womb.

Dendrite A short fiber that extends from a nerve cell (neuron). It carries incoming electrical signals from other nerve cells.

Deoxyribonucleic acid (DNA) A long molecule found inside the nucleus of body cells. DNA contains coded instructions that control how cells work and how your body grows and develops.

Digestion The process that breaks down food into tiny particles that your body can absorb and use.

Digestive enzyme A substance that speeds up the breakdown of food molecules.

Disease Any problem with the body that may make a person feel unwell. Diseases caused by germs are called infectious diseases. Many are spread from person to person, for example by coughs or sneezes.

Dopamine A chemical released in your brain when you feel excitement or pleasure. Dopamine is a type of neurotransmitter—it travels across the tiny gap between neighboring nerve cells to pass a signal on.

Embryo The name given to a developing baby between the time it arrives in the womb and eight weeks after fertilization.

Emotions Inner feelings that are produced by the brain, including joy, fear, and anger.

Endocrine gland A type of gland, such as the pituitary gland, that releases hormones into your bloodstream.

Enzyme A substance that speeds up a particular chemical reaction in the body.

Epiglottis A flap of tissue that closes your trachea when you swallow food to stop the food from entering.

Feces Another name for poo. The solid waste made up of undigested food, dead cells, and bacteria that is left over after digestion and expelled from your anus.

Fat A substance found in many foods that provides energy and important ingredients for cells. The layer of cells just under the skin is full of fat.

Fertilization The joining together of a female egg (ovum) and male sperm to make a new individual.

Fetus The name given to a developing baby from the ninth week after fertilization until it is born.

Fever A rise in body temperature above the normal range.

Genes Instructions that control the way your body develops and works. Genes are passed on from parents to their children.

Genome The DNA contained in a set of chromosomes. In humans, there are 46 chromosomes.

Germ A tiny living thing that can get into your body and make you sick. Bacteria and viruses are types of germs.

Gland A group of specialized cells that make and release a particular substance, such as an enzyme or a hormone.

Glucose A simple type of sugar that circulates in the bloodstream and is the main energy source for the body's cells.

Gravity The force that pulls objects toward the ground.

Gray matter Brain tissue that consists largely of the cell bodies of neurons. The outer layer of the brain is gray matter.

Hippocampus A part of the brain that helps store long-term memories.

Hormone A chemical produced by glands in order to change the way a different part of the body works. Hormones are carried by the blood.

Hypothalamus A small structure in the base of your brain that controls many body activities, including temperature and thirst.

Immune system A collection of cells and tissues that protect the body from disease by searching out and destroying germs and cancer cells.

Infection If germs invade your body and begin to multiply, they cause an infection. Some diseases are caused by infections.

▼ MESSAGE CENTER *Your brain is your body's communication hub. Signals are received from and sent to your body through your nerves.*

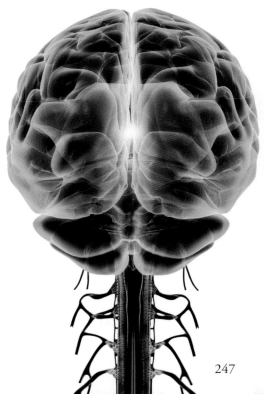

Joint A connection between two bones.

Keratin A tough, waterproof protein found in hair, nails, and the upper layer of your skin.

Ligament A tough band of tissue that connects bones where they meet at joints.

Limbic system A cluster of structures inside your brain that are vital in creating emotions, memory, and the sense of smell.

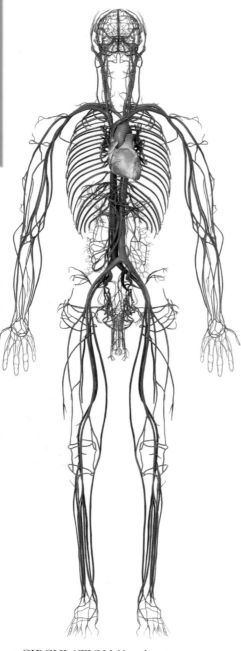

▲ CIRCULATION *Your heart pumps blood around your body through a vast network of tubes called blood vessels.*

Lymphatic system A network of vessels that collect fluid from body tissues and filter it for germs, before returning the fluid to the bloodstream.

Lymphocyte A white blood cell that specializes in attacking a specific kind of germ. Some lymphocytes make antibodies.

Macrophage A white blood cell that swallows and destroys germs such as bacteria, cancer cells, or debris in damaged tissue.

Magnetic Resonance Imaging (MRI) A scanning technique that uses magnetism, radio waves, and a computer to produce images of the inside of the body.

Melanin A brown-black pigment that is found in your skin, hair, and eyes and gives them their color.

Metabolism A term used to describe all the chemical reactions going on inside your body, especially within cells.

Mind The thoughts, feelings, beliefs, ideas, and sense of self that are generated by the brain make up what we call the mind.

Mineral A naturally occurring solid chemical, such as salt, calcium, or iron, that you need to eat to stay healthy.

Mitochondrion (plural **Mitochondria**) A tiny structure found inside cells that releases energy from sugar.

Mitosis The division of a body cell into two new, identical cells.

Molecule A single particle of a particular chemical compound. A molecule is a cluster of atoms (the smallest particles of an element) bonded together permanently.

Motor neuron A type of nerve cell that carries nerve impulses from your central nervous system to your muscles.

Mucus Slippery liquid found on the inside of your nose, throat, and intestines.

Muscle A body part that contracts (gets shorter) to move your bones or internal organs.

Muscle fiber A muscle cell.

Nerve cell *See* neuron.

Nerve impulse A tiny electrical signal that is transmitted along a nerve cell (neuron) at high speed.

Neuron Another word for a nerve cell. Neurons carry information around your body as electrical signals.

Neurotransmitter A chemical created by nerve cells (neurons) that relays signals across the tiny gaps (synapses) between one neuron and another.

Nucleus The control center of a cell. It contains DNA-carrying chromosomes.

Nutrients The basic chemicals that make up food. Your body uses nutrients for fuel, growth, and repair.

Organ A group of tissues that form a body part designed for a specific job. Your heart is an organ.

Organelle A tiny structure inside a cell that carries out an important role. The nucleus is an organelle that contains genetic information.

Ovum Also called an egg, this is the female sex cell, which is produced by, and released from, a woman's ovary.

Oxygen A gas, found in air, that is vital for life. Oxygen is breathed in, absorbed by the blood, and used by cells to release energy from glucose (a simple sugar).

Pathogen A microorganism that causes disease. Pathogens are also called germs and include bacteria and viruses.

Peristalsis The wave of muscular squeezes (contractions) in the wall of a hollow organ that, for example, pushes food down the esophagus during swallowing.

◄ BLOOD CELLS *Your blood contains red blood cells that take oxygen from your lungs to all parts of your body. It also contains germ-fighting white blood cells.*

Proteins Vital nutrients that help your body build new cells. Food such as meat, eggs, fish, and cheese are rich in proteins.

Red blood cell A disk-shaped cell that contains hemoglobin (a protein that carries oxygen and makes your blood red).

Reflex A rapid, automatic reaction that is out of your control, such as blinking when something moves toward your eyes.

Retina A layer of light-sensitive neurons lining the back of each eye. The retina captures images and relays them to the brain as electrical signals.

Saliva The liquid in your mouth. Saliva helps you taste, swallow, and digest food.

Scanning Any technique used to create images of soft tissues and organs inside the human body.

Sebum An oily liquid that keeps your hair and skin soft, flexible, and waterproof.

Sensory neuron A type of nerve cell (neuron) that carries impulses from your sense organs to the central nervous system.

Sensory receptor A specialized nerve cell or the end of a sensory neuron that detects a stimulus, such as light, scent, touch, or sound.

Sex chromosome One of two chromosomes present in each body cell that determine whether you are male or female.

Sperm The male sex cells, which are made in, and released from, a man's testes.

Sphincter A ring of muscle around a passageway or opening that opens and closes to control the flow of material, such as urine or food, through it.

Spinal cord A column of nerve cells (neurons) that runs down your backbone and connects your brain to the rest of your body.

Spinal nerve One of 31 pairs of nerves that branch out from your spinal cord.

Sweat A watery liquid produced by glands in the skin. Sweat cools down the body as it evaporates.

Synapse The junction where two nerve cells (neurons) meet but do not touch.

System A group of organs that work together. Your mouth, stomach, and intestines make up your digestive system.

Tendon A cord of tough connective tissue that links muscle to bone.

Tissue A group of cells that look and act the same. Muscle is a type of tissue.

Toxin A poisonous substance released into the body by a disease-causing bacterium.

Trachea (Windpipe) The main airway leading from the back of your throat to your lungs.

Ultrasound An imaging technique that uses inaudible, high-frequency sound waves to produce pictures of a developing baby in the womb or of body tissues.

Vein A blood vessel that carries blood toward your heart.

Vellus hair One of the millions of fine, soft hairs that grow all over your body.

Virus A kind of germ that invades cells and multiplies inside them. Diseases caused by viruses include the common cold, measles, and influenza.

Vitamin One of a number of substances needed in small amounts in your diet to keep your body healthy.

Vocal cords The small folds of tissue in your voice box that vibrate to create the sounds of speech.

Voice box (Larynx) A structure at the top of the trachea that generates sound as you speak. The sound is created by folds of tissue that vibrate as you breathe out.

White blood cell Any of the colorless blood cells that play various roles in your immune system.

White matter Brain tissue made up mainly of the axons (long fibers) of nerve cells. The inner part of the brain consists largely of white matter.

X-rays A form of radiation that reveals bones when projected through the body onto photographic film.

Index

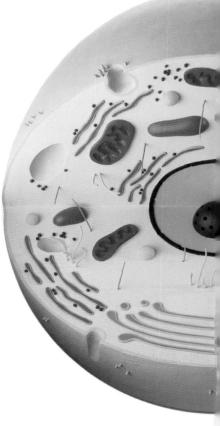

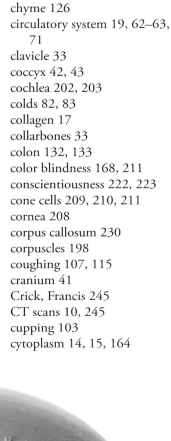

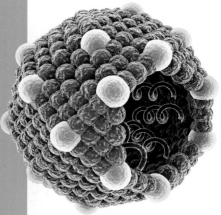

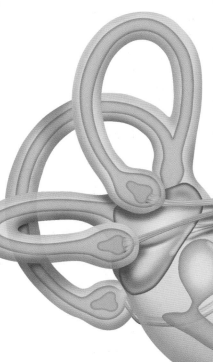

REFERENCE SECTION

skeletal system 30–45
skeleton 23, 32–33, 46
    see also bones
skin 17, 18, 24–25, 28–29,
    63, 85, 97, 140, 163
skin sensors 183, 198
skull 32, 33, 36, 39, 40–41,
    67, 179
sleeping 79, 184–185, 229,
    230
sleepwalking 185
smallpox 245
smell 200, 201
smell receptors 200
smiling 52, 53, 225, 233
sneezing 59, 82, 114
snoring 115
sound 116, 117, 182,
    202–203
space travel 58–59
spatial intelligence 220,
    240–241
sperm 14, 156, 157, 159, 161
sphincters 126, 127, 145,
    150, 151
spinal cord 42, 43, 174,
    177, 179, 186,
    186–187
spine, *see* backbone
spleen 10, 90
starch 120, 121, 136
stem cells 12–13, 100
sternum 32, 33, 43
stethoscopes 77, 243
stings 97
stomach 8, 10, 19, 121, 122,
    123, 126–127, 191
stomach acid 84, 123
sugars 120
suntans 25
suprachiasmatic nucleus
    (SCN) 228
surgery 99, 103, 244, 245
survival instincts 201, 224,
    225
sutures 40
swallowing 107, 125, 187
sweat 24, 25, 152, 191
sweets 121, 201
synaspses 177
syringes 244

T
talking 116–117, 162, 182,
    204
taste 200, 201
taste buds 200, 201
tears 85, 190
teenagers 137, 163, 194,
    230–231
teeth 10, 40, 121, 122, 124,
    125
temperature 24, 47, 66, 85,
    134, 184
temporal lobe 218, 219
tendons 17, 46, 48, 54, 57
testes 156, 192
testosterone 192, 193, 222,
    223
thighbone 32, 34–35, 37
throat 84, 124, 125
thumbs 38, 54, 168
thymus gland 90
thyroid gland 19, 192
tibia 32
tissues 13, 17, 18–19, 33, 35,
    68, 152, 202
    connective 18, 19, 71
    epithelial 18, 19
    muscle 18, 19
    nerve 18, 19
toes 26, 39, 56, 57, 161, 175
tongue 47, 117, 122, 124,
    125, 200
tonsils 91
touch 25, 26, 174, 183,
    198–199
toxins 82, 123, 134
trachea 106, 107, 110, 112,
    113, 115, 245
transplants 74, 101, 145,
    245
trepanning 103

triceps 47, 48, 49
tuberculosis 89
tumors 99
twins 161, 165, 223

U
ulna 33
ultrasound 10, 11, 161, 245
umbilical cord 160, 161
urea 149
ureters 144
urethra 144, 150
urinary system 21, 144–145
urine 144, 145, 147, 148, 49,
    150–151
uterus 157

V
vaccinations 93, 243, 245
vagina 156, 157
valves 70, 74, 77, 90, 132
van Leeuwenhoek, Antonie
    14, 243
vegetables 120, 136, 140
veins 62, 63, 69, 70, 71, 74,
    134, 144

vertebrae 33, 42
vertigo 205
Vesalius, Andreas 242
villi 129, 120
viruses 82, 83, 85, 93, 94, 98
visual cortex 225
vitamins 120, 121, 132,
    134,136, 140–141, 145
vocal cords 116, 117
voice box 106, 116, 117
voice 41, 106, 116, 163, 217
vomit 123, 127, 141

W
walking 57
washing 98
waste removal 66, 67, 109,
    123, 132, 144–145, 149,
    160
water 120, 132, 149, 151,
    152–153
    spa water 103
Watson, James 245
weight 32, 41, 42, 56
weightlessness 58, 59
Wernicke's area 117
womb 157, 160, 161
worms 82, 91
wounds 17, 66, 71, 85, 86
wrists 39

X
X-rays 10, 11, 33, 37, 65,
    195, 244

YZ
yawning 115

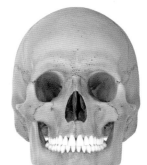

Acknowledgments

Dorling Kindersley would like to thank Jolyon Goddard and Wendy Horobin for additional writing and editing, Ralph Pitchford and Peter Radcliffe for additional design, Jane Yorke for proofreading, Carron Brown for the index, and John Searcy for Americanization.

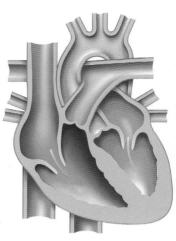

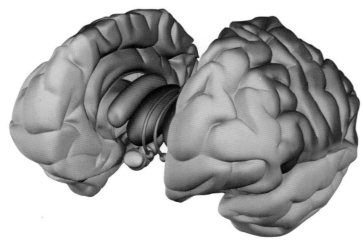

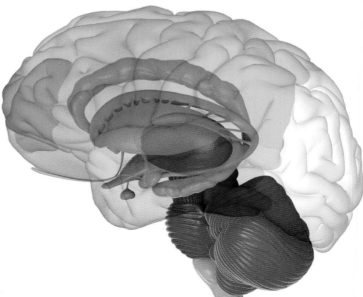

Steve Gschmeissner (cr). **114 Science Photo Library:** Damien Lovegrove. **117 Getty Images:** TTH / a. collectionRF (bl). **Science Photo Library:** Welcome Dept. of Cognitive Neurology (c). **118-119 Corbis:** Atlantide Phototravel. **119 Science Photo Library:** Alain POL, ISM (tr); USDA (tl); Eye of Science (tc). **120-121 Science Photo Library:** Maximilian Stock ltd.. **121 Corbis:** Bettmann (cra). **Getty Images:** Eric Audras (br). **Science Photo Library:** Biophoto Associates (tc). **123 Science Photo Library:** USDA (br). **125 Science Photo Library:** Photo Insolite Realite (tr); Eye of Science (cr). **126 Science Photo Library:** Dr. K.F.R. Schiller (tc). **127 Corbis:** Bettmann (tr). **Science Photo Library:** Steve Gschmeissner (bl). **129 Science Photo Library:** Eye of Science (cra). **130-131 Science Photo Library:** Steve Gschmeissner. **132 Science Photo Library:** Professors P. Motta & F. Carpino / Univer- Sity "La Sapienza," Rome (b). **133 Science Photo Library:** Alain POL, ISM (br). **134 Science Photo Library:** A. Dowsett, Health Protection Agency (br). **135 Science Photo Library:** Prof. P. Motta / Dept. of Anatomy / University "La Sapienza," Rome (cra). **137 Getty Images:** Alex Cao (crb). **138-139 Corbis:** Steven Vidler / Eurasia Press. **140 Corbis:** the food passionates (bc). **141 AlltheSky.com:** Till Credner (tl). **Corbis:** Layne Kennedy (c). **142-143 Science Photo Library:** 3D4Medical.com. **145 Corbis:** Juice Images (cl). **Getty Images:** Buena Vista Images (t). **Science Photo Library:** Life in View (br). **146-147 Mary Evans Picture Library:** Interfoto / Sammlung Rauch. **149 Corbis:** Digital Art (l); Ian Hooton / Science Photo Library (cr). **150 Getty Images:** Steve Gschmeissner (cr). **151 Corbis:** John Lund / Annabelle Breakey / Blend Images (tl). **Getty Images:** Alex Cao (c). **152 Corbis:** Tetra Images (cr); Warren Morgan (bl). **153 Corbis:** Clouds Hill Imaging Ltd. (bc); Photo Quest Ltd / Science Photo Library (bc/brown image). **Getty Images:** Bartosz Hadyniak (cl). **154-155 Corbis:** 3d4Medical.com. **155 Science Photo Library:** Christian Darkin (tc). **157 Science Photo Library:** Christian Darkin (tc); D. Phillips (tl); Dr. Yorgas Nikas (tc/Morula); Dr. Yorgos Nikas (tr). **158-159 Science Photo Library:** Don Fawcett. **161 Getty Images:** UHB Trust (c). **165 Alamy Images:** Inmagine (tr). **Getty Images:** AFP (br). **Science Photo Library:** Pasieka (bl). **166-167 Science Photo Library:** L. Williatt, East Anglian Regional Genetics Service. **168**

Corbis: Hola Images (clb). **168-169 Corbis:** 3d4Medical.com. **169 Getty Images:** altrendo images (br); Image Source (tc). **170 Science Photo Library:** David Parker (l); Philippe Plailly (cr). **171 Science Photo Library:** Jan Van De Vel / Reporters (tl). **172-173 Science Photo Library:** Claus Lunau. **173 Corbis:** Imagemore Co., Ltd. (tr); Zena Holloway (tc). **Science Photo Library:** Nancy Kedersha (tl). **174 Corbis:** Kim Kyung-Hoon / Reuters (cr). **Getty Images:** Time & Life Pictures (bl). **176-177 Dreamstime.com:** Sebastian Kaulitzki. **176 Corbis:** Charles O'Rear (br). **Science Photo Library:** Sciepro (bc). **177 Science Photo Library:** Gary Carlson (c); Jacopin (t). **178 Corbis:** Sprint (cr). **Science Photo Library:** D. Roberts (b). **179 Getty Images:** Roger Harris (br). **Science Photo Library:** Pasieka (cr). **180-181 Science Photo Library:** Nancy Kedersha. **183 Corbis:** Visuals Unlimited (cr). **Science Photo Library:** Patrick Landmann (tc); Natural History Museum, London (bl). **185 Corbis:** Peter Ginter / Science Faction (tr). **187 Corbis:** Zena Holloway (bl); Bob Krist (br). **188-189 Science Photo Library:** Mehau Kulyk. **190 Corbis:** moodboard (tr); Ocean (b). **Science Photo Library:** Henning Dalhoff (crb). **191 Alamy Images:** imagebroker (cla). **Corbis:** Imagemore Co., Ltd. (br). **193 Corbis:** Luc Beziat / cultura (bl); Robert Michael (cr). **Science Photo Library:** Lea Paterson (tc). **195 Corbis:** Bettmann (br). **Science Photo Library:** (tr); Steve Gschmeissner (bl); AJ Photo (tl); Pasieka (cl). **196-197 Corbis:** Suren Manvelyan / Visuals Unlimited. **197 Corbis:** Radius Images (tl). **198 Getty Images:** Mary C. Legg (b). **199 Corbis:** Ondrea Barbe (bl/Heat and cold); Dewitt Jones (bc); Radius Images (br/Faint touch). **Getty Images:** Paul Piebinga (bl). **Dr. Hunter Hoffman, U.W.:** Ari Hollander / www.vrpain.com (cl). **The Natural History Museum, London:** Natural History Museum, London (tl). **200 Science Photo Library:** Steve Gschmeissner (c); Dr. Richard Kessel and Dr. Randy Kardon / Visuals Unlimited, Inc. (bc). **201 Corbis:** Envision (clb); David Ponton / Design Pics (tr); Annika Erickson / Blend Images (br). **203 Corbis:** Radius Images (tl); Image Source (bc); Robert & Linda Mostyn / Eye Ubiquitous (bc/Pneumatic drill). **Getty Images:** Stephen Strathdee (br). **Science Photo Library:** Dr. David Furness, Keele University (cr); Susumu Nishinaga

(tr). **205 Corbis:** Dave G. Houser (cl); Mike Kemp / Tetra Images (br). **Getty Images:** jld3 Photography (cr). **206-207 Getty Images:** Tyler Stableford. **209 Getty Images:** Junior Gonzalez (tr). **Science Photo Library:** Omikkron (cl). **211 Corbis:** moodboard (cl). **Getty Images:** Thinkstock (tr). **212 Fotolia:** Tristan3D (clb). **Getty Images:** Juergen Richter (tr). **212-213 Ian Loxley / TORRO / The Cloud Appreciation Society.** **213 Getty Images:** (tl). **214-215 Corbis:** Sean Davey / Australian Picture Library. **215 Corbis:** Doug Berry / Blend Images (tr). **Getty Images:** Tek Image (tc). **216 Getty Images:** (bl). **217 Getty Images:** Russell Sadur (bc); Jonathan Storey (tl). **219 Corbis:** Imagemore Co., Ltd. (bl); Edith Held (crb); Lisbeth Hjort / cultura (br). **Getty Images:** Dennis Kitchen (c). **220 Dreamstime.com:** Natalia7 (cl). **Getty Images:** Nick Dolding (crb). **221 Alamy Images:** Eileen Langsley Gymnastics (bc). **Corbis:** Bettmann (tl). **222 Getty Images:** Digital Zoo (cra). **223 Getty Images:** Ian McKinnell (cla). **224 Corbis:** Fabio Cardoso. **225 Corbis:** Strauss / Curtis (cla); FBP / Tetra Images (ca); Lawrence Manning (cra). **Getty Images:** Tek Image (br); Andreas Kuehn (tc); Anna Summa (tr). **226-227 Corbis:** Randy Lincks. **229 Corbis:** Peter Ginter / Science Faction (tl); Alain Nogues / Sygma (bl). **230 Corbis:** Ocean (b). **231 Corbis:** Doug Berry / Blend Images (cr). **Getty Images:** Red Chopsticks (bc). **234-235 Science Photo Library:** Pasieka. **235 Corbis:** CDC / PHIL (tr). **242 Corbis:** Bettmann (tc, br); Ocean (cb) (br/Cerebrum); Gianni Dagli Orti (cra, cla). **Getty Images:** Leemage (bc). **242-243 Getty Images:** Leemage (c). **243 Corbis:** Bettmann (cla) (tc). **Getty Images:** Gaston Melingue (br); French School (cr). **Science Photo**

Library: (cb); Sheila Terry (ca, tr); Adam Hart-Davis (bl). **244 Corbis:** Bettmann (cra, bl, bc); Image Source (tc); Leonard Gertz (crb). **Getty Images:** Wilhelm Roentgen (cb); English School (clb). **Science Photo Library:** (cla, tl); St. Mary's Hospital Medical School (br). **244-245 Corbis:** CDC / PHIL (t). **245 Corbis:** Scott Camazine / Visuals Unlimited (cr); Skip Nall (cb). **Getty Images:** NY Daily News via Getty Images (tc); Imagemore Co., Ltd (cla). **Science Photo Library:** A. Barrington Brown (bl); Henning Dalhoff (bc). **246-247 Alamy Images:** John Schwegel. **247 Corbis:** 3d4Medical.com (br). **250 Getty Images:** London Scientific Films (cr)

Jacket images: *Front:* **Corbis:** Micro Discovery bc, Pasieka / Science Photo Library bl, Image Source bc / (Boy); **Getty Images:** Roger Harris / SPL tc; **Science Photo Library:** Scott Camazine br; *Back:* **Corbis:** 3d4Medical.com tc; **Dept. of Fetal Medicine, Royal Victoria Infirmary:** bc/ (Baby); **Science Photo Library:** Simon Fraser bl, Patrick Landmann tr, Martin Oeggerli br.

All other images © Dorling Kindersley
For further information see:
www.dkimages.com